CLASSICISM AND THE CONSTRUCTION OF CAPITAL CITIES

Bloomsbury Studies in Classical Reception

Bloomsbury Studies in Classical Reception presents scholarly monographs offering new and innovative research and debate to students and scholars in the reception of Classical Studies. Each volume will explore the appropriation, reconceptualization and recontextualization of various aspects of the Graeco-Roman world and its culture, looking at the impact of the ancient world on modernity. Research will also cover reception within antiquity, the theory and practice of translation, and reception theory.

Also available in the series
Alexander the Great in the Early Christian Tradition: Classical Reception and Patristic Literature, Christian Thrue Djurslev
Ancient Magic and the Supernatural in the Modern Visual and Performing Arts, edited by Filippo Carlà and Irene Berti
Ancient Greek Myth in World Fiction since 1989, edited by Justine McConnell and Edith Hall
Anne Carson/Antiquity, edited by Laura Jansen
Antipodean Antiquities, edited by Marguerite Johnson
Classical Antiquity and Medieval Ireland: An Anthology of Medieval Irish Texts and Interpretations, edited by Michael James Clark, Erich Poppe and Isabelle Torrance
Classics in Extremis, edited by Edmund Richardson
Faulkner's Reception of Apuleius' The Golden Ass in The Reivers, Vernon L. Provencal
Frankenstein and Its Classics, edited by Jesse Weiner, Benjamin Eldon Stevens and Brett M. Rogers
Gender, Creation Myths and their Reception in Western Civilization: Prometheus, Pandora, Adam and Eve, edited by Lisa Maurice and Tovi Bibring
Greek and Roman Classics in the British Struggle for Social Reform, edited by Henry Stead and Edith Hall
Greeks and Romans on the Latin American Stage, edited by Rosa Andújar and Konstantinos P. Nikoloutsos
Greek Tragedy in 20th-Century Italian Literature: Translations by Camillo Sbarbaro and Giovanna Bemporad, Caterina Paoli
Homer's Iliad and the Trojan War: Dialogues on Tradition, Jan Haywood and Naoíse Mac Sweeney
Imagining Xerxes, Emma Bridges

Julius Caesar's Self-Created Image and Its Dramatic Afterlife, Miryana Dimitrova
Kinaesthesia and Classical Antiquity 1750–1820: Moved by Stone, Helen Slaney
Once and Future Antiquities in Science Fiction and Fantasy,
	edited by Brett M. Rogers and Benjamin Eldon Stevens
Ovid's Myth of Pygmalion on Screen, Paula James
Performing Gods in Classical Antiquity and the Age of Shakespeare,
	by Dustin W. Dixon and John S. Garrison
Reading Poetry, Writing Genre, edited by Silvio Bär and Emily Hauser
Sex, Symbolists and the Greek Body, Richard Warren
The Ancient World in Alternative History and Counterfactual Fictions,
	edited by Alberto J. Quiroga Puertas and Leire Olabarria
The Classics in Modernist Translation, edited by Miranda Hickman
	and Lynn Kozak
The Classics in South America: Five Case Studies, by Germán Campos Muñoz
The Codex Fori Mussolini, Han Lamers and Bettina Reitz-Joosse
The Gentle, Jealous God, Simon Perris
The Persephone Myth in Young Adult Fiction: From Girl to Woman,
	Cristina Salcedo González
*The Thucydidean Turn: (Re)Interpreting Thucydides' Political Thought Before,
	During and After the Great War*, Benjamin Earley
Translations of Greek Tragedy in the Work of Ezra Pound, Peter Liebregts
Truth in the Late Foucault: Antiquity, Sexuality and Psychoanalysis,
	edited by Paul Allen Miller
Victorian Classical Burlesques, Laura Monrós-Gaspar
Victorian Epic Burlesques, Rachel Bryant Davies
Virgil's Map: Geography, Empire, and the Georgics, Charlie Kerrigan

CLASSICISM AND THE CONSTRUCTION OF CAPITAL CITIES

LONDON, ATHENS AND ROME IN THE NINETEENTH CENTURY

Richard Alston

BLOOMSBURY ACADEMIC
LONDON • NEW YORK • OXFORD • NEW DELHI • SYDNEY

BLOOMSBURY ACADEMIC

Bloomsbury Publishing Plc, 50 Bedford Square, London, WC1B 3DP, UK
Bloomsbury Publishing Inc, 1385 Broadway, New York, NY 10018, USA
Bloomsbury Publishing Ireland, 29 Earlsfort Terrace, Dublin 2, D02 AY28, Ireland

BLOOMSBURY, BLOOMSBURY ACADEMIC and the Diana logo are trademarks of
Bloomsbury Publishing Plc

First published in Great Britain 2025

Copyright © Richard Alston, 2025

Richard Alston has expressed his right under the Copyright, Designs and Patents Act, 1988,
to be identified as Author of this work.

Cover image: Leo von Klenze, *The Acropolis at Athens*, 1846. Oil on canvas, 103 × 148 cm.
Neue Pinakothek, Munich. Peter Horree/Alamy Stock Photo

All rights reserved. No part of this publication may be: i) reproduced or transmitted in any form, electronic or mechanical, including photocopying, recording or by means of any information storage or retrieval system without prior permission in writing from the publishers; or ii) used or reproduced in any way for the training, development or operation of artificial intelligence (AI) technologies, including generative AI technologies. The rights holders expressly reserve this publication from the text and data mining exception as per Article 4(3) of the Digital Single Market Directive (EU) 2019/790.

Bloomsbury Publishing Plc does not have any control over, or responsibility for, any third-party websites referred to or in this book. All internet addresses given in this book were correct at the time of going to press. The author and publisher regret any inconvenience caused if addresses have changed or sites have ceased to exist, but can accept no responsibility for any such changes.

A catalogue record for this book is available from the British Library.

A catalog record for this book is available from the Library of Congress.

ISBN: HB: 978-1-3504-4531-4
ePDF: 978-1-3504-4532-1
eBook: 978-1-3504-4533-8

Series: Bloomsbury Studes in Classical Reception

Typeset by RefineCatch Limited, Bungay, Suffolk

For product safety related questions contact productsafety@bloomsbury.com.

To find out more about our authors and books visit www.bloomsbury.com
and sign up for our newsletters.

CONTENTS

List of Illustrations — viii
Preface — x

Introduction: An Essay on the Reception of Classical Architecture — 1

1 London: A Civil Society, 1800–1820 — 19
2 Athens: The Colonization of Greece, 1830–1846 — 69
3 Rome: City of Unity, 1870–1911 — 121
4 Fascist Rome: Scenes of Fantasy, 1922–1943 — 157

Epilogue: Classicism and Authoritarianism — 181

Notes — 185
Bibliography — 189
Index — 211

ILLUSTRATIONS

0.1	The east façade of the Louvre, as engraved by Jean Marot (1676) from the Bibliothèque municipal de Valenciennes	11
0.2	Laugier's Hut: the origins of architecture (Laugier 1753: Frontispiece)	13
0.3	Gilly's Friedrichsdenkmal, Berlin (https://en.m.wikipedia.org/wiki/File:Gilly_Denkmal.jpg)	15
0.4	The Parthenon in elevation from Stuart and Revett (1787)	16
0.5	The Parthenon in Athens from Stuart and Revett (1787)	16
0.6	The Tower of the Winds from Stuart and Revett (1787)	17
1.1	London's census population: 1801–31	20
1.2	Map of London in 1806 (detail from Mogg 1806)	22
1.3	*Bird's Eye View of a Design for a Triumphal Bridge* (© Sir John Soane's Museum, London)	27
1.4	Soane's entry to Downing Place (from Elmes 1827)	27
1.5	Soane's entry to Lothbury Court, Bank of England (© Sir John Soane's Museum, London)	32
1.6	*Architectural Ruins: A Vision* (Joseph Gandy 1798) (© Sir John Soane's Museum, London)	35
1.7	Map of Bloomsbury and the West End in 1806 (from Mogg 1806)	39
1.8	Britannia Triumphant (Flaxman 1799)	47
1.9	Decimus Burton's entry to Hyde Park	48
1.10	Soane's design for a palace at Constitution Hill (© Royal Collection Enterprises Ltd 20024 | Royal Collection Trust)	49
1.11	Soane's designs for gates into Hyde Park (Yale Centre for British Art; https://collections.britishart.yale.edu/catalog/tms:12035)	49
1.12	Regent's Park Villa (Elmes 1827)	50
1.13	Waterloo Place (Elmes 1827)	51
1.14	Wilkins's Main Building, University College London	53
2.1	Map of Greece	77
2.2	The Fauvel plan of Athens (1787)	96
2.3	Kleanthis and Schaubert's plan for Athens, 29 June/11 July 1833	96
2.4	Kleanthis and Schaubert's plan for Athens, late 1833	97
2.5	Detail from the von Klenze plan of Athens	101
2.6	Schinkel's palace on the Acropolis (from Schinkel 1840)	104
2.7	Von Klenze's design for the Royal Palace (from Sechs Lithographien n.d.)	109
2.8	The Royal Palace, Athens (Bain News Service: Library of Congress: https://www.loc.gov/pictures/item/2014691079/)	111
2.9	The estimated population of Athens: 1809–40	114

2.10	Villa Ilissia	116
2.11	The Academy, Athens (Dimboukas at Wikimedia Commons: https://creativecommons.org/licenses/by-sa/3.0)	118
3.1	'A Roman Cobbler' (Bersezio 1872)	127
3.2	Rome's population 1860–78 (from Castiglioni 1879)	132
3.3	*Piano regalotore* of 1873	135
3.4	The Ministry of Finance	138
3.5	*Piano regalotore* of 1883	139
3.6	Piazza Vittorio (from Claude van der Grift, at Wikimedia Commons, CC BY-SA 4.0: https://creativecommons.org/licenses/by-sa/4.0)	143
3.7	Koch's Galleria Esedra	144
3.8	Palazzo Koch	145
3.9	Palazzo dell'esposizioni nazionale di belle arti	146
3.10	Palazzo di Giustizia (from Calderini 1918)	148
3.11	Sacconi and Maccagnani's design for il Vittoriano	151
3.12	Il Vittoriano	154
4.1	The Italian Pavilion at the Chicago World Fair, 1933	163
4.2	Façade at the *mostra della rivoluzione fascista*	163
4.3	Stazione Ostiense in 1940 (Wikipedia: https://en.wikipedia.org/wiki/File:Stazione_Ostiense_1940.jpg/*Il Messaggero*, 26 November 1940)	168
4.4	*Mussolini Wields the Pick* (Achille Beltrame) (© Bridgman images (asset 2778334))	171
4.5	Brasini's (1925) plan for piazza Colonna	172
4.6	The Foro Italico (Foro Mussolini 1937)	174
4.7	Stadio dei marmi (Foro Mussolini 1937)	174
4.8	Colonnade of the museo della civiltà romana, EUR	176
4.9	Vista from the Basilica dei Santi Pietro e Paolo	177
4.10	La terza Roma relief, EUR	178
4.11	Palazzo della Civiltà italiana, EUR	179

PREFACE

It was a time ago that I first went to Rome. It was a time later that I moved to London. And it was a time after that that I made it to Athens. All three places are important to me.

I first started thinking and writing about cities when I was working on Egyptian urbanism in the Roman period. As part of that project, I read a lot about modern cities. I realized, and this now sounds extremely naïve, that there was no easy method to understand cities. Cities are notable in their variety and their complexity. Simplification, ideal types, economic models and much early social theory do little to explain that variety and complexity. I soon realized that this characteristic evasion of regularities was common to urban communities, whether they be ancient or modern. I wrote about the cities of Egypt in the Roman and Byzantine periods and reflected on their cultural, social and economic complexities. And I hoped that I would eventually get to write about modern cities. This book is a realization of that hope after more than two decades.

That is a long gestation for any project. I made various false starts. I moved on to other projects. I gave talks at conferences. I read about city planning. I explored the intellectual traditions of urbanism and read perhaps more nineteenth-century utopian tracts and anarchist political theory than is healthy. I searched for a theme. I visited Rome and spent time in the British School's library. I met the late Terry Kirk, who kindly pointed me to so much that I did not know, interloper that I am. And eventually it seemed necessary to start again. But I had found a theme: the Classical in the imaginary of the modern city. I engineered some time. Everything else could wait.

A global pandemic struck. My responsibilities to my wonderful students and my dear colleagues could not be paused. Everything else was more important and nothing could wait. The project was put aside again until a measure of normality was restored. And then, I had six months. The bulk of the book was written in that time. It took another year to reduce the sprawl. And here it is. There is no definitive, last word on this subject. There is no end to the reading about or the seeing of these cities that could be done. I am painfully conscious of how incomplete any study of three such fascinating cities must be. But there is an end to a book.

Many debts have been accumulated, predominantly to people who have sat politely and listened to my obsessions: the colleagues who have tried to find supportive questions and the students who have at least pretended interest and to Bloomsbury and the lovely people there who have guided this project through its publication stages. I owe much to the casual conversation, to the mentions of buildings that have left little trace in the literature, and to those who have talked to me about towns and cities which have found no place in this literature. In following this interest, I have wandered so many cities and met kindness. The urban histories of alienation that form such an important part of the London chapter have not been my experience.

But the most intense debts are to those closest. My sons have often wondered why we are looking at this building, in this square, in this weather, but had the good grace not to complain too often or too loudly. Or at least, I didn't hear them.

I have wandered the many streets of these cities with Efi. Doing so has made me happy beyond measure. Born in central Athens and a citizen of the world city that is contemporary London, she torments me from time to time with the suggestion that we should leave the city for the countryside and a supposed rural idyll. In the hope that we will forever put off that day, I offer this book to her.

INTRODUCTION: AN ESSAY ON THE RECEPTION OF CLASSICAL ARCHITECTURE

Methods and approach

This book is about places, politics and culture. It starts from an observation. At the historical moment when economies, cultures and social values were transforming and the European nations were becoming imperial, the cities of this new, modern world were dressed in Classical architecture. Many cities laid claim to their modernity by adopting an antique style. One can make a long list of examples: Paris, Berlin, Vienna, Washington, Brussels, Naples, Munich, London, Edinburgh, Newcastle, Liverpool, Rome, Athens and most of the cities of the young United States. Through European colonialism, the Classical style traversed the globe, from South America to Africa to India to Australia. The neoclassical was the preferred style of the nineteenth-century urban revolution. My focus is in on the political ideologies underlying those aesthetic decisions.

Large-scale urban architectural projects are inevitably political. Public architecture situates citizens spatially in relation to each other and within social and economic systems. The metaphor of 'one's place in the world' is a significant acknowledgement of the influence of space on our social lives and identities. Architecture also operates as a system of signs which transmits the meaning of a built environment. The relationship between architectural signs and the social organization of space shapes the lived, everyday experience of the city. Major public architecture makes claims as to how the contemporary city is to be understood. The modern adoption of Classical architecture offers a historical interpretation of ancient urbanism and ancient societies, and situates the modern in relation to the Classical. This reception of a Classical past is formative in the construction of the city of modernity. It informs our experience and understanding of the built environment and situates that understanding in an interpretation of history. My focus is on politics of that reception.

The Classical reception of architecture is not straightforward. The prominence of neoclassical architecture in nineteenth-century cities demonstrates the ideological importance of the Classical. Major urban projects brought the Classical into the everyday lives of cities and the Classical legacy became an element in the politics of place. Contemporary political understanding of the legacy of the Classical fed into the remodelling of nineteenth-century cities. The Classical had been central to the political imaginaries of the West for centuries before *c.* 1800 (the starting point for my analysis) and has continued to be influential into the late twentieth century. The nineteenth-century understanding was specific to the intellectual and political circumstances of the time and is not necessarily shared by earlier or later thinkers. The reuse of Classical architectural forms had a value specific to the period and place of that reception. Even a supposedly close copy of a Classical building carried very different meanings in its modern environment from that of the original.

Classicism and the Construction of Capital Cities

The redeployment of Classical architectural forms was a global phenomenon. The West defined itself in large part through its cultural appropriation of the Classical. That appropriation was both general to European intellectual culture and specific to local environments. Classicism was a European aesthetic which intersected with local cultures, traditions and environments. Historical cultures are often considered within national and linguistic boundaries, but such parochialism makes little intellectual sense. Architectural discourse is profoundly international and has been so since the seventeenth century. Architecture happens locally, but specific places are made in a reception of ideas and in relation to socio-economic changes that know few borders. It is misleading to separate the histories of particular national urban developments from intellectual, political and aesthetic trends in Europe and elsewhere. To understand the phenomenon requires honouring both the European intellectual movements and the historical specifics of places.

My approach to this task is to focus on case studies: London, Athens and Rome. I could have chosen other cities. The choice is personal and academic. I live in London. I visit Athens most years. Rome is a city that I have found fascinating for as long as I can remember. The case studies also allow my narrative to cross the nineteenth century, from the urbanistic developments from Charing Cross to Regent's Park in London, to the creation of modern Athens in the 1830s and 1840s, to the post-1870 transformation of Rome into a national capital.

The cities present contrasts and similarities. All three were remodelled to represent their respective nations. London, though, was built as a city divided by social class with Classicism marking the territory of the upper orders. Athens corresponded to a colonial model with the Bavarian regime appropriating Classicism to justify their rule. Rome was developed as a modern technocratic city which turned away from Classicism and monumentalism until there was a perceived need for a major national monument around which the nation could be unified. Nationalism and class figure centrally in all three instances. These developments were to varying degrees authoritarian: there was an imposition of a particular model of society on a pre-existing and complex urban society. Those models reflected the views of political and social elites.

The studies end with fascist Rome. I end with the fascists in part because fascism captures in extreme form many of the contradictions of neoclassical urbanism and in part because every neoclassicism after 1945 exists in the shadow of the fascist and Nazi appropriation of the Classical. This long shadow is also cast into our understanding of the nineteenth-century city. Yet, as I shall argue in the epilogue, the reception of Classical architecture is not a teleological process in which modern neoclassicism found its inevitable culmination in fascism. The case-study approach allows full weight to be given to the historically specific nature of each reception and its interaction with a particular politics of place. As tracing the origins of fascist thought back into the Enlightenment does not constitute an argument that all Enlightenment thought is fascist, so fascist architectural aesthetics do not determine the interpretation and meaning of earlier neoclassicisms. In reverse, earlier neoclassicism does not render the fascist version any less authoritarian. Honouring the specifics of each instance of reception allows for

Introduction: An Essay on the Reception of Classical Architecture

difference and the fascist relationship with the Classical past was particularly intense and peculiar.

Nevertheless, there is a shared authoritarianism in these instances. The aesthetic carries a particular and common conception of history, society and political order. One can argue that the models of Roman imperial architecture carry an authoritarian and imperial weight that is necessarily repressive. The use of Classical styles in colonial environments reinforced that authoritarianism. As the nineteenth century progressed, the style became more closely associated with Western cultural authority, bourgeois and aristocratic cultural values, and social regimentation. It enhanced a common European and American association of Classicism with 'high culture', elitism, and class and racial prejudices. That is the history which this book aims to write.

I write as a social and intellectual historian rather than as an architect or an architectural critic. The least comfortable part of writing this book is attempting to transmit the aesthetic impact of buildings. That impact is both intensely personal and culturally determined. People may feel differently about particular buildings. They may care far more about the technical details and the minute differentiation of neoclassical styles. Those details were important in the same way that grammar and diction are important to literary production. The number of studies focused on defining the architectural orders attest to their significance. These were the rules. And yet, the academic elements were also a means of gatekeeping and exclusion. The grammatical may be important, but it is in service to other functions of a literary work. Similarly, architectural orders serve a cultural, political and historical aim that goes beyond a set of formal aesthetic rules. I focus on those aims rather than the technicalities. To those aghast at such temerity, I apologize.

The structure of the book is straightforward. In the remainder of the introduction, I consider issues of Classical reception with a focus on urbanism, the politics of Classical architectural forms in the modern city, and the social utopianism of major architectural interventions in the urban landscape. In the final section of the introduction, I trace the reception of Classical architecture from *c*. 1415 to *c*. 1800. This sets the scene for the following chapters. The first chapter treats London, *c*. 1800. It argues that the redevelopment of London was a response to uncertainties brought about by the rapid social and economic change of the period. The aim was to establish London as a bourgeois community and identify that community with nation, empire and civilization. The second chapter focuses on Athens and the Bavarian regime's attempt at an Athenian renaissance. The endeavour was inherently colonial and in conflict with the values of much of contemporary Greek society. That conflict arguably remained a feature of Greek cultural politics for generations but the rapid transformation of Greek society in the post-revolutionary period allowed a reappropriation of the Classical tradition. The third chapter focuses on Rome post-1870. The incorporation of Rome into the Italian state and the imposition of a new vision of the city as a modern capital displayed colonial dynamics. Although Classical forms were employed, it was not until the building of il Vittoriano that Classicism and nationalism were united in the city. The torrid history of that monument reflects an ambivalence inherent in the relationship of Classicism, bourgeois culture and Italian nationalism. In the final chapter, attention is turned to fascist Rome. The extremity of fascist ideology produced an architecture and an urbanism which promoted an ultranationalist mythic understanding of time and history. The architecture was symbolic, fantastical and deeply embedded within fascist ideology. Although it draws on similar cultural and intellectual elements, the extremity and the totalitarian symbolic aspirations were significantly different from the other earlier instances of urban development. Finally, in a brief epilogue, I consider the politics of Classicizing urbanism, arguing that the architectural style has reactionary and authoritarian connotations that were reinforced through its repeated modern usages. Classicism is in part a denial of historical change in favour of a particular arrangement of urban society that is supposedly timeless, rational and of universal benefit. The attempts to create fixity against the processes of history and render permanent a particular social hierarchy were hubristic, authoritarian and bound to fail.

Classical reception and architectural forms

Large-scale urban architecture is inherently ideological. It represents an urban community and an understanding of history and heritage as the powerful would like it to be. The major urban projects in London, Athens and Rome were aspirational. They looked to a future rather than to a current social or political reality. Architecture was seen as having metaphoric power to turn ideology into reality. There were elements of the new architectural visions that aimed at bringing to the fore an essential and supposedly hidden quality in the community. London was given the appearance of imperialist gentility that supposedly reflected its achievements. Bavarian Athens was an assertion of a 'real Greece' that the Greeks themselves could not perceive. Fascist Rome claimed to represent something fundamental, innate but previously scarcely visible about Rome and the Italian people. Even so, the architectural projects were laced with a speculative utopianism in which the powerful hoped or assumed that their urban interventions would generate their preferred societies.

Architectural forms influenced social interactions. The bourgeois cities of the nineteenth century required new spaces that allowed the bourgeoisie itself to come into existence. Cause and effect were intertwined. Changes in class structure gave greater prominence to the bourgeoisie. They required spaces of sociability that made their class visible to itself and to other social participants (Borsay 1989). They found those spaces in theatres, parks, promenades, museums, art galleries, churches, clubs, cafés, concert halls, libraries, assembly halls, lecture halls, universities, learned societies, arcades and shops. Journals and newspapers and various didactic and fictional guides to respectability provided the textual models for behaviour for the new and uncertain middle orders, while the new spaces provided the places in which those behavioural codes could be projected, performed and learnt (see, *exempli gratia*, Habermas 1991; Davidoff and Hall 1987; Harvey 1997).

Introduction: An Essay on the Reception of Classical Architecture

The increasing prominence of the bourgeoisie in eighteenth- and nineteenth-century cities was contemporary with the intensification of nationalism. The new bourgeois elites aimed to take control of increasingly complex state economic and administrative systems and reap the benefits of those systems. The nation was often appropriated by and associated with bourgeois values and cultural forms, particularly in capital cities. Complex, large and diverse societal groupings, such as nations and classes, depend on the voluntary adherence of individuals to the signs and behaviours that signify the group. That associative process is inherently flexible, capacious, contentious and responsive to individual circumstance. Such flexibility makes social class difficult to define closely and allows debate as to associated cultural values (Joyce 1991: 6–8). Manners, dress, education, linguistic choices and other social elements could be seen as markers of class. Further, markers of national identity overlapped with markers of class. Rather than associating national identity with the markers mostly widely shared in the political community, cultural markers of the nation were often inherent to a particular social group or class. Even language as the most widespread national cultural marker was divided by accent, diction and grammatical form to enforce class distinctions. Such associations were always contentious and political actors had an interest in disputing and enforcing the markers that defined identity groups. Whereas many cultural markers are ephemeral, architecture transmits an impression of stability and historical depth such as to make the markers of identity seem long-lasting and concrete.

Architecture derives meaning both from the symbolic associations of a style and the lived experience of social interaction. It provides for socio-economic functions and shapes and controls interactions on an everyday basis. It does not, however, determine those social interactions since they are also shaped by multiple economic and social circumstances. There is a dialectic between the macro-scale of urban design and its social intent and the micro-scale of behaviours in everyday interactions. Even if urban designers sometimes behave as if architecture will determine society, it does not. Major projects are rhetorical simplifications of the complex processes of social and cultural formation. In the absence of effective tools to produce an ideal social form, however, major architectural interventions are advanced in the fond hope that if the new city is constructed, the new society will follow.

Since architectural forms were normally built to be long-lasting, the socio-cultural relations associated with these forms were thereby given a patina of permanence. This permanence can be contrasted with the contingent and precarious social and economic relations that sustained individuals' social status in everyday social interactions. In London, Athens and Rome, the architectural developments reinforced social and ideological orders which were, to varying degrees, new, precarious and haunted by the prospect of revolutionary socio-political unrest. In a nationalistic ideology, the durability of a capital's architectural form attempted to represent the nation's transcendence of history. This had evident appeal in the context of rapid political, social and economic changes and the threats of revolution.

The Classical provided the signification for such durable, utopian spaces. It was associated with Enlightenment values and hence with modernity in its early forms. The turn to the Classical was a reaction against medievalism. It was connected to citizen politics and civic republicanism. In the early nineteenth-century, civic Classicism was also an appropriation of the style of the great houses and conjoined old aristocratic and new bourgeois values. Classicism positioned societies within an emerging civilizational discourse. That discourse was colonial in drawing distinctions between European societies and the rest of the globe and historical in finding an origin myth for European colonialism in Greece and Rome. It also laid claim to rationalism through an association with Enlightenment rationality.

Even though it seems unlikely that anyone could have believed that the new cities were close reconstructions of their Classical forebears, the symbolism pointed to the type of urban societies to which their political leaders aspired. They were also reactions against other models of urbanism. Bavarian Athens differentiated itself from the Ottoman city it replaced. Rome post 1870 set itself against the medievalism of the Papal city. For London, the fear was the city of proletarian crime, violence and revolution. The Classicizing city was set against the rapidly changing urban environments of modernity.

These modern cities sucked the children of villagers into a new urban world and swept away the imagined certainties of traditional societies. The green fields of social convention became dark oceans of tempestuous relations. Such cities were wonders that inspired horror. The poorest areas of Manchester were, in the pithy sentiments of Friedrich Engels (1892: 53), 'Hell upon Earth'. Such imagery finds echoes throughout Charles Dickens, especially *Hard Times* (1854), in Elizabeth Gaskell's *Mary Barton* (1848), Thomas Carlyle's *Past and Present* (1843) and William Blake's *Jerusalem* (1808) with its satanic mills. Victor Hugo's *Les Misérables* (1862) was, among other things, a great novel of the precarity of modern urban life. James Parton (1868: 21) in an essay for *Atlantic Monthly*, described a smoke-ridden, perpetually darkened Pittsburgh as 'Hell with the lid taken off'. Fear of the satanic nature of the industrial city ran deep in nineteenth-century culture.

The Classical was a means of holding off that vision in favour of an absolute, eternal cultural excellence. The columns would resist the chimneys. Grandiose Classicism fortified the new cities whether it be in the Greek purity of St George's Hall, Liverpool, or Theophil Hansen's Parlamentsgebäude in Vienna, or the Classical frontages of Newcastle. Train stations, the very epitome of modernity, often adopted aggressively Classical styles, perhaps the most famous examples being Euston Station, London, and Grand Central, New York. The American Republic housed its state and national institutions in neoclassical grandeur. Classicism was an attempt to prove that in modernity some elements of the changing social, economic and political landscape could be resisted by eternal, transhistorical values.

Classicism symbolized a modernity that was educated, rationalistic, bourgeois and eschewed revolutionary fervour. Those values were associated with citizen politics, but not with a specific constitutional arrangement. It could apply to the citizen republicanism of revolutionary America and France, the oligarchic monarchy of imperial Britain, the colonialism of Bavarian Athens, or the totalitarian populism of fascist Italy and Nazi Germany. The Classicizing modern city was an assertion of the ambitions of a social and political order to historical importance and to represent timeless political and cultural values.

Generating the new society

From a historical distance, the Classicizing utopianism of the nineteenth century appears conservative, but that is in part the nature of utopianism. Few utopian dreams transcend the generations. Much nineteenth-century utopian literature seems startlingly outmoded to modern readers (Beaumont 2012; Raban 1976: 1–11; Claeys 1997; 2008). Inevitably, utopian thought draws on the contemporary political imaginary and makes use of the intellectual resources at its disposal to imagine a new and different society (Jameson 2005). Those resources are frequently derived from history.

Architecture transmits a view of how a future community could be. That view needs to be sufficiently hegemonic to acquire the financial and political support for the construction of the imagined landscape. Inevitably, that landscape would need to appeal to political elites. Once built, the architecture encouraged those of a similar sensibility to engage. The new city provided opportunities for new social elements to relocate and become more visible. Thus, architecture could enhance processes of social change and in each of our instances, the new cities had some success in generating the societies for which they were planned.

Architecture's influence on social behaviours is subtle. Pierre Bourdieu's (1979; 1990) semiotic reconstruction of the Kabyle house demonstrated, for all its faults, the complexities of social thought that could be written into domestic space. Gaston Bachelard's (1958) musing on the poetics of spatial arrangements connected cultural and spatial forms in a web of signification that allowed the reading of a society's history, culture and social relations from its domestic space. Cultural values were naturalized by their representation in the built environment. For both Bourdieu and Bachelard such codings are deep structures, resistant to change. Whereas Bachelard's poetics require a learned interpreter (a poet), Bourdieu's spatial signs operate at a near subconscious level to inculcate social expectations and rules of behaviour. Those rules make sense because of a perceived relationship to supposedly fundamental values, such as gender, cosmology, and status.

Yet, the nexus of architectural forms and social ideologies is sensitive to change (Lefebvre 1991). The specific socio-economic and cultural system that gives rise to an urban form might theoretically be stable, but most modern cities are characterized by change. The potential for dissonance between architectural signs, intended social form and the individual in the cityscape is enhanced by historical change. The ability of the individual to read the environment can generate a sense of belonging or, conversely, alienation. Belonging generates social integration and identification with dominant ideologies. Alienation has the opposite tendency.

Any major architectural intervention is disruptive of a pre-existing environment. Such disruption is felt through this nexus of architecture and ideology. In our examples, architecture was often a manifesto for change. Since architectural design is utopian, there is already a distance between the intended social-cultural form of the city and the city as was. If the city develops along a contrary course, the possibility of alienation is increased. The city might be left with what seem like relics of an older failed, idealized and unreal representation of the community. Architectural forms do not determine political and social structures and cannot fix them against the winds of history.

Cities have their rhythms, the curious dances across time and space by which populations manage urban complexity (Lefebvre 1996). Such rhythms give the city a sense of individual continuity amidst the movement and provide individuals with a measure of order (Chakrabarty 1992a). They might not be obvious to the non-resident, for whom the continuous movement seems chaotic and to whom the regularities of the city are opaque (de Certeau 1984: 91–110 and see pp. 56–78 for the incomprehensibility of London).

These layered and multiple experiences of the city are always in tension with normative impositions. It is easier to create an aesthetic vision and trust that it will generate the ordered utopian city than to change deep-seated social complexity (Scott 1990). In an absence of spaces that acknowledge diversity, new cities can appear totalitarian in their uniformity and normativity and a reflection of the vast political and economic power of the elites that created them. A city that exhibits diversity and reflects the multiple periods of its creation has within it the ghosts of other social orders. These offer remembrances of historical processes and show the transitory nature of the present hegemonic social and economic orders. Potentially, such diversity creates spaces that resist the current order (Agnew 2010). The presence of such spaces can, however, generate anxiety. The nineteenth century saw not just grand display of the bourgeois public, but also a fear of the urban abyss and the spaces and people supposedly left behind by modernity (Walkowitz 1992).

Urban complexity, diversity, change and economic and social precarity generate anxiety. One response is an anti-urbanism that seeks fixity and certainty through an association with supposedly timeless values. This fixity could be found in the countryside, the nation or Classicism. Anti-urban movements reacted against the modern city and sought social and economic certainties in the conservatism of the small community or even with the isolationism of the bourgeois household (Alston 2012). Urban designers often built the countryside into the city. In London, the picturesque formed a link between city and country in the *rus in urbe* of the great parks. Villa architecture brought the values of the country to the town and the style of the town to the country.

The use of the Classical in large urban centres runs counter to any understanding of the city as a focus of change and multiplicity. The Classical lays claim to an absolute value that transcends the shifts of historical time. It is in denial of the contingencies of a cultural or social order. The Classical style depicted a singular vision of the city as an achievement for the ages. As such, its modern emergence represented a return to and an end of history. With history complete, all that was left was a continuous now in which the current social and political order would be forever maintained. As a reaction to a society and economy in flux as never before, this is both comprehensible and fantastical. History ends in a transcendent rule of reason. That reassuring narrative was made concrete in Classicism.

The rediscovery of Classical architecture

Classical architectural theory was transmitted to the modern world through text, most notably the ten books of Vitruvius' *De Architectura*. There is a mythic tale of the discovery of a manuscript of Vitruvius in the library of St Gallen in 1416 by the indefatigable Renaissance scholars and manuscript hunters Poggio Bracciolini and Cencio Rustici (Krinsky 1967). Yet, the manuscript tradition for Vitruvius is broad, especially for a technical text. Vitruvius survived in summary forms and within collections of mathematical and technical literature. Before 1400, there were forty-eight known manuscripts of Vitruvius in various libraries. Vitruvius was widely referenced by scholars from the ninth century onwards, though the work appears to have had no influence on architects before 1415 (Clarke 2002).

The first printed text of Vitruvius was 1486, but Vitruvius had inspired a growing body of architectural theory before that date (Krinsky 1967). Leon Battista Alberti wrote a Vitruvian architectural textbook, *de re aedificatoria*. Early versions were likely circulating from the 1460s before a much wider distribution from the 1470s (Kruft 1994: 41–50; Clarke 2002). By the late fifteenth century, ideas of a (utopian) model city were becoming more popular, perhaps influenced by Florentine urban experiments, and Vitruvius' audience was no longer limited to philosophers, mathematicians and antiquarians. Artists and architects were applying his techniques in the 1450s and 1460s notably in Florence and Urbino.

The sixteenth century saw a flourishing of Vitruvian architectural theory and practice. Most prominent was Andrea Palladio's (1570) *I quattro libri dell'architettura* which established the Palladian aristocratic villa as a new fashion. Sebastiano Serlio's (1987 [1584]) *I sette libri dell'architettura* had been circulating in preliminary versions after a partial publication in Venice in 1537. Serlio drew inspiration from Roman remains as well as Vitruvius. He was an architectural practitioner and advised on the building of Fontainebleau. Parts of the text were circulating in French by 1545 in Pieter Coecke van Aelst's translation (Serlio 1545). Van Aelst, a notable artist himself, was also responsible for translations into Flemish and German, and Serlio's text moved into English from Flemish. It was translated into Latin by 1569.

In late-seventeenth-century France, Vitruvian Classicism became entangled within a ferocious and politicized cultural debate. The Quarrel of Ancients and Moderns (*Querelle des Anciens et Modernes*) followed from the foundation of the Académie française in 1634. The Académie associated cultural value with the king. It was the ambition of the French political establishment to be seen as at least the equals of their Classical forebears. The Classical tradition was revered, but it could also be surpassed. Translations and adaptations of literary and theoretical works were seen as improving the originals. The most prominent polemic in favour of the moderns was Charles Perrault's (1687) poem, *Le Siècle de Louis le Grand*. Charles Perrault is now chiefly famous for his collections of French folktales, an interest that foreshadowed more nationalistic approaches to European culture. The contentious reaction to Perrault's claims for Louis's golden age led to a reassertion of his argument in his *Parallèle des Anciens et des Modernes*, published in several volumes from 1692 to 1693.

Architecture was central to this learned debate. Much of the focus was on highly technical matters, such as architectural orders, questions of ornamentation and the mathematics of perspective. Yet, what was at stake in such debates was France's position within a civilizational hierarchy. For the moderns, France needed to surpass ancient architectural and urban models. The Académie royale d'architecture was founded in 1671 as an advisory board and a discussion forum to facilitate Louis XIV's architectural endeavours. The ambitions of the regime were to be achieved by educating a generation of architects. François Blondel (1675) delivered and published a *Cours d'architecture*, which maintained an art-historical focus and eschewed practicality. It was based on Roland Fréart de Chambray (1650), *Parallèle de l'architecture antique et de la moderne* which was translated into English by John Evelyn by 1664. Fréart and Blondel were traditionalists and maintained that Vitruvian architecture was an absolute standard.

This perspective came under pressure from the 'moderns', most obviously represented by Claude Perrault, brother of Charles (Garnham 2013: 3–5). Claude Perrault's position reflected the complexity of contemporary French receptions of the Classics. To favour the moderns was not to reject the Classical, but to innovate and develop from within a generally accepted Classical aesthetic. Claude Perrault was a translator of Vitruvius. His key work of architectural theory, *Ordonnance des cinq espèces de colonnes selon la méthode des anciens* (1683), studied both Classical and contemporary designs. Instead of relying on an art-historical method, Perrault engaged with the physics of perception and issues of mathematical proportion. By relying on natural science, the epistemological basis of his architectural theory became a claim to absolute value. Even as he sponsored a contemporary reinvention of Classical form, he proclaimed the Classical as superior not because of cultural associations, but because it was scientifically better.

Claude Perrault's connections, in part through Charles, enabled him to put his theories into action in the east façade of the Louvre (1667–74). The façade is Vitruvian, borrowing from temple architecture and displaying a mathematical balance in which double columns provide a regular and ordered variety. This purist Classicism was to be cited repeatedly over the following century. The focus on mathematical regularity influenced Edmund Burke's (1998: IV 13) view of the sublime as resting in the optic response to order, repetition and variation, rather than in cultural associations. Marc-Antoine Laugier, *Essai sur l'architecture* (1753: 3), to be discussed below, made much of the emotional affect produced by the architectural work of art. This affect was attained by Perrault, mastered by the Greeks, and was a natural, scientific response to architectural form.

This understanding influenced architectural theorists for at least the next 150 years. By the middle of the eighteenth century, Classicism was symbolic of rationalism and was

Introduction: An Essay on the Reception of Classical Architecture

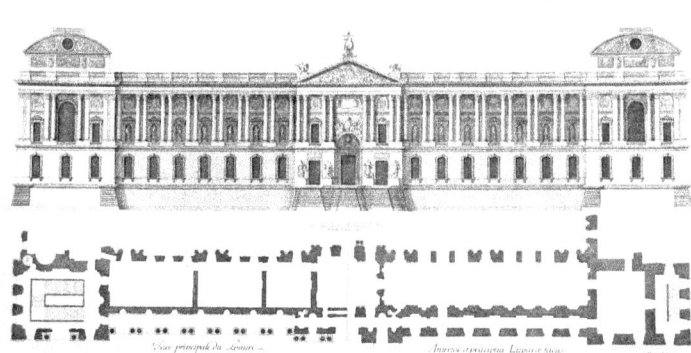

Figure 0.1 The east façade of the Louvre, as engraved by Jean Marot (1676) from the Bibliothèque municipal de Valenciennes.

seen as a natural and ideal form. That ideal jumped via a metaphoric transference from the aesthetic to the socio-political. The natural, excellent order of architecture was associated with a natural, excellent order of society. The regulated columns of Classical orders spoke of socio-aesthetic discipline and hierarchies which were transhistorical. In French thought, the promise of an ordered Classical community was to be set against the political, architectural and social disorder of Paris. As Laugier put it:

> Our cities are always what they were, a heap of houses, heaped together confusedly, without economy, without design. No part of this disorder is more sensible, more shocking, than in Paris. The center of this capital has not changed almost at all for three hundred years: we see there every day the same number of little streets, strait, winding, which breaths nothing but disorder and smells.
>
> *Laugier 1755: 234–5*

Paris had a centralized authority and a city architect from 1769. This institutional provision allowed architects to dream of large-scale urban interventions. These were mostly fanciful redesigns that rejected dense urban environments in favour of aristocratic parks (Vidler 1990: 136; Bergdoll 2000: 48–50). Claude-Nicolas Ledoux (1736–1806) was one of the more successful of these city improvers. He made his name designing Palladian hôtels set in parklands so that his patrons could experience a form of urbane rurality. He later became involved in the development of a new customs boundary for Paris, where the authorities could tax goods coming into the city. He designed forty-two of the gatehouses. These designs deployed variants of Classical styling (Vidler 1990). Since there was a charge on wine, Parisians were accustomed to travel through the barrier on Sundays to enjoy the benefits of cheaper alcohol. Consequently, Ledoux also designed suburban taverns and at least one brothel (Ledoux 1804). After 1771, as Commissaire des Salines, he planned a new model settlement at the Saline de Chaux, near Besançon in

11

eastern France. The scheme for the village features a geometric plan and Classical architectural styling as was common in contemporary Enlightenment utopianism (Chouquer and Daumas 2008). The village was set in a productive rural parkland. It was an idealized aesthetic and social architecture, though the exact mechanics of its social ordering are opaque (Baridon 2008).

Marc-Antoine Laugier was the most influential eighteenth-century architectural theorist. His *Essai sur l'architecture* was published in 1753. There was already an English translation by 1755. He drew a distinction between the architectural modernization of the grand houses and the neglect of the city:

> the taste of embellishments is become general ... [but] this taste should not be confined to houses, it should extend itself to entire cities. The most part of our cities have remained in a state of negligence, of confusion and disorder, wherein the ignorance and rusticity of our forefathers have put them.
>
> *Laugier 1755: 234*

His solution was ambitious:

> Paris is already one of the greatest cities of the world. Nothing can be more worthy for so brave a nation, so ingenious, so powerful as the French nation, as to undertake upon a new design to make of it one of the finest cities of the universe.
>
> *Laugier 1755: 252*

Laugier (1753: 3–7) followed Perrault in viewing architecture as rationalistic and scientific. He derived architecture from natural forms and considered Greek Classical architecture preeminent through its naturalism. His position drew some support from Vitruvius whose origin myth for architecture found its original forms in male and female bodies (*De Architectura* 3.1), and the primitive hut (*De Architectura* 2.1; Bergdoll 2000: 11–12). Laugier saw the essence of architecture in its origins:

> the little rustic cabin ... is the model upon which all the magnificences of architecture have been imagined, it is in coming near in the execution of the simplicity of this first model, that avoid all essential defects, that we lay hold on true perfection. Pieces of wood raised perpendicularly, give us the idea of columns. The horizontal pieces that are laid upon them afford us the idea of entablatures. In fine the inclining pieces which form the roof give us the idea of the pediment ... It is in the essential parts that all the beauties consist; in the part, added thereto by caprice, consist all the defects'.
>
> *Laugier 1755: 11–12*

Such naturalism fed into Laugier's ideal of the city. Cities should resemble forests or parks in which beauty is made through a multitude of wide avenues, in which the whole

Introduction: An Essay on the Reception of Classical Architecture

Figure 0.2 Laugier's Hut: the origins of architecture (Laugier 1753: frontispiece).

exhibited order and symmetry, as well as variety and contrast (Laugier 1755: 248–9, compare Sennett 1994).

Not all were so convinced. Durand (2000: 82) complained that 'if the architects who invented the orders were seeking to imitate the hut, they imitated it extremely badly' and pointed out that a hut was not a natural object. For Durand (1817) architecture was primarily geometry. Its aesthetic value lay in its simplicity and functionality, characteristics which were, in his view, ahistorical.

Yet, Durand appears to have been in the minority. There was an evident desire in the eighteenth and early nineteenth centuries to connect architecture to nature, nature to political and social structures, and society to history in a chain of associative reasoning. Laugier (1753: 4) claimed that Greek architectural perfection stemmed from their position as a 'nation priviligiée' which was translated as 'a free nation'. In 1802, Ledoux (1847: xiii) proclaimed that 'the blood of Pericles stirs in my veins'. William Chambers (1791: i–ii) saw architecture as a key element in the improvement of society, allowing for 'a well-ordered commerce and the display of grandeur and pre-eminence'. His treatise was written to 'diffuse the love of vertu' (1791: iv). Sir John Soane (2000: 38–9) related the achievements of Greek architects to political freedom and artistic decline to their loss of that freedom. He associated great architecture with statesmanship and civic improvement and asserted the universal historical truth that architecture shapes the mind, though he leaves it to his readers to work out how (Soane 2000: 39–41; 1827: preface). Thomas Hope (1835: 1–44) expressed similar views. For him, architecture sprang plant-like from soil and climate and was a manifestation of a nation. The Greek achievement was to

13

preserve architectural truth through a freedom that was transmitted via architectural forms that maintained conformity with the naturalism of the hut.

The ideal and natural form of architecture emerged in conjunction with an ideal and natural form of politics and society. A free citizen would live within a natural social order and there would seem to be an assumption that a lack of freedom would be observable in a deviation from the ideal and natural architectural form. Thus, if a city gave the appearance of Classicism, it was intrinsically free. Analogy and association traversed the logical gaps in this argument. It is evident, for instance, that there was no association of the Classical and a free society, and yet that association was useful for authoritarian regimes. By the late eighteenth century, the use of Classical architecture was not a purely aesthetic choice or a reverential rediscovery of a Classical heritage. It was a political and cultural claim for the rational or natural status of a particular social and political order.

The association with the Classical laid claim to the values and virtues of that social and political order transcending historically specific socio-economic arrangements. It was utopian in conception. The model was not of a society finding representation for its cultural and political systems in a particular architectural aesthetic, but of the acquisition of an absolute value or virtue as the best, most natural society in or through the Classical architectural forms. Such distinction was threatened by the historical processes of decline and fall as experienced in the erosion of Greek cultural excellence and the traumas of Roman Republican collapse. Socio-economic processes of historical change, normatively seen as decline and fall, were to be resisted from this cultural citadel. Arguably, this has been the fundamental political stance of Classicism throughout modernity.

Enlightenment architectural discourse was European. The centres of architectural development, teaching and publication were networked through the movement of people and of texts. The focus of activity shifted over the seventeenth and eighteenth centuries from northern Italy to Paris.

Young, ambitious architects travelled. Most spent considerable time in Italy. Many studied in Paris. All read the French architectural theorists (Bergdoll 2000: 128–32). Paris was the intermediary through which the modern Classical was transmitted. Many of the key texts were translated into multiple languages with notable rapidity. Advances in printing allowed images to be distributed. Palladian influences fed into English country house designs. These ideas returned to Europe through the published plans in *Vitruvius Britannicus* (Campbell 1715–25). Some of the major British architects had huge libraries (see pp. 28–30; Watkin 1996: 98–130). Julien David Le Roy's *Les ruines des plus beaux monuments de la Grèce* of 1758 and Stuart and Revett's *Antiquities of Athens* of 1762 and later were European intellectual sensations that made the architecture of Classical Greece accessible.

Friedrich Gilly, who can be seen as a founding figure in German neoclassicism studied in Paris in 1799. His tutor, Langhans, had attended the Paris architectural school. Gilly had also visited London (Bothe 1979). On his return to Berlin, he founded an architecture club which was rapidly transformed into the Berliner Bauakademie, the first professional architectural institution in Germany. He equipped it with his personal library, which featured the major French theorists: Laugier, Blondel, Briseux, Peyre and de Quincy (Neumeyer 1994). Gilly, who died aged twenty-eight in 1800, had taken on Karl Friedrich

Introduction: An Essay on the Reception of Classical Architecture

Schinkel as a pupil in 1797. Schinkel was influenced by Durand (Goalen 1991). He became the leading architect of his generation, training among others Eduard Schaubert and Stamatios Kleanthis, who were presiding influences in the development of Bavarian Athens (Kühn 1979; see pp. 92–107). Leo von Klenze worked with Gilly and spent time in Paris before finding a position in Munich from where he was called in to advise on the plans for Athens (Hamdorf 1986). Friedrich von Gärtner also studied in Paris under Durand before he was summoned to Athens (Hederer 1976: 10) and the Danish architects Christian and Theophil Hansen studied in Paris and were influenced by Schinkel before they went to Athens (Schwarz 2003; Badema-Phountoulake 2001: 35; Haiko 2013) and later to Vienna. Networks of learned architects relied on networks of patronage within the very small aristocratic cliques that ruled Europe.

This international exchange of styles and ideas had paradoxical aspects. In an age of burgeoning nationalism in which divergent national identities and cultures were being discovered and invented, the architectural forms of many of the leading cities were becoming similar. Moreover, the predominant Classical style was by its very nature at some distance from the vernacular and localized forms common in those separate nations. The authorities were also competitive and emulative: London, Berlin and Munich competed with Paris. The rulers of Athens and post-1870s Rome aspired for their cities to meet the standards of other international capitals. The capacity of architecture to make places of specific cultural and historical resonances was conflated with neoclassical internationalism and the cross-cultural rationalism of the Enlightenment.

Such Classicism frequently positioned itself at distance from the contemporary and every day. Gilly was noted for his stylistic simplicity, stripping away unnecessary decoration. Neumeyer (1994) argues that his architecture attempted to materialize the aesthetic Absolute in which beauty was defined in the separation from the finite of the everyday. That otherworldliness is captured in a design for a Tempel der Einsamkeit of 1799/1800 and in his most famous design, that for the Friedrichsdenkmal, which was to be situated at the Potsdam Gate precisely because that was one the quieter points of the city and thus a suitable place for reflection and contemplation (Gilly 1994: 129–38).

Potts (1991: 47–55) argues that Schinkel's architecture similarly sought the aesthetics of freedom in which beauty and the sublime stepped beyond the material into the realm

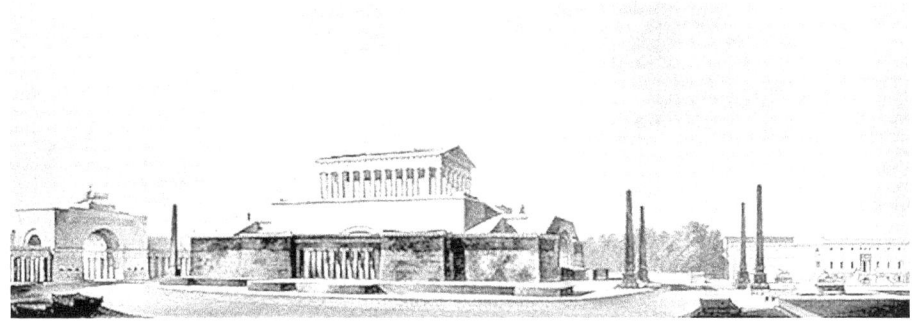

Figure 0.3 Gilly's Friedrichsdenkmal, Berlin.

Classicism and the Construction of Capital Cities

Figure 0.4 The Parthenon in elevation from Stuart and Revett (1787).

of pure thought. He was influenced by his contemporary Berliner philosopher, Fichte. Friedrich Schiller also perceived freedom as a psychological state embedded in a pure aesthetics and separate to any specific environment (Schiller 2016; Güthenke 2008: 34–5). The Greek achievement was to have established an art beyond culture. In consequence, the emulation of Greek art was a reproduction of a pure aesthetic and an ethic of freedom that was fundamentally individual rather than political or social.

This denial of the everyday can be seen in Stuart and Revett's (1787) ground-breaking drawings. They began Volume II with a plan of the Acropolis that elided the non-antique buildings. The first plate depicts the Parthenon in its contemporary surroundings but is followed by a restored elevation from which all traces of history and ruination have been removed (Mallouchou-Tufano 1994). The rest of the presentation features architectural detail and drawings of restored aspects. It is a pattern repeated in the treatment of the various antiquities. Local picturesque sets the scene for the clarity of an architectural

Figure 0.5 The Parthenon in Athens from Stuart and Revett (1787).

16

Introduction: An Essay on the Reception of Classical Architecture

Figure 0.6 The Tower of the Winds from Stuart and Revett (1787).

drawing that severed those ruins from any understanding of place. We thus have two ways of seeing the buildings: the Tower of the Winds in the Capuchin monastery is a spectral presence within a Christian tradition. But as a technical drawing it becomes a pure aesthetic model. Removing such structures from their urban context was preparation for their transference to Western European discourse.

It is in this reduced form that we now experience the Parthenon, in large part due the efforts of the Bavarian regime's architects and archaeologists (see pp. 103–8). As an architectural form, the Parthenon could be anywhere: in Berlin as a representation of Enlightened monarchy; in Regensburg to sacralize German cultural achievement; in London as an adornment of the imperial centre; or in Edinburgh as a monument to the Scottish war dead (Borbein 1979; Kondaratos 1994; Cleghorn 1824). The aestheticization of the architectural form separated the monument from the specifics of place, making it the common architectural currency of Western Europe and the Enlightenment.

In what follows, I explore the processes by which those purified aesthetic forms were put into specific spaces, given new meanings and cultural and political associations, and employed to make new places.

CHAPTER 1
LONDON: A CIVIL SOCIETY, 1800–1820

Introduction: A new society

London and Paris have claims to be the earliest modern cities. They were the first capitals to be transformed in the modern processes of urbanization. London was the first European city since Ancient Rome to house a million inhabitants. Paris was rather better equipped than London to meet the challenges that modern growth posed. British eighteenth-century monarchs were politically weaker than their French counterparts and closely bound by parliamentary institutions. London had no centralized civic authority. There had been interventions in the urban fabric, most notably after the great fire of 1666, but London's governance was politically and institutionally fragmented. Eighteenth-century monarchs built, but their attention shifted between multiple palaces beyond the fringes of the city, such as Richmond, Windsor and Hampton Court, and Central London residences, such as St James's Palace, Carlton House and later Buckingham House. These were not, at least before the later development of Buckingham Palace, imposing presences on the cityscape. Architectural guides tended to focus more on the great church complexes of St Paul's and Westminster Abbey than the royal centres and the twin cities of London and Westminster were more multifocal than Paris.

From *c.* 1550 to *c.* 1650, London entered a period of rapid growth in which the population rose from about 70,000 to 400,000, an increase of 470 per cent. Over the next century, the increase slowed but the population reached about 675,000 by 1750 (increase of 68 per cent) and 900,000 by the time of the first census in 1801 (34 per cent in fifty years). London's population was about 7 per cent of the English total in 1650 and 11 per cent in 1750.[1] We have more reliable statistics from 1801 after the institution of the national census. London's population in the century after 1801 rose by 5,400,000, an increase of approximately 490 per cent. For the period 1801–31, on which we focus, the rise was to 1,878,229 or about 71 per cent. London was a demographic and economic hub, and its influence was made greater by the mobility of the population; many people passed through the city without residing there permanently.

Population figures for large cities have an arbitrary quality. Defining the boundary of a city is not straightforward and administrative boundaries often do not reflect the realities of urban form. Some residents also have an interest in not appearing in any official registers. The author of *The Ambulator* (1782: x) thought the population in 1782 was between 725,000 and 1,000,000, but if one included the periphery that population would be 1,500,000. *Leigh's New Picture of London* (Leigh 1830: 30) advanced the surprisingly low figure of 1,263,595 in 170,000 houses.[2] *The Great Metropolis* (Grant 1836: 3) and Robert Ainslie's (1836: 1) sermon on London reported that the population was likely in excess of 2,000,000 in 250,000 houses. London was not only the largest city

Classicism and the Construction of Capital Cities

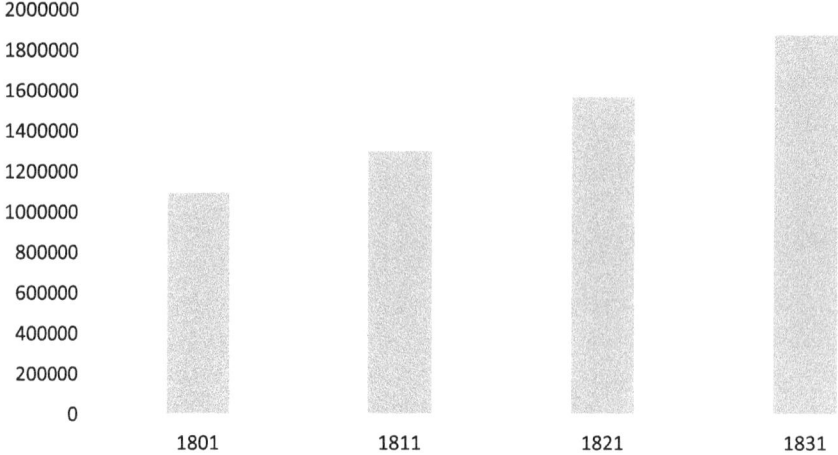

Figure 1.1 London's census population: 1801–31.

in the world (overtaking Beijing in around 1800), but it was growing at a rapid rate, putting demands on housing and civic infrastructure.

This expansion was driven primarily by the economic changes sweeping Britain. Those changes can be associated with the Industrial Revolution and with the increased trading related to Britain's imperial expansion. The first modern metropolis provided considerable economic opportunities. It is difficult to imagine that it did not inspire Adam Smith's *Wealth of Nations* (1776) and the growing eighteenth-century understanding that they were living through revolutionary times.

This new social and economic order was not limited to London. Provincial market towns, such as Chester, acquired new spaces of sociability by the mid to late eighteenth century. These served new class identities formed in the shifting of social hierarchies and a new distribution of wealth. The new spaces were sometimes purpose built and sometimes developed from existing buildings such as inns. They included assembly rooms, where dances could be held, theatres and, notably, shops (Stobart 1998). 'Polite' retail involved browsing the goods, buying on credit and social recognition, and had been an increasing part of an urban renaissance in the smaller towns and cities (Borsay 1989; Berry 2002; Hann and Stobart 2005). The sector's existence depended on a wider distribution of disposable wealth and a growing consciousness of fashion. The gentry did not disappear but the 'respectable classes' broadened and increasingly sought to find their place and space in society.

The eighteenth and early nineteenth century saw a concentration of wealth in the upper echelons of society (De Vries 1993). The gentry and middling landowners experienced a sustained boom in agricultural incomes with consequent beneficial effects on their spending power and consumption of goods. Rents on agricultural lands had been relatively stable from 1630–9 to 1715–19 (rising about 20 per cent over the period). By 1765–9, rents had risen a further 30 per cent on the 1715–19 level and fifty years later, by 1815–19, rents were a further 130 per cent higher.[3]

Opportunities in trade and manufacture allowed a fortunate few of lower origins to amass fortunes sufficient to allow them to pass among the higher born. In London especially, merchant wealth met landed wealth in a new, enlarged and prosperous elite (Colley 1992: 155–93). Such social mobility caused significant anxiety. For the wealthy and aristocratic there were issues of reliably in recognizing one's peers. For the aspiring, there was the problem of adhering to unfamiliar social *mores*. The micro-divisions of the upper orders were maintained, but this new elite was largely integrated. That integration took place in the new social spaces of the capital. London was a national stage on which elites asserted identities and on which, consequently, broad class divisions were drawn. London provided the spaces which made possible a dense network of elite social interactions. This intensity of social interaction and the socially exclusive nature of those interactions remade and reinforced elite class identity. The spaces in which this occurred came to be marked by Classical architectural forms.

London was institutionally, politically and socially divided. There were two primary units: the City of London and the City of Westminster. The City of London was densely developed and there was an established social and economic divide between the East and West Ends, which mapped loosely onto these administrative divisions. The East depended heavily on trade and housed the old institutions of London. The docks spread thickly across the northern banks of the Thames especially and the port's business was rapidly intensifying to service imperial trade networks. The port, the merchants and trading houses, and the growing manufacturing industries were pulling a working population into the East End. The West End, by contrast, served the court and the political-legal establishment. Westminster had been less intensively developed than the City and there was consequently more open space nearer the centre. The lands around Westminster tended to be part of noble estates that had been established in proximity to the court in the aftermath of the Restoration of 1688. The north of London was characterized by a mix of villages and estates, the lands of which were rented out for small farming.

The most aristocratic area was in the vicinity of St James's Square and St James's Street. These were close to the old royal palaces of St James and Carlton House and the new palace in Buckingham House as well as to Parliament. This area became a zone of male sociability. Clubs and theatres catered for the new and old wealth.

The demographic expansion of London created a requirement for new housing. Provision was mostly unplanned as a city level but was far from chaotic. The major later eighteenth-century developments came mainly to the north and west of the city on the estates of the nobility. These areas became Farringdon, Bloomsbury, Marylebone and the West End. Initially, aristocratic individuals were prepared to live relatively modestly in London while displaying their wealth and status in their country seats. The Bloomsbury squares provided for a mix of the established wealthy and the rising middle classes. The new housing was socially zoned. Working-class areas may have been adjacent, but the new squares were topographically distinct.

Even in the early eighteenth century, London was a problem for the English. Its size and diversity meant that it was different from other cities. By the end of the century, those problems had multiplied. Accounts of London from this period manifest many of

Classicism and the Construction of Capital Cities

Figure 1.2 Map of London in 1806 (detail from Mogg 1806).

the concerns that we would associate with modern urbanism, particularly around social recognition, community cohesion, trust and criminality. There was a fear of precariousness and the reduction of social bonds to financial transactions. The old moral and social order seemed to be in decay amid a tornado of immorality. Concerns focused, inevitably, on sex and money. The old representative Englishman, John Bull, who opposed French tyranny through a continual consumption of beef, was a creature of the countryside, but whether he was a comfortable resident of London was less clear.

From the middle of the eighteenth century, there was a growing desire to improve London. By *c.* 1800 politicians were aiming to make London a metropolis worthy of Britain and a rival to Paris. The most significant development came with the building of a new north–south route through the city from Pall Mall and Charing Cross to what became Regent's Park. New Street, later named Regent Street, was a conscious topographic division of the city which was meant to restrict the access of the working classes to the West End. It allowed the wealthier classes to establish a social and topographic exclusivity in their movements between the new park and Westminster and through the various clubs, theatres and shops. The development provided the space and opportunity for the extensive monumentalization of nation, monarchy and Empire.

Many of the new buildings and the design of the Regent Street development from Charing Cross to Regent's Park employed Greek revival or Roman styles. Classicism was used for new structures of sociability and culture, such as the British Museum, the National Gallery and educational institutions, such as University College London. It was also used for more private institutions, the clubs and villas. Monuments also were established in Classical Greek and Roman imperial styles.

The Classical had carried radical political resonances drawn from the American and French revolutions. However, in the remodelling of London, that revolutionary energy was diverted. Classicism had been extensively employed within aristocratic houses as a mark of cultural and educational distinction. In the late eighteenth and early nineteenth centuries, it became the architecture of the 'public'. This 'public' was a class-based formation that included the bourgeoisie and aristocracy and excluded the working classes (the 'mechanics' in contemporary descriptions).

Class differentials were central to the contemporary experience of London. Members of the rising bourgeoisie were anxious to understand themselves in the context of the nation and the city. Architecture provided a reassuring marker of an orderly and comprehensible social topography. It reinforced an already emerging class-based topography and provided spaces of social interaction in which class identities could be learnt and performed. Although such social zones were porous, particularly for men, the reshaping of the city encouraged the development of class-specific locations of sociability that reinforced class identities.

In what follows, I explore the development of the class-divided city in early nineteenth-century London in its interaction with Classical architectural forms. As in France and Germany, architecture became a learned profession with a predominant aesthetic that was increasingly closely identified with the Classical. Much of the architectural discourse was imbued with political values. The Classical was associated with an ordered, hierarchical and disciplined community, often in explicit contrast to the disorderly nature of aristocratic behaviours and the city of the lower classes. Concern with the mechanics expressed anxiety over the possibility of revolutionary uprisings and, more broadly, a fear of a potential loss of social control in the complex, growing metropolis.

The new, broader elite expressed its identity via a network of political ideas that encompassed the public and the nation. Classical architecture allowed that public and nation to become visible. Elements of those ideas, notably citizenship and empire, were derived from the Classical. The Classical was a mode by which those ideas could be appropriated by the elite and by which that elite could be rendered distinct from the lower classes. It was also an appropriation of a previously aristocratic style for the new public in a manner which paved the way for a symbolic unification of the rising bourgeoisie and old aristocratic orders. That unity was reinforced in the celebration of notions of nation and empire.

These strands of thought established an ambivalent view of London. The city was a source of wealth and culture and the scene of national display. It was also discomforting, confusing and socially threatening. The changes sweeping the nation were nowhere more visible than in the capital. Classicism had an absolute and timeless value that promised to restrain the forces of historical and social change. Its appeal was aesthetic and political. In late-eighteenth-century architectural theory, the Classical was reassuringly blended with the landscape: town was to meet country in urban aesthetics as traditional rural hierarchies were to meet urban class politics. Social and political harmony was to be generated in an oneiric aesthetic hegemony of the neoclassical.

In the first section, I consider the theory of this development through contemporary architectural discourse. The second section looks at the imposition of these theories in the Regent Street and Regent's Park developments. The third section considers the evident and widespread social anxiety engendered by London society. Finally, I explore the political and architectural assertion of a 'respectable city' to represent and define the nation. Classical architecture allowed the English (and increasingly the British) to self-define as a republican citizen and imperial nation. The prestige of nation and empire was appropriated by the elite. The working-class city was a place of excitement and danger but was construed as an internal other in ways that echoed the colonial system which that same elite was imposing on the world.

Architectural imaginations in London

In this section, I examine the development of architectural ideas in London from the mid eighteenth century onwards and their engagement with the Classical. The predominance of ecclesiastical and aristocratic buildings was already shifting by the middle of the eighteenth century when the architect and engineer John Gwynn pressed for a public architecture of magnificence. Magnificence was associated with the Classical. That desire intensified over the next fifty years and the ambition for a magnificent public architecture was delivered by a new generation of learned British architects. These men were fluent in contemporary European architectural theory and in the Classical legacy. They and their patrons not only produced a new urban aesthetic for London but developed the spaces and aesthetic markers for a new society.

In 1766 John Gwynn decried the state of London. He wrote that:

> The English are now what the Romans were of old, distinguished like them by power and opulence, and excelling all other nations in commerce and navigation. Our wisdom is respected, our laws envied, and our dominions are spread over a large part of the globe.
>
> *Gwynn 1766: xv*

And yet, there was a want of public magnificence in London and Westminster. Gwynn condemned the irregularity of the streets (1776: 6). He complained about the ruined nature of many of the buildings, even at the centre of the city. He was particularly savage on the Palace of St James, which he saw as:

> an object of reproach to the kingdom in general, it is universally condemned, and the meanest subject who has seen it, laments that his Prince resides in a house so ill-becoming the state and grandeur of the most powerful and respectable monarch in the universe; a Prince whose supreme happiness consists in promoting the good and welfare of his subjects, who is himself a lover of the arts, and under whose happy auspices artists of every denomination or real merit and ingenuity can never doubt of obtaining patronage and encouragement in a manner adequate to their respective abilities.
>
> *Gwynn 1776: 10*

Gwynn compared mid-eighteenth-century Britain to Rome in its imperial dominion and its commercial and economic power. Yet, there was no public monumentality to represent the magnificence of nation and king.

This was a radical agenda. Magnificence had, Gwynn claimed, been seen as the equivalent of luxury and therefore undermining of moral value. However, magnificence brought wealth and power through the work it generated. It refined taste, produced true elegance in the nobleman, and cleanliness and decorum in the mechanic. Magnificence made the citizen and affirmed and displayed social order (Gwynn 1776: 1–2).

His viewpoint echoed Bernard Mandeville's *The Fable of the Bees* (1724: preface) in which he argued for the social necessity of vices and corruption in establishing the dynamic for the raising of 'vast, potent and polite Societies, as they have been under several great Common-wealths and Monarchies that have flourished since the Creation'. For Mandeville, the filthiness of London was a measure of its success and although men might prefer the sweetness and repose of the garden, the city was essential for the generation of wealth and power. This comparison of garden and city was a religious argument, contrasting an egalitarian religious pastoralism with a hierarchic secular civilization. If the garden was the divine offering, urban civilization was the historical achievement of men.

In Gwynn's vision, London needed buildings to represent order and nation. He did admire some contemporary architecture, such as the church of St Martin-in-the-Fields, with its magnificent Classical portico, and New Church (St Mary le Strand) on the Strand. He saw in the Earl of Burlington a contemporary Maecenas of architecture (Gwynn 1776: 47). Burlington's primary architectural achievement was Chiswick House (1729), a very early example of Palladian architecture in Britain. Gwynn distinguished between religious and secular architecture but did not envisage a public sphere separate from the aristocratic houses. Royal and aristocratic palaces could provide the Roman magnificence he craved.

Eighteenth-century country houses achieved magnificence through Classical styling, as can be seen in Holkham Hall, Norfolk, built by Thomas Coke from 1727 onwards and designed by Matthew Brettingham (see Brettingham 1761), Marble Hill House, Twickenham (1729), Houghton Hall, Norfolk (1722) and in the many designs collected by Colen Campbell (1715–25) in *Vitruvius Britannicus*. At the same time, English aristocrats were collecting Classical artefacts and transporting them to Britain to decorate their houses. Classicism was an expression of the landed elite's political, social and economic power. Although Roman political theory had been important to the English radicals of the previous two centuries, country-house Classicism symbolized the vast wealth, elevated social standing and cultural authority of the landowners. Those values were acquired through an elite education and the fundamentally aristocratic experience of the Grand Tour. The houses referenced imperial Rome's leisured aristocratic villas rather than the spaces of contentious citizen politics.

Status was connected to an aesthetic order that could only be appreciated by the educated. Paradoxically, that order was presented as both natural and contrived. In Edmund Burke's understanding, the effect of the architectural arrangement was innate to the building (the vibrations hitting the eye) and existed separately to issues of taste. His architectural theory linked trees and pillars and admired the ordered ranks of planted avenues (Burke 1998: IV 23). Ordered beauty was natural and scientific (see pp. 12–15). Taste, however, was important. People could acquire taste, allowing them to appreciate the truly beautiful (Burke 1998: IV 68–70).

Architecture, then, could only be appreciated fully by the learned, and consequently the Classically educated and informed aristocrat required a Classically-trained architect to build his villa. Gwynn complained that the most active architects of his day were moonlighting from their primary profession as coffin-makers (1766: 68) and thus lacked the necessary education to provide public magnificence, but that situation was already transforming, with a new and educated architectural profession emerging with knowledge of contemporary French and Italian architectural theory and the Classical tradition.

The need for architectural education fuelled and funded a rush of archaeological expeditions and publications. In the mid-eighteenth century, there was very little direct knowledge of Greek architecture. Julien-David Le Roy published *Les ruines des plus beaux monuments de la Grèce* in 1758. An English version was published in 1759. The Society of Dilettanti sponsored James Stuart and Nicholas Revett's trip to Athens in 1751. Publication was delayed. The first volume was published in 1762, but with a limited circulation.[4] Later volumes followed in 1787, 1794 and 1816.[5] But their findings were circulating sufficiently to be mocked in William Hogarth's 1761 etching *The Five Orders of Periwigs* (Crook 1972: 14–15; Watkin 1982: 18). The Society of Dilettanti also funded Richard Chandler's travels and survey in Ionia (Chandler 1769). Robert Wood's *The Ruins of Palmyra* (1753), and his *The Ruins of Balbec* (1757) increased knowledge of the Classical architecture of the Middle East. Wood's *Palmyra* especially caused a stir in antiquarian and architectural circles and his Palmyran scenes were painted as a backdrop at Vauxhall Gardens in 1754 (Watkin 1999).

Many of the major architects spent time studying in Rome, including William Kent, Matthew Brettingham, Nicholas Revett and James Stuart. Robert Adam was in Italy for several years in the late 1750s, despite receiving a thorough architectural education from his father, William Adam. James Gibbs, the architect of St Martin-in-the-Fields, was also trained in Rome. Few of the leading architects of the period were 'gentlemen architects' in the style of the Earl of Burlington, and most had relatively humble origins or grew up in the trade.

The extraordinary John Soane (1753–1837) provides insight into the architectural culture of *c.* 1800. Soane's relationships with other architects were sometimes difficult. Many of his more imaginative proposals did not get built, surviving in elaborate drawings which were in themselves art works (Soane 1827). He had a fondness for grand public architecture. Alongside his Bank of England, there were designs for a west entry to London at Hyde Park, modelled on the propylaia to the Acropolis; a vast new royal palace for London notable for its multiple Classical arches, central square, with obelisks and fountain, and temple-like entry into the main palace building; new law courts; two designs for a new 'Senate', the first imagined in an innovative triangular form in park land

Figure 1.3 *Bird's Eye View of a Design for a Triumphal Bridge.*

Figure 1.4 Soane's entry to Downing Place (from Elmes 1827).

with three separate temple-like porches with three rows of columns supporting the entry points, linking vast colonnades and a central domed building, and the second as a central building with two vast flanking courts with temple-like and triumphal arch entrances and vast curved porticoes; a 'triumphal bridge' which was accessed through extended triumphal arches and associated buildings and centred on a large domed building; and an equally grand entry into Downing Street from Whitehall, complete with triumphal arch and extended colonnade. Much of this was fantasy architecture, visions of what a utopian city might look like. Yet, though unreal, impractical and, one presumes, vastly expensive, Soane offered a vision of what an unconstrained architectural imagination could create.

Soane was one of several architects of the period whose professional skills allowed social mobility. He was the son of brick-maker from Reading. He had early practical building experience but was without the educational advantages that might have followed from a more elite parentage. He won a travel scholarship in 1778 which enabled him to visit Italy. He was a jobbing architect, following the money, and initially the money was in the country estates rather than more prestigious civic developments. Ptolemy Dean (2006) estimates that nearly two-thirds of his work was on country estates rather than on public projects or in London. Soane was appointed to the Surveyorship of the Bank of England in 1788 and presided over the rapid expansion and development of the site. His designs for the frontage were heavily influence by Hadrian's villa at Tivoli (Elmes 1827: 128–31). He had previously worked on interiors and a whole host of smaller projects; perhaps his first major public project was the Dulwich Picture Gallery (opened in 1815). His Council Office (1826) was supposedly a reconstruction of the Temple of Jupiter Stator in the Roman Forum, known only from texts. He was appointed as Professor of Architecture at the Royal Academy in 1806 replacing George Dance, who had the distinction of never delivering a lecture in his seven years in the role. Soane's lectures as reconstructed by David Watkin (Soane 2000; Watkin 1996: 9) provide us with a 'textbook account' of architecture in the early nineteenth century.

Soane was an educator who found inspiration in intellectual debates. His library was vast. He had 6,857 volumes (Harris and Savage 2004). The printed *Catalogue* (1878) runs to 414 pages. The books are mostly in English, French and Italian. There were a few texts in Latin, but he accessed Classical texts mostly through translations. He had some 30,000 architectural and topographical drawings including a hugely important collection of Renaissance designs (http://collections.soane.org/home; Fairburn 1998). It was a compendious resource all of which was crammed into his house on Lincoln's Inn Fields. Dana Arnold (2000: 112) compares the jumble of inspiration in Soane's house to the artistic and architectural encounter with the disorder of contemporary Rome.

Soane had multiple copies of the key texts, of which the main inspiration remained Vitruvius. He had texts of Vitruvius or compendia drawn from Vitruvius in French (4), Italian (3), Latin (2) and English (6). He had one copy of the more specialist Frontinus *De aquaeductu Urbis Romae*. Andrea Palladio's *I quattro libri dell'architettura* was represented by three Italian editions, four English editions, two French and eleven volumes of selections and studies. He possessed five versions of Leon Battista Alberti's *Della architettura*. The Blondels were represented in two works by François and three by Jacques François. There were treatises from Jean Nicolas Durand, Louis le Brun's *Théorie de l'architecture*, and C. A. Jombert's *Architecture moderne*. The library had Laugier's *Essai sur l'architecture* in six copies, three in French and three in English, and his *Observations sur l'architecture* in another three copies. Charles Ledoux, whose publications were more complicated, is represented by *L'architecture considérée*. Claude Perrault's abridgements of Vitruvius and his *Ordonnance des cinq espèces de colonnes* appear in French and English along with some minor writings. He also had various volumes on the Classical architectural orders, a subject of extended debate in the period. Alongside Perrault, his collection included Marie-Joseph Peyre's *Oeuvres d'architecture*, Riou's *The Grecian*

Orders, D. de Rossi's *Studio di architettura civile* and Giacomo Barozzi da Vignola's *Regola delli cinque ordini d'architettura* in six Italian and French versions and two English.

Much of the contemporary debate on architecture turned on comparison with the ancients and focused heavily on Roman and Italian examples. Soane had a collection of academic architectural studies focused on this issue, including eight works by G. B. Falda on the architecture of Rome; Just Fréart's *Parallèle de l'architecture antique et moderne* in two French versions and five English translations; three volumes of Giovanni Cipriani's architectural drawings; F. Milizia's volumes on Italian architecture, civil architecture and the lives of architects in Italian and English translations; Giofreddo's *Dell'architettura;* V. Scamozzi's *Dell'idea della architettura universale* and the *Notitia architectonica Italiana* by J. Gwilt. He had a vast collection of publications on Italian antiquities, both ancient and later. These included Inwood's volumes *Le Antichità di Ercolano* as well as multivolume reports of the finds at Herculaneum. He had numerous catalogues of Italian art and antiquities including G. J. Rossi's various works on Roman temples, villas, and designs, and a copy of F. de Rossi's *Ritratto di Roma moderna*. Alongside Ruggieri's *Studio d'architettura civile*, he also had Ruggieri's studies on the architecture of Florence. Perhaps more notably, there were twenty-two folios of the works of Francesco Piranesi and Giovanni Battista Piranesi, sometimes in multiple copies, and Winckelmann's *Monumenti antichi* together with his *Geschichte der Kunst des Alterthums* in French translations: there is almost nothing in German in the library.

He also collected the work of leading British architects. The catalogue lists fifteen works by William, Robert and James Adam; four versions of Matthew Brettingham's designs for Holkham Hall; two copies of Campbell's *Vitruvius Britannicus* and Richardson's *New Vitruvius Britannicus*; eight works by Sir William Chambers in multiple copies and with some translated into French; John Evelyn's *A Parallel of the Antient Architecture with the Modern* in five copies; seven folios of George Dance's designs; James Elmes's lectures on architecture and his *Metropolitan Improvements*; James Gibbs's sketches and four printed works on architectural ornamentation; four copies of Goodwin's *Domestic Architecture*; and his *Historical Description of St Paul's*; John Gwynn's *London and Westminster Improved*; William Halfpenny's *Practical Architecture* and *The Modern Builder's Assistant*; collections of the designs of Inigo Jones; four volumes by the English architect Roger Morris, published between 1728 and 1759; Augustus Pugin's essay on Gothic architecture; and Robert Smirke's *Specimens of Continental Architecture*. There was also a considerable technical literature on finances, mathematics, aesthetics, perspective, and on roads and numerous treatises on chimneys, which, of course, had no Classical parallel to which the moderns could refer. The library also contained Soane's own publications and notes.

Alongside the focus on ancient and Italian architecture and its contemporary reception, he had books on British and French antiquities, including books on Merlin and on Stonehenge as well as material on London and other English and French towns and cities. There was also a good collection of early archaeological works or travellers' accounts from Greece such as Charles Cockerell's studies of Athenian antiquities and *The Temple of Jupiter Olympus at Agrigentum*; the Dilettanti Society's *Ionian Antiquities* and their *Unedited Antiquities of Attica*; Dodwell's *Views in Greece* and *A Classical and Topographical Tour through Greece*; Inwood's study *The Erechtheion at Athens*; Le Roy's *Les ruines des plus beaux monuments de la Grèce* in four copies under Le Roy and five copies under Roy. Quatremère de Quincy was represented by seven works on Roman, Greek and Egyptian architecture and a partial translation by Soane himself of his book on Egyptian architecture. There were three copies of Stuart and Revett's *Antiquities of Athens*, including a French translation. There were also studies of 'Greek' architecture from further afield, such as William Wilkins's *The Antiquities of Magna Graecia*; Robert Wood's *The Ruins of Palmyra* in English and French, and Wood's *Ruins of Balbec*.

In addition to works which might be thought of as constituting a bibliography of art, architecture and archaeology, he had two copies of the thirty-three volume *Encyclopédie* (1765); three copies of Edmund Burke's *Philosophical Enquiry into the Origin of our Ideas of the Sublime and Beautiful*; Gibbon's *Decline and Fall*; the essays of Montaigne, Montesquieu and Locke; an extensive collection of the works of Rousseau; Schlegel's art history; Adam Smith's *Wealth of Nations*; and works by Voltaire.

Soane's vision for architecture was intellectual, historical and aesthetic. In this, he followed his patron in the profession, William Chambers (1791: 7–9), who wrote in his 1759 treatise on decorative architecture that the architect needed to be healthy, vigorous, a good pen man, good at maths, be able to run an office and of good moral character, proficient in French and Italian (he does not reference German or Latin), a genius, and educated in Ancient history, fable and mythology. Chambers studied in Paris with Blondel and spent several years in Italy and was evidently a crucial link between French intellectual traditions and the academic architectural groups in Britain. In his first pages on the history of architecture, Chambers has an extended quote from 'Father Laugier', even before he references Vitruvius.

In Soane's first lecture after his 1806 appointment as the Royal Academy's Professor of Architecture (2000: 41), he assured his distinguished audience that architecture was not a mere mechanical art. He drew a distinction between the various builders who had employed practical skills in the development of contemporary architecture and the skilled and learned architects whom he was hoping to educate. He was also making a point about social class: the mechanicals were the working-class from whom Soane was differentiating himself and his fellow architects.

His lectures to the Royal Academy (Soane 2000) take an initially historical approach. He begins with the Egyptians before moving rapidly to the Greeks. The first five lectures follow the history of architecture as far as his present day. From lecture six onwards, he concentrates on architectural themes, such as arches and decorations (lecture 6), villas (lecture 7), chimneys, windows and staircases (lecture 8), doors and roofs (lecture 9), ornamental buildings and gardens (lecture 10), external and internal decorations (lecture 11), refinement and taste, bridges and obelisks (lecture 12).

In his introductory lecture on Egypt and Greece, Soane offers a theory of architecture familiar from Laugier.[6] Soane's collection of artefacts includes a model 'hut', used to illustrate the origins of Classical architecture and architectural elements, such as the pediment and columns. He also had a second version in which the model hut had more of the attributes of a Greek temple.[7] He developed Laugier to draw a connection from architecture to wonder to psychology to political form:

> From such simple [Greek] ideas and almost imperceptible changes we owe all the beauty, scenery, and enchantment in the forms of the great Grecian edifices whose stately structures, whose elegant forms and magnificent appearance, have been for ages the delight, wonder, and admiration of the most refined minds of all countries, and will continue to be so as long as any knowledge of pure art remains, or superior intellect is cultivated and respected ... When the Grecian states lost their liberty and became colonies to their successful rivals, the Romans, they likewise lost in a great degree their love for the arts, but not entirely as long as the empire of their conquerors continued ... The buildings of ancient times show the splendid effects of architecture, and its power to affect the mind ... The influence of architecture on the minds of men appears to have been general to all ages.
>
> *Soane 2000: 38–9*

The key evaluative terms of 'beauty' and 'enchantment' relate to a natural aesthetic which transcends history and culture. Like Burke, Soane saw architecture as influencing the mind. Yet, this excellence is an aesthetic manifestation of freedom. Architecture is then both of public benefit in improving the minds of men and is associated with and a product of a free society. Quite what Soane understood as constituting a free society is not clear. Such a society might have princes and powerful statesmen (Soane 2000: 41) and in lecture 2, imperial Roman architecture is seen as unsurpassed in splendour (43).

Although London did not possess buildings to rival the sublime qualities of Mediterranean Classical remains or even the buildings of Paris (he sees St Paul's as failing to achieve those heights), he hoped for circumstances which would lead to a revival of Greek excellence:

> Grecian art may be concealed as fire under embers, but be assured my young friends, on the first favourable opportunity it will burst forth like the glorious sun from behind clouds of darkness and show itself in all the splendour of eternal truth, and again become the admiration of mankind.
>
> *Soane 2000: 124*

This revival might happen in England:

> ... let us hope, the magic powers of architecture will be called into action to raise structures for use, and magnificence, in grandeur and extent, commensurate with the national glory and character, and such as may vie with the proudest monuments of our art. No longer let foreigners reproach us with the total want of great national monuments; let us, in this respect, imitate our Gallic neighbours, let us look at their Pantheon, an edifice dedicated exclusively to the honour of great men. This superb Fane, calculated to immortalize the memory of its architect, Soufflot, will

ever be ranked amongst the finest specimens of modern art that Europe can boast. In the portico and the interior of this superb structure the classical elegance and refined graces of Grecian architecture are united with all the intricacy, variety, and pleasing effects of the finest examples of our Gothic cathedrals. The erection of a few such buildings in this country ... would soon raise the art to its ancient glory.

Soane 2000: 173

This English Renaissance was to compete with the best in Parisian architecture and express the eternal truths of Greece. If his theory was embedded in the Enlightenment, Soane's expression tends to the Romantic. His vision was picturesque. The more fanciful architecture unified landscape and architecture, corresponding to his theoretical position that architecture emerged from nature and in representation of nature. Nevertheless, London could host Grecian and Parisian neoclassical architectural forms.[8]

Soane's aesthetics represent a set of values that were widely shared among the architects and builders of early nineteenth-century London. John Billington, for example, asserted that Classical Greece showed superiority in architecture and sculpture over that of other nations since 'Greece ... [was] blessed with a mild and beautiful climate, and enjoying political and civil institutions the most favourable to genius'. Beauty and nature were inherently connected to architecture and civil institutions. Architecture declined the further it was abstracted from nature (Billington 1834: 15, 22, 39).

Greek revival architecture was not merely an early-nineteenth-century consumer preference. It reflected an understanding of architecture and of rationality and of society and politics. The aesthetic codified certain class values and was best appreciated by the refined and educated. Consequently, the architect needed to be learned and was not,

Figure 1.5 Soane's entry to Lothbury Court, Bank of England.

whatever his social origin, one of the 'mechanics'. Billington (1834: 282–4) stressed the importance of discernment and of taste: the beautiful was only to be understood by the educated and after long study.

Soane's desire for a new public architecture to rival that of Rome was expressed through the rhetoric of nationalism. Paris was the immediate rival. His choice of Soufflot's Pantheon as an exemplification of French superiority was significant. The Pantheon was aggressively Classical and as a monument to the republican heroes of France, it was also a representation of public values. A republic enabled men to become great and then honoured them in public monuments.

The emergence of the public national space was a process which undermined the exclusively aristocratic nature of good society. Billington associated republican politics with public splendour rather than private magnificence, providing a more Classical understanding of luxury than we see in Gwynn and Mandeville.

> When the acquirement of power and the possession of riches afford men the means of obtaining luxuries, the simplicity of the style adopted in the habitations of their fellow citizens is rejected; they will no longer inhabit constructions which designate them as being mortals, but they raise for their dwellings, temples and other similar edifices. At Athens, the dwellings were simple, and the public edifices sumptuous. Rome also retained, for a long period, this same moderation in the residences of individual.... If we consider the antique cities, where the arts took up their abode, how modest and unassuming appeared the residences! But how immense were their public edifices; how their temples, tribunals, &c., majestically distinguished themselves from the adjacent habitations! It was in them that the public pride and enjoyment was placed, being considered as the property of each citizen; and the fame and pleasure attached to their magnificence, was not individual, but national.'
>
> *Billington 1834: 292–4*

Magnificent public spaces represented the virtuous nation and Billington draws a political, aesthetic and moral contrast with the aristocratic nation.

This was, however, no return to the Classically-inspired English radicalism of the sixteenth and seventeenth centuries. Instead, it reflected a particular understanding of the British political and social order as having successfully blended a citizen republic and the traditions of aristocracy and monarchy. James Elmes dedicated his *Metropolitan Improvements* to the king, a common performance of political loyalty at the time, and offered a paean to England under George IV.

> The power of England, concentrated by peace and directed by wise counsels, extends its general influence over a greater portion of the habitable globe, than did ever that of Rome by the demoralizing influence of the sword. And under the benign reign of your Majesty, we must derive more advantages from the liberal cultivation of the arts of peace, than did any other people, from the most triumphant consequences of successful war.

In Rome the few were prodigiously rich, and the mass of the people as wretchedly poor; in Britain the converse of this unhappy condition prevails: and the majority of your Majesty's subjects are in the secure enjoyment of liberty, prosperity and happiness. This state of prosperity arises principally from a due regard for the honours of a noble ancestry; from active commerce, industrious trade, skilful manufactures, agriculture, arts, science, literature, and those magnificent rewards, which are ever the solace of genius and talents, from a patriotic sovereign and enlightened people.

Elmes 1827: iv–v

The Georgian paradise depended on social order and good governance, and provided liberty, prosperity and happiness for the majority. The Enlightened people spread their wisdom across the globe while George IV cleared 'pestilential alleys and squalid hovels, 'substituting rich and varied architecture and park-like scenery' so as 'to render London, the Rome of modern history'. The Georgian present is 'THE AUGUSTAN AGE OF ENGLAND' (Elmes 1827: 1–2; cf 4). In 1816, the author of *Remarks on the Buildings and Improvements in London and Elsewhere* had hoped for an Augustan sponsor for London to 'give a becoming beauty and magnificence to the seat of government, and to the capital of so mighty an empire' (Remarks 1816: 7). For Elmes, London had found its Augustus in George IV (see Arnold 2000: 55).

Elmes depicted London's new architecture as a manifestation of a utopian regime. The social and political triumph of the age was prosperity and unity, which found its architectural representation in the West End and Regent's Park. That analysis was extended to locate Britain as Rome's superior in the history of civilizations and to proclaim the British's Empire's beneficial contribution to the world. The association with the Augustan period linked politics, culture and empire in a utopian consensus of world-historical significance.

The demand for a London which was worthy of its imperial age was a trope of architectural writing of the period. Even George Griffin Stonestreet, who was hostile to any expenditure on architectural monumentality, demanded the improvement of London on the grounds of its imperial success:

The Metropolis of the British *Empire*, consolidated, invigorated, extended as it stands; the envy of its rivals, the admiration of the world: – the Metropolis of such a nation, ought to suitable to its dignity, its wealth, its population, and its magnitude: Possessing the highest advantages of situation and capability, much yet remains to be done to give it all the splendour and conveniences to which it is entitled.

Stonestreet 1800: 3

Such imperial confidence was inevitably haunted by the end of Empire. The Romantic engagement with Rome stressed ruination. English architectural aesthetics had engaged with the aesthetic of ruins in the eighteenth century, though much of this was in an architectural display of learning and culture within the parklands of estates.[9] William Chambers, for instance, constructed a ruined arch in Kew Gardens in 1759.

Soane also engaged with the aesthetic of ruination. He had a major collection of the sketches of Piranesi, but he also envisioned the potential ruination of London. His collaborator, Joseph Gandy (1771–1843), produced a famous painting of his Bank of England as a cutaway axonometric representation that recalls an urban field of ruins akin to Pompeii.[10] Gandy also painted a vision of the rotunda of the Bank of England in ruins (*Architectural Ruins: A Vision*) and Soane had it hung next to John Martin's 1831 *The Fall of Babylon* which depicts a vast metropolis being struck down, complete with multiple distressed women in very fashionable early-nineteenth-century dress.[11] One of the strangest parts of Soane's house is a ruined hermitage built into the basement. In a low period in his personal and professional life, he imagined his own house as a ruin and what an antiquarian would have made of the multifarious collection of antiquities that would have been preserved in the archaeology.[12]

Alongside imperial confidence, there was psychological insecurity and a fear of the collapse of civilization. This fear spans the period. Henry Fielding's (1751) pamphlet on poverty and crime is haunted by the fall of Rome, which was supposedly brought about by moral decay consequent upon luxury. Rather than propose a repression of contemporary luxury, he suggested that the rich were capable of sustaining their moral and societal values in spite of temptation, and it was the poor whose suppression was required (xxxi–xxxii). Class conflict and fear of the lower orders disturbed the wealthy even before the French Revolution gave weight to these fears. One might see the

Figure 1.6 *Architectural Ruins: A Vision* (Joseph Gandy 1798).

celebration of the unity of the British elite and the Georgian golden age as a triumphant denial of revolutionary worries.[13]

The most eloquent testimony to this political psychology comes (as often) from outside, from Chateaubriand. François de Chateaubriand, Duc d'Enghien (1768–1848) was a victim of the French Revolution and in 1792 found himself exiled and destitute in London. As a prominent member of the French aristocracy, he was extraordinarily well connected among the refugees and the English aristocracy but was without a viable income. His history of his first period in London illustrates the thin line between riches and starvation (Chateaubriand 1849: III 154–77). Thomas de Quincey (2013) produced a similar account of his near starvation on the streets of London in 1803. Chateaubriand's experience of personal precarity was entangled with his pervasive fear of societal collapse.

On his return to London in 1822 as ambassador, Chateaubriand dined with his friend Lord Liverpool.

> I made to my host an elogium on the solidity of this English monarchy pondering on the equal balance of liberty and power. The venerable lord, lifts and stretching his arms, showed me the city and said to me, 'What is so solid in these enormous towns? One serious insurrection and all is lost'. It seemed to me that I completed a course in England like that I had had other times in the ruins of Athens, in Jerusalem, and Memphis and at Carthage. In calling before me the centuries of Albion, in passing from the renowned to the renowned, in seeing them perish one by one, I experienced a moment of sorrowful dizziness/vertigo. … All this is finished; the superior and the mediocre; hates and loves; fortunes and miseries; oppressors and the oppressed; torturers and victims, kings and peoples, all sleeping in the same silence and the same dust.
>
> *Chateaubriand 1849: IV 155*

Britain was the undisputed global power of the age and London was proudly asserting its status as a global city. Yet, Lord Liverpool, the Tory Prime Minister, was gripped by the frailty of the regime, conscious that the suppressed masses of London might follow the revolutionary path of Paris.

Chateaubriand's reaction was one of dizzying Romantic reflection on the passing nature of the individual in the face of the long histories of civilizations. His sense of self was shaken before the experience of time. He was too good a Classicist not to be aware of the associations with Scipio Aemilianus watching and weeping as his troops were sacking Carthage since this was the eventual fate of Rome, as it had been of Troy,[14] and so London would one day fall and all would be dust.

This spectre of ruination seems not so much to be a counterpoint to the power of the imperial nation as a psychological association. The distinctive and somewhat solipsistic association of the status of the individual and the stability of society is a feature of Romantic engagements with Classical ruination (see pp. 124–31). It differs from the ruin-gazing of later periods and the *mimesis* of imperial Rome (Hell 2019). At the very moment of imperial triumph, the masters of the world are possessed of visions of their own temporal and historical limitations.[15] And yet their visions turned ruination from a traumatic and life-threatening experience in which society came unbound and death stalked the streets to a touristic drama to be vicariously enjoyed by the rich and powerful.

Visions of ruination did not undermine the imperial ambitions of the nation, but were an undertone of fear that everything, even the most powerful of imperial civilizations, lacked solidity. The vision of ruination has limited power if the to-be-ruined society is not at its height. Thus, Gandy's imagining of the ruination of Soane's triumphant Bank of England is an expression of the financial and artistic power of Georgian London whose only rival was Classical Athens and Augustan Rome. Despite their confidence in the absolute value of their politics, society and architecture, the end of the Classical world was a spectre haunting Georgian feasts. The Fall of London would be a tragedy to compare with the Fall of Rome. It was to be resisted through social and political discipline and loyalty to the established utopian order. If the Romans were moved to unity by the fear of their enemies (notably the Carthaginians), the Georgian enemy were the mechanics who skulked to the east of the city.

Imperial ambitions and national confidence were represented in London's architecture. That architecture was not thought of as merely symbolic but was also seen as generative. In this perception, the architects of London followed their French theorists.[16] Their architectural theory fused ideas of community, class, history and the Classical inheritance. Their architecture built a national, bourgeois public sphere. It glorified the Georgian achievement of a political order that united the monarchy, nobility and the rising bourgeoisie, and asserted the city's timeless cultural values. And yet, as Lord Liverpool's dramatic gesturing made clear, the great cities of the nineteenth century posed an existential challenge. The sweeping power of economic and social change threatened the established order. Revolution was an ever-present threat, justifying repressive and protective measures. Rome itself had fallen and the new society was haunted by the fate of its precursor.

Building the class city: The Regent's Park developments

The late eighteenth-century expansion of London saw increased class differentiation in the city. London attracted the wealthy from the provinces. Trade and industry were making fortunes for a new prosperous middle class. These people needed homes. George Stonestreet (1800: 19) complained that the merchant classes were being forced away from their work in the City of London to the new squares in the west. The wealthy and respectable required housing that matched their status and this was only available in the new developments. The consequence was increasing residential separation by social class.

Housing was constructed along the northern edge of London, through the modern areas of Clerkenwell, Farringdon and Bloomsbury. Bloomsbury Square was laid out as early as 1661 by the Earl of Southampton. It set a template for later expansion. Queen

Square was laid out from 1716. Bedford Square was built after 1775. Mecklenburgh and Brunswick Squares were begun in 1792 and 1795. Russell Square was built from 1804. Tavistock Square was under development from 1806 and Gordon and Woburn Squares in the 1820s. The major developments were on land owned by the Foundling Estate (east of Russell Square), the Bedford Estate, the Skinners' Company Estate and Edward Lucas. The motivation for the developments was primarily commercial. As a result, they were piecemeal, extending when and where the opportunities arose.

The house building was speculative: there was no resident identified before building started. Consequently, developments required considerable capital investment without guaranteed returns. This was enabled through agreements between landowners and builders and financed through a combination of the builder's own capital, capital advances from the estates, loans and peppercorn rents for the builders. The risk was held mostly by the builder who needed confidence that there would be an available renter on completion of the building works. Although there were varying grades of houses, they were mostly taken up by the relatively prosperous. There was also an incentive to keep expenses low by both cutting down on unnecessary ornamentation. Mostly, the houses and were stripped down and utilitarian.

Much of the land was owned by large estates. For the estates, the houses and squares were a long-term investment. They contributed some capital and perhaps faced short-term reductions in income from the peppercorn rents and during the period of construction, but the asset value of their property was considerable increased. The initial investment could be sustained on the expectation of vastly increased incomes as the houses were relet at higher lease and rental values. These financial arrangements proved attractive and James Burton's building firm alone built 1,762 houses in Bloomsbury between 1792 and 1814 (Arnold 2005: 15–51).

The Russell family owned much of what became Bloomsbury though the estate was divided between two branches of the family, the Dukes of Bedford and the Marquises of Tavistock in 1760. In 1733, the Bloomsbury estate brought in an income of £4,517 per annum, which rose to £7,187 by 1751. In 1775, with the estate divided, the Marquis of Tavistock's Bloomsbury properties produced £9,055. Ten years later, the income was £13,653. By 1811, it had reached £20,273 and income crossed £25,000 by 1816. By 1819, the Duke of Bedford's London estate was matching his rural income in producing £48,413 per annum. Direct comparison is difficult, but it looks as though the property was producing an income ten times greater by 1830 than in 1760. Fortunes were being made (Olsen 1964: 220-2).

James Malcolm (1803: 6–8) saw the Bloomsbury development as a great improvement. Bedford Square's neat houses and trees 'made that part of London pleasing and respectable'. The new Brunswick Square had the same effect while the on-going build in Russell Square was expected to be 'very elegant'. 'Neatness', 'respectability' and 'elegance' were terms loaded with assumptions of social status. Russell Square gardens were designed by Humphrey Repton, the leading landscape gardener of the day (Arnold 2005: 3–6). This brought some aristocratic gloss to the Square. What was being built for the prospective residents was not just domestic space but a style of life.

Figure 1.7 Map of Bloomsbury and the West End in 1806 (detail from Mogg 1806).

The money being made through these developments attracted the attention of the Crown. The leases on Mary-le-bone Park were up for renewal in 1811 and the Crown's representatives, the Treasury and the Commissioners of His Majesty's Woods, Forests and Land Revenues, saw an opportunity. On 13 June 1812, the Commissioners presented the *First Report of the Commissioners of His Majesty's Woods, Forests and Land Revenues* to Parliament on 13 June 1812 (*First Report* 1812). At that point, the total income from Crown lands was £283,160 per annum of which £40,000 came from the London properties.

The Commissioners were presented with two plans for the development of the Regent's Park. The first was from the firm of Leverton and Chawner and the second was from the architect John Nash (1752–1835). The Commissioners recommended Nash's plan. In addition to the development of the park, the Commission proposed the construction of a new straight north-south route from Pall Mall to the park, which was to become first New Street and then Regent Street. The route had been in the planning for some years, but the key to advancing the scheme was that the Regent's Park houses would seem more attractive if there were good communications to the West End.

Leverton and Chawner's proposal appeared in *First Report* 1812: Appendix 12A. The park was 540 acres and vastly larger than any of the areas developed over the previous century. That posed a financial challenge since no individual builder would be able to meet the costs of leasing the land. The Crown would have to seek multiple builders and Leverton and Chawner envisaged a gradual development of Bloomsbury-style squares, starting in the south of the park, and thus closest to the fashionable areas of the town. They doubted that the development would be such as to fill the entire area and envisaged that two-thirds of the park would be taken by the squares with spaces left for villa development and service provision in the northern third. They proposed to follow closely the model for development established by the Dukes of Bedford and Portland through Bloomsbury with the proviso that the public interest would be best served if the designs of the houses be subject to the approval of the Crown authorities. The perceived danger was that any poorly constructed residences would bring down the value of the whole.

Leverton and Chowner gave little detail on the development of New Street. In a letter of 27 December 1808, they estimated the cost of the clearance for a new broad road to be £290,000 of which £236,000 would be immediately recouped from the resale of the demolition materials. Their proposal thus envisaged an initial outlay of £54,000 which was justified by the public benefit the new street would bring, the increased asset value of the Crown land, and the prospect of vastly increased lease incomes once speculative building had taken place.

The Nash scheme (*First Report* 1812: Appendix 12B) was more radical. As he summarizes the purposes of his report:

> The principles on which this Report, and the designs accompanying it, are formed, and the objects proposed to be obtained, are, that Mary-le-bone Park shall he made to contribute to the healthfulness, beauty, and advantage, of that quarter of the Metropolis; that the Houses and Buildings to be erected shall be of that useful description, and permanent construction, and possess such local advantages, as shall be likely to assure a great augmentation of Revenue to the Crown at the expiration of the Leases; that the attraction of open space, free air, and the scenery of Nature, with the means and invitation of exercise on horseback, on foot, and in Carriages, shall be preserved or created in Mary-le-bone Park, as allurements and motives for the wealthy part of the Public to establish themselves therein; and that the advantages which the circumstances of the situation itself present shall be improved and advanced, and that markets, and conveniences essential to the comforts of Life, shall be placed in situations, and under such circumstances, as may induce Tradesmen to settle there.
>
> *First Report 1812: 85*

Nash's argument was primarily economic. He considered that a Bloomsbury-style development would entail risk since if the builders could not find a higher class of tenant, then they would inevitably seeker poorer tenants who would not maintain the buildings with the required care. Instead, he proposed seeking high-class tenants and continuing the development not on the model of Bloomsbury, but of the West End around St James's Square. Three consequences followed. The first was that housing would be less dense and grander in design. The park would have to be developed as a respectable promenade on the model of Hyde Park. The third consequence was to reinforce the need for a connecting route from Regent's Park to the Court and Parliament and to the various entertainments in the West End.

Nash's proposal was for an urban parkland, a *rus in urbe* which would sustain the illusion of a country estate. Houses were set in varying amounts of land and organized so that they would not overlook each other. Grand terraces were established whose view would be into the park and not to another line of houses. The tenants would have easy access to the park where they could go walking or driving in their coaches.

Nash calculated that the wealthy would pay far more for these urban country houses than could be extracted from the bourgeois renters of Bloomsbury-type properties. He estimated an annual revenue from the park development of £45,268 15 shillings (*First Report* 1812: 116). This was a revision of an initial estimate but was higher than the rentals assumed by his rivals. The initial outlay was estimated at £12,115. When the leases were to come up for renewal, his estimate for the value of the leases was £187,724 (*First Report* 1812: 10), 467 per cent of the pre-1811 Crown revenues for London. The Commissioners were faced with a proposal which considerably increased revenue, required limited expenditure, vastly increased the value of the Crown's holdings, and provided high quality housing of the sort that might be attractive to the very Parliamentarians who overlooked the plans.

The most radical part of the plan was the development of New Street.

> THE new Street direct from Charing-cross to Mary-le-bone Park, proposed in your Instructions to me, would be of such advantage to the Crown Lands of Mary-le-bone Park, by the additional value it would give to that property as alone to justify the Crown in carrying it into execution, and of such advantage to the Nobility and Gentry occupying the principal houses in the West and North-west quarters of the Town, in their communication with the Houses of Parliament, the Courts of Law, the Treasury, Admiralty, and other public offices in the lower parts of Westminster, that I have considered it under three distinct heads: its Utility to the Public; Beauty to the Metropolis; and the Practicability of the Measure.
>
> *First Report 1812: 88*

Nash saw Regent's Park as providing a point of attraction for the wealthy of the city and improving access between the streets and squares of the west and the fashionable society therein to Regent's Park, Pall Mall and Westminster would make the houses of the park area more desirable. He opposed the line for a north-south street proposed in 1808 since this would leave a number of working-class streets and establishments on the western side of the new street. In his plan:

> there would be no Opening on the East side of the new Street all the way from the Opera-house to Piccadilly, and that the footpath consequently would be uninterrupted by Crossings; and the inferior houses, and the traffic of the

Hay-Market, would be cut off from any communication with the new Street ... It will also be seen by the Plan that the whole Communication from Charing-cross to Oxford-street will be a boundary and complete separation between the Streets and Squares occupied by the Nobility and Gentry, and the narrow Streets and meaner Houses occupied by mechanics and the trading part of the community.

First Report 1812: 89

The intended beneficiaries from this class division were the Crown and the wealthy residents of the West End. The Crown's benefit was financial. By catering to the interests of the wealthy, their properties became of greater value. The residents of the West End saw improvements to their parts of the city, which enhanced the social exclusivity of their experiences and the ease with which they moved through their city. The requirement for exclusivity provides more context for Nash's opposition to the Bloomsbury-style developments: not only might the renters not have maintained their property, but lower-class renters would be close to the wealthier elements and thus reduce the attractiveness of a property to those wealthier tenants. Social exclusivity created a vision of 'respectable life' that Nash could sell.

The losers were the 'mechanics and trading part of the community'. Although their losses were not mentioned in the First Report and may not even have been considered, the economic impact on their businesses was considerable. In February 1817, a Parliamentary Committee heard a petition from the traders and inhabitants of Norris Street and Market Terrace, an area that was primarily a meat market. Located on the fringes of the West End, the traders were well-positioned to serve the great houses to the west, but their access to that area was cut by New Street. They met with Nash and asked for access points to New Street. Nash refused. He stated that the request 'cannot be complied with, because persons in riding up and down the main street, will look upon the market, and will see offal or something of that kind' (*Report from the Committee on the Petition of the Tradesmen* 1817: 4). The insulation of respectable society was essential to his vision of the city. As a consequence, profitable businesses were ruined, and the traders were rendered destitute.

Nash was selling social exclusivity. Under examination by another Parliamentary Committee (*Report from the Select Committee* 1828: 74), he explained that the curve in the street accomplished by the rotunda, one of the most admired architectural elements of the plan, was not to keep the street on land owned by the Crown, but rather to isolate the less respectable streets to the east.

In his initial report (*First Report* 1812: Appendix 12B), Nash offered a vision of the society to be created along his new street. His comparison was Bond Street, which was at the time the most fashionable street in London. New Street was to have pavements of fifteen feet deep and a wide carriageway. These proportions were double those of Bond Street. The street fronts housed retailers within a light colonnade to protect the shoppers from the rain and to provide covered spaces for social interchange. The colonnade was to support balconies with balustrades accessible from second-floor apartments. These were intended for single gentlemen or occasional visitors and would provide a platform from which they could interact with the society of the street and 'add to the gaiety of the scene' (*First Report* 1812: 86).

Nash envisaged his street as a stage. The fashionable gentlemen were on display in their elevated residences. The spaces of retail allowed the movement of women through the city. The whole was designed for the promenades and social exchanges of the respectable classes. These peripatetic ladies and gentlemen were expected to move through a socially controlled environment. Nash gave considerable attention to the architectural unification of the two West End districts to the north and south of Oxford Street. This was to be achieved by a circus structure at the crossing of New Street and Oxford Street.

The planners were anxious to avoid unexpected or unpleasant encounters. The Act of 10 July 1813 made provision for the closing of the new street. Iron gates were erected at the north end and porters' lodges built at the junction with New Road (Euston Road as it now is). The porters were to prevent 'Stage Coaches, Mail Coaches, Hearses, Waggons, Carts, Drays, or other Vehicles for the carriage of goods, merchandize, manure, soil, or other articles; or Droves of Oxen, Cows, Horses, or Sheep',[17] from passing down the street.

This social exclusivity was marked architecturally and monumentally. Nash (*First Report* 1812: 89) envisaged façades of beautiful architecture along each street which would culminate in a monumental crescent or square at Charing Cross (which became Trafalgar Square) with a large central equestrian statue and monumental government buildings. The broad spaces of the new development were to be lined with Classicizing architecture and adorned with Classicizing monuments. Although Nash was responsible for a limited number of the buildings, all the plans were approved by his office and he was able to generate a measure of aesthetic unity.

Much of the subsequent political debate turned not on the aesthetics or the social engineering, but the costs (see Pitt 1818). The Select Committee report of 1828 commented that:

> the appearance and convenience of the parts of this Metropolis to the North of Pall Mall and Piccadilly, have been much improved by the grand line of Regent Street, and the buildings leading to and connected with it; of which the general design and many of the details are excellent.
>
> *Report from the Select Committee* 1828: 8

For James Elmes, the development of Regent's Park and Regent Street delivered a new Augustan Age:

> Augustus made it one of his proudest boasts, that he found Rome of brick, and left it of marble. The reign and regency of George The Fourth have scarcely done less, for the vast and increasing Metropolis of the British empire: by increasing its magnificence and its comforts; by forming healthy streets and elegant buildings, instead of pestilential alleys and squalid hovels; by substituting rich and varied architecture and park-like scenery, for paltry cabins and monotonous cow-lairs; by

making solid roads and public ways, scarcely inferior to those of ancient Rome, which have connected the extremest points of the empire, and have brought its provinces and seaports, many days journey nearer the Metropolis ...; and, by beginning, and continuing with a truly national perseverance, a series of desirable improvements, that bid fair to render London, the Rome of modern history.

Elmes 1827: 1–2

The costs, however, far exceeded initial estimates. Nash's first estimate for the costs of the street came in at £290,000 but with the defrayal of various costs and certain incomes from rental to builders, the overall investment was just £54,000. This expense could be met from two years of rentals (*First Report* 1812: 13). By 1816, Nash's estimate for the costs of New Street had risen to £462,527 with an estimated annual revenue of £36,831 (*Second Report* 1816: 17–19). By 1828, the Select Committee on the Office of Works reported a final cost of £1,535,688 and 16 shillings. In this period, the total revenue of the Exchequer was about £57 million. Expected rental incomes were also higher and the asset value of the Crown Estate was vastly increased, but Regent Street was far short of repaying the Crown's investment.[18]

Nash's estimates were so wrong principally because of the payment of compensation to those whose businesses were destroyed. Nash had not estimated for those costs nor was he likely to have had the means to make such estimates. In defence of his conduct, Nash pointed out that a vinegar maker had received £34,000 and four shopkeepers in St James's Market who had been offered compensation of £260 settled for £2,621 (Pitt 1818: 77, 130). Nash's case seems to have been generally accepted, but the result was that the Crown made a vast, uncommercial investment in improving of the living conditions of the richest segment of London society.

It is tempting to imagine that Nash was selling an illusion.[19] The carefully aligned villas and terraces in the park aimed to generate an arcadia in London. The closed-off, gated Regent Street to control access for the working-classes, the hiding away of the unpleasantness of butchery that put meat on the heavily burdened Georgian tables and the unsightly services that made the city function abstracted the respectable ladies and gentlemen from the realities of their provisioning. The Classicizing architecture, the monumentalized cityscape and the performances of aristocratic ladies and gentlemen exercising their gentility through the colonnades or swapping pleasantries from the balconies were disconnected from the city to the east. This disconnection was key to the political support that the scheme commanded.

Urban forms are both representative of social ideology and generative of social behaviours. The architectural 'improvements' expanded and unified the West End of London to create a distinct class identity for an area which stretched from Charing Cross, Buckingham House and Hyde Park to the south to Regent's Park in the north. Regent Street was an area of social interaction, like many of the other fashionable retail streets of the city. It was a place to buy the latest fashions and thus acquire the uniforms and styles of the aristocracy. It was a place to be seen and to interact and to form or reinforce social bonds. Nash's projection of the gaiety of the scene of well-dressed young gentlemen discoursing with their friends on the street is a vision of sociability and of the formation of a high society that was also being fashioned in the theatres, clubs and parks that made up the public arena of the West End.

The territory of the London elite was differentiated from the labyrinthine alleys and streets of the rest of the city.[20] The arcadian developments in Regent's Park advertised an attachment to the country house which was less of a pastoral reaction to the satanic mills of the industrial city than an attempt to make real the picturesque vision of a union of architecture and landscape. Classicism was a component of that picturesque. It also marked the territory of the learned and refined. It made the imperial link to the Augustan Age, and it associated the West End with the modern and rationalist values of the Enlightenment. The Georgian elite used these associations to perform the astonishing trick of persuading themselves that the building of an exclusive wealthy quarter was a public good and of manifest benefit to the nation.

The Regent Street development enabled the city to be read as a landscape of class. The early nineteenth century saw the increasing identification of an internally coherent elite with the nation (Colley 1992: 149–97). Nash's scheme furthered the association of Crown and elite and imperial grandeur and national identity and marked this union with the aesthetics of Classicism.

Monumentality and the expansion of the public

At the end of the eighteenth century, there was little enthusiasm for London architecture. Comparisons with Paris were unfavourable for London. There were few architectural wonders to amuse and amaze visitors. *The Ambulator* (1782), a guide to London, describes some architectural features near Charing Cross, Berkeley Square, Burlington House, Chiswick House, Kensington Palace and Gardens, and Vauxhall Gardens, but much of the guide focuses on the private art collections in the great houses. Feltham's (1802: 14) *Picture of London* admits that 'London does not excel in the number of buildings celebrated for grandeur of beauty . . . this metropolis is distinguished by an appearance of neatness and comfort'. The guide sees the glory of the city in the shops and their 'unrivalled aspect of wealth and splendor'. Feltham listed several significant buildings, most notably St Paul's and Westminster Abbey (34–54), other churches (54–7), royal palaces and parks (58–71), the Palace of Westminster (71–8), the Tower of London (78–91), and a selection of offices and commercial buildings (92–112). A guidebook to *The Wonders of the British Metropolis* (*Wonders* 1810) listed just the Royal Exchange, Newgate Prison, St Bartholomew's Hospital, Somerset House, Carlton House, Horse Guards, the Palace of Westminster and the Foundling Hospital. Ackerman's *Microcosm of London* was similarly slight, adding the British Museum, the Coal Exchange, the Magdalen House (for former prostitutes and destitute women), the Pantheon and Vauxhall. His sights of London were as much social tourism as architectural: he spends a considerable time deploying Classical imagery to describe a brawl between women in Billingsgate (Ackerman 1808–10: esp. 62–8).

Two decades later, *Leigh's New Picture of London* (Leigh 1830) was deprecating about contemporary London but only in comparison with Classical Rome. Instead of lamenting public architecture, he stressed the bourgeois comforts of retail and domesticity:

> London will not excite much admiration in the minds of those whose ideas of the beauty and grandeur of a great town are formed upon the notions they have obtained from the remains of Greek and Roman architecture. The dull uniformity presented by rows of brick buildings, of the same general form and appearance, possess very little attraction for the eye; but with respect of the inside of the dwellings of the metropolis, they are unrivalled for grandeur, elegance, and convenience, according to the respective ranks of those to whom they belong: in short, nothing is wanting to convey an adequate conception of the opulence, ingenuity and industry of great capital. The shops are also unrivalled, both in external appearance, and the riches and variety of the articles on sale ... [although] London may be inferior to Rome, and some other cities for architectural splendour, it is more than compensated by the comfort and convenience which it has derived from increasing information and practical science.
>
> *Leigh 1830: 29*

Even so, Leigh's listing of notable buildings is more extensive, starting with St Paul's and Westminster Abbey (116–32) and including, among other things, the Regent's Park houses (166–8), Soane's Bank of England (183) and Council Offices (197), Smirke's Post House (192–4), and the various private members' clubs in the West End (203–5). The *Original Picture of London* considers monuments in Hyde Park, Regent's Park, many of the new squares, Regent Street, the British Museum and a host of learned societies and their buildings, art galleries and libraries, theatres and clubs (*Original Picture* 1826: 80–338, 350–64).

The expansion of the coverage in the guides reflected the rapid enlargement of the public sphere. In what follows, I examine monuments, real and imagined, by which London posed as an imperial centre of global historical significance, the development of parkland and the *rus in urbe* aesthetic, and then follow Elmes's tour of London. I examine the major public institutions forming in this period, such as University College London and the national museums. I finish our tour in Clubland and the spaces of male sociability. These buildings, spaces and places existed in a dense network that formed the built environment for respectable society. The network provided spaces of sociability, from shops to clubs to theatres to museums to universities, for the new citizen community. It symbolized the unity of that community through a shared Classical aesthetic. That aesthetic offered meaning to the community through Classical social and political resonances and via a monumentality which coupled Classicism with nation and Empire. In the density of social interaction, these spaces were educational, allowing the performance and replication of social rules, spreading fashions and forming polite society.

This public sphere contained an increasing number of monuments. Some of the grandest proposed monuments, some of which were built, related to the Napoleonic wars. In 1799, John Flaxman wrote to the Committee that was seeking to raise a pillar to commemorate the Battle of the Nile. His proposal was for a

> STATUE of Britannia Triumphant, with its pedestal and basement, 230 feet high; the pedestal decorated with the Portraits of His Majesty, and the Naval Heroes, Howe, St. Vincent, Duncan, Nelson, &c. with Wreaths of Laurel on the altars, at the corners of the basement, to contain the names of Captains, &c.
>
> *Flaxman 1799: Explanation of the plates*

The statue was to be situated at the summit of Greenwich Hill from where it would be visible to all entering the city along the Thames and from the south-east. The case for such gigantism was 'to present the noblest Monument of National Glory in the world' (Flaxman 1799: 8). This genius of the British Empire was to compete with the colossus of Rhodes and the Pharos of Alexandria, be worthy of the grandeur of the country, and to attest to the skills and excellence of artists, mechanics and builders, as well as providing 'a lasting memorial of the Magnanimity, Virtue and Wisdom of the Country' (11). Flaxman's grandiosity made clear the Empire's claim for world historical importance.

The triumphal arch was a favoured monumental form. Decimus Burton designed the Wellington Arch which was constructed from 1825. It was originally at the conjunction of Hyde Park and Buckingham House and was one of a pair with the Marble Arch designed by Nash. Marble Arch was designed for the court in Buckingham House and was a core ceremonial feature in the extensive remodelling of the House in the 1820s that transformed it into Buckingham Palace. Both celebrated Wellington's victories.

Burton's arch was set to face his screen entrance to Hyde Park (1828). At this time, the westward development of London was limited by the royal parks so that Hyde Park marked the entry to the city from the west. The park itself was a significant social space.

Figure 1.8 Britannia Triumphant (Flaxman 1799).

Figure 1.9 Decimus Burton's entry to Hyde Park.

It was the scene of the London *passeggiata* where the residents of the West End would ride in carriages or on horses or go for walks. In Pierce Egan's fictionalized account of upper-class male life in London (see below), Hyde Park is one of the first places the knowing Corinthian Tom takes his acolyte, Jerry Hawthorn (Egan 1822: 148–9). The park was a place for the performance of respectability, display and sociability.

Burton's screen consists of three thin Classical gateways linked by ionic columns. The central gateway had a scaled-down reproduction of the Parthenon frieze, which would, one imagines, recall for viewers the controversial appropriation of the marbles and reference London's claim to be a city of world culture. Other than the Parthenon quotation, the screen is simple and disciplined in its design. Burton's design was remarkably close to an unexecuted design for a screen by James Adam from 1778 that is in the Soane collection.[21] The Adam design has the same tripartite form, but the central gate was a triumphal arch on top of which was a Britannia. The Burton screen was Classical but discrete and less imposing. It was more in keeping with bourgeois sociability than imperial aspirations.

Sir John Soane also made proposals for an entry point to Hyde Park. One proposal was an elaborate and fantastical royal palace, shifted slightly from Buckingham House.[22] A gate design from 1817 has an initial court formed by two aligned triumphal arches. A third side of the court is composed of yet another triumphal arch structure. This third arch is smaller and simpler.[23] A scheme of 1826 is formed by a central triumphal arch and eight flanking plinths (four on each side) which enable the entrance to be screened. The arch was topped with an inscription and an equestrian statue.[24] Another scheme, also of 1826, was much more elaborate. It also had a tripartite form with low gates linked to three open neoclassical elements, two elaborate columns seemingly modelled on Trajan's Column in Rome, flanking rotunda structures supporting equestrian statues, and almost every surface covered with friezes.[25] The fantastical elements of Soane's vision suggest an overarching imperial aesthetic.

Regent's Park was also gated and ornamented. The northern park was an alternative open space of socialization for the residents of the West End. James Elmes provides us

London: A Civil Society, 1800–1820

Figure 1.10 Soane's design for a palace at Constitution Hill.

Figure 1.11 Soane's designs for gates into Hyde Park.

with a laudatory description in his *Metropolitan Improvements*, quoted above. His utopian vision is of a dominated by 'rich and varied architecture and park-like scenery' (Elmes 1827: 1–2) and 'stately streets ... palaces and mansions, ... elegant private dwellings, ... rich and costly shops, filled with the products of every clime' (1–2). Regent's Park is celebrated as an extreme gentrification of London that has created 'a rural city of almost eastern magnificence' (7). Elmes sets the beauty of the architecture in its 'sylvan' location (19–20). The new gentrified urbanism of London was arcadian and, as Arnold notes, the 'aesthetic vocabularies of antiquity and arcadia were appropriated and a new syntax formulated to create an effective national visual language with encoded meanings for the educated classes' (2005: 1).

Classicism and the Construction of Capital Cities

The concept of the villa was derived from the rural luxury housing of the Roman Empire. It was sufficiently new as an architectural form in nineteenth-century England that Elmes felt the need to define the concept and to differentiate the English version from the Roman and from the nobleman's country house. The country house was a 'residence of state', having importance in the community. The English villa, however, was private and a residence for the bourgeois citizen.

> All the elegancies of the town, and all the beauties of the country are co-mingled with happy art and blissful union. They surely must all be the abodes of nobles and princes. No, the majority are the retreats of the happy free-born sons of commerce, of the wealthy commonality of Britain, who thus enrich and bedeck the heart of their great empire.
>
> *Elmes 1827: 20.*

Regent's Park provided a very controlled and polite rurality, suggesting that the countryside Elmes had in mind was less that of agricultural villages and more a sylvan arcadia of Classical myth. The combination of the delights of town and country unified landscape and architecture and the city and the countryside to add to national identity and power.

In his description of the villas and the terraces, Elmes (1827) comments repeatedly on the Classical architectural elements, contrasting the Doric and Italianate features of Chester Terrace (22), the 'richness and correctness' of Cornwall Terrace (19), and the 'pure Greek' of Grove House (30). The deployment of minarets in Sussex Place comes in for some criticism (48) whereas Nash's Hanover Terrace with its more uniformly Classical style is praised (48–9) and the quotations from Classical Athenian architecture, notably the Tower of the Winds, is noted at the villa of the Marquess of Hertford (51).

After leaving the park, Elmes's walking of tour of London takes his visitor south towards Regent Street and the river. Looking back to the park from Langham Place:

Figure 1.12 Regent's Park Villa (Elmes 1827).

The vista is one of the finest in this fine part of the metropolis, finished as it is, by the paradisiacal views of the park. It is an inclined plane of architectural beauty, rising from the spot where we are viewing it, to a climax of scenic perfection, in the distance, that cannot be paralleled in Europe; whether we consider the wealth that it embodies, the salubrity of the site which surrounds it, or the optical beauty that results from this charming combination of architecture, sculpture and landscape gardening.

Elmes 1827: 96

The city was to be understood as a visual phenomenon. Regent's Park was a symbol of national wealth and power. The success of the nation was to be represented by the magnificence of the private houses of the wealthiest. The houses of the poor were to be hidden and forgotten.

Turning to the town, Elmes (1827) stresses the life and bustle of the streets. The 'broad and showy shops' (Elmes 1827: 98) and the opulence of the scene. The wealth of London and the quality of the district is seen in the shops and in the culture of consumption. His architectural commentary focuses on the Classicism. Cockerell's Chapel of St George (now demolished) is noted for its quotation of the choragic monument of Thrasyllos in Athens (Elmes 1827: 101). Corinthian columns on Regent Street give way to Ionic columns at Waterloo Place. Nash's style is criticized for its lack of Greek purity since the pure Greek is the only acceptable standard (Elmes 1827: 102, 121–2). Elmes is horrified by the heresy of Crockford's Club House, not because of the wickedness of the gambling for which the club was notorious, but for the mixing of Ionic and Corinthian elements (140–1).

The architecture and the landscaping created a stylistic unity that brought together town and country and asserted national ambition. Regent's Park was a city as garden for the rich merchant princes. The commercial opulence and the bustle of Regent Street were a celebration of London's trading success. Elmes's utopian London was urban and

Figure 1.13 Waterloo Place (Elmes 1827).

commercial and restricted to a respectable, wealthy public. Nash and his fellow architects, notably Decimus Burton, had delivered a topographic separation of the upper orders of society from the rest of the community.

This public had developed an institutional sphere. At the smaller scales, its institutions were the shops so regularly identified in the architectural tours. There were places of assembly and conviviality, most notably the many clubs that proliferated through the West End. And there were the major civic institutions, the galleries and museums, and the university.

The main building of the University of London, now University College London, was designed by William Wilkins. Wilkins epitomized his generation of learned (Classical) architects and was at the forefront the Greek revival. He published major antiquarian works on Athens and the archaeology of southern Italy (Wilkins 1807; 1816; 1837). Wilkins's London buildings included the National Gallery, and he was largely responsible for the planning of what later became Trafalgar Square. University College, in both its institutional formation and ambition, and its architecture, embodied a new understanding of the civic and public.

The intellectual roots of the University of London lay outside England. The driving forces behind its creation were Scottish, Thomas Campbell and the MP Henry Brougham. Fellow Scots among the founders included Joseph Hume, a radical MP and social reformer from Aberdeen; Zachary Macaulay, a notable abolitionist, from Inverary; James Mackintosh, a lawyer who came to fame through a defence of the French Revolution and who was from near Inverness. The Scots brought an understanding of education that stemmed from their experiences of the universities of Edinburgh and Aberdeen. The intellectual scene in Edinburgh especially had been significantly more radical than that in England and had prospered in the Scottish Enlightenment. Direct inspiration came from the religiously open University of Bonn and Jefferson's University of Virginia.

The English universities, Oxford and Cambridge, were still religious institutions and excluded those from outside the Church of England. They were not well-suited to adopt the new European modes of learning, both scientific and civic, that had been developing through the eighteenth century. London University had a different vision for the public benefit inherent in a university. Rather than a religious institution, it looked to models of citizenship and the public good which drew on Utilitarianism and ultimately on Classical models of citizenship. It was aggressively secular and open to all, regardless of faith. The institution committed to a broad scientific and Humanities education, excluding theological study.

The founders were a relatively tight network of friends, social reformers, political figures, intellectuals and radicals. Financial support came from a number of shareholders including the Jewish financier, Isaac Goldsmid. Nonconformists and dissenters made significant contributions, including Henry Waymouth, a leading dissenter and abolitionist who was also a founding member of the Anti-Slavery Society, the prominent nonconformist Francis Cox, and the dissenter MP and London merchant Benjamin Shaw.[26] Catholic interests were represented by the Duke of Norfolk, whose family were perhaps the most influential Catholics of the age, and Lord John Russell, who was a leading campaigner for Catholic emancipation.

The founders drew on some of the most significant intellectuals of the era, such the philosopher James Mill, the liberal historian of Ancient Greece, George Grote, the educationalist and medical doctor, George Birkbeck, who was committed to spreading education beyond the elite, and the mathematician, Olinthus Gregory, who was the son of a shoemaker. Jeremy Bentham was an influence and a supporter and gave further philosophical and intellectual prestige to the foundation but had a limited practical role.

In its avowedly modern, rationalist and civic approach to education, the founders looked to Classical traditions. For their main building, they were attracted to the Greek revivalism that was at the height of fashion. William Wilkins won the competition in 1826, somewhat before the finance was in place. His plan centred on a large domed building accessed from a wide staircase and through an elevated temple-like portico. The entry is formed by ten Corinthian columns supporting the pediment. Two wings decorated with a second-storey colonnade lie to the side of the central dome.

Wilkins also designed the National Gallery. In 1824, Parliament bought a private art collection to form the core of a national collection. Housing that collection required a new gallery to which Parliament committed in 1831. The National Gallery was located in the royal mews, close to the site of the recently demolished Carlton House. Half the building was picture gallery and half housed the Royal Academy. It was in a high Classical style with a design which was extremely close to that used for University College (Martin 1971). The decision to invest in public art and a national gallery was a competitive response to the Louvre galleries. It also moved art beyond the great aristocratic collections, which were often open to visitors, to the public sphere.

The British Museum was also as a national public benefit and a public space. The building was designed by Robert Smirke in 1823 to house an increasing national collection of antiquities, including, of course, the Parthenon marbles. The King's library, comprising George III's collection, was donated by George IV in 1823 and was to form the core of the British Library, though the library had heavily restricted access into the 1850s.

Figure 1.14 Wilkins's Main Building, University College London.

The guides of the period paid considerable attention to the clubs of the West End. *The Great Metropolis* devoted fifty pages to a discussion of the clubs. There were two main types: subscription houses and group-owned houses. The most important clubs often had clear political allegiances. Brooks's was a Liberal club (founded 1762) and had a distinguished aristocratic membership including the Marquis of Cholmondeley, the Duke of Queensbury and the Prince Regent, as well as the politician James Fox and the playwright Sheridan (Grant 1836: I 109–11). The Tories had Boodle's (founded 1762) and the Carlton Club (founded 1832). Other prominent clubs included White's (founded as a chocolate café in 1693), the Reform Club (1836), Crockford's (1823), the Athenaeum (1824), the Clarence Club (1826), the Oxford and Cambridge Club (1830), the Oriental Club (1824), the Travellers' Club (1819), the Union Club (1800), the United Service Club (1815), the Junior United Service Club, Arthur's Club (1827) and the Windham Club (1828).

The clubs had varied origins, some beginning as chocolate or coffee houses catering for the wealthy and then gradually providing additional services. Some were set up as gambling houses with dining and social facilities on a commercial basis. Others were established as shared houses in which a group of wealthy men would band together. They offered communal dining, drinking and gaming facilities. Many had libraries. Some of the houses were purpose-built and all were designed to meet the standards of the great country houses. They allowed the networks of homosociality and the various cliques within the London elite to flourish. They were important ways in which male elites could be blended and influence secured. Political decisions were influenced by the informal networks of opinion in the clubs.

The membership of clubs could be large. In *c.* 1836, the Carlton Club had 950 members. Its house was valued at £25,000–£30,000 and it was rumoured to have contributed £500,000 to a Tory election campaign. The Athenaeum was larger with 1,300 members and a house that cost £40,000, a library worth £4,000, and tableware worth £2,500 (Grant 1836: I 113–25). Many built and equipped their houses on borrowed money, but the demand for membership and the wealth of the membership ensured financial viability and a spectacular growth in the number of clubs.

The clubs were popular since they offered social opportunities, entertainment and important connections. They also provided elegant living. For those whose main residence was outside London, clubs allowed the adoption of an aristocratic mode of life even if they maintained relatively modest London households. Some clubs provided apartments for their members (Rendell 2002: 63–85). But even for those with more elaborate London abodes, the social connections and networks of finance and political and social influence made clubs irresistible. Sociability depended on informal social connections and an adherence to rules of etiquette. It allowed the performance of class identities. Exchanges of favours drew men closer into networks. Club owners regularly advanced cash or credit to their members. There was an evident tension between the values of respectable domesticity, increasingly associated with women, and the excesses of male sociability, particularly the eating, drinking and gambling, Clubs were seen as a place of male refuge from domestic disciplines.

> If a husband spends too much of his time in the clubs, the fault is that of his spouse, and not his own … there must be misgovernment, if not absolute despotism at home, when a husband prefers the clubs, as a place of resort, to his own house.
>
> Grant 1836: I 157

The clubs were concentrated in a very small area north of Pall Mall and around St James's Square and Regent Street. By 1826, there were twenty-one recognized club or subscription houses, ten of which were on St James's Street (*Original Picture* 1826: 364–5). There were also numerous gambling houses and coffee houses concentrated within the same area. Many of the clubs were designed and decorated by the leading architects of the day and advertised their contemporary taste. The Union Club and the Junior United Service Club were designed by Smirke, the University Club by Gandy and Wilkins and decorated with copies of friezes from the Parthenon, the United Service Club by Nash, Crockford's by the Wyatts, and the Athenaeum by Burton, with more Parthenon friezes (Leigh 1830: 203–4). They formed part of Elmes's (1827: 140–56) architectural tour and a close link was maintained between Classical aesthetics and the spaces of the upper orders.

The late eighteenth and early nineteenth centuries saw a transformation of London's society. The developments through the West End created spaces for elegant sociability. These spaces were public (notably the streets and parks), institutional, and semi-private in the case of the clubs, though even the public was a policed and exclusive space. These spaces were intersecting and topographically integrated within a relatively small area of West London. People would move between club, institution, street and park. All these spaces were marked by Classical architectural elements enhancing an association of this socially exclusive public with Classical ideals of citizenship and sociability. The Classical had class associations in referencing a culture of refinement and particular forms of elite learning. The architectural development increased class differentiation and encouraged elite sociability which reinforced class bond and boundaries and affected the formation of the social and political elite.

The period sees both architecture with monumental aspects, such as Buckingham Palace and University College, and purely monumental architecture, as in the numerous arches and gateways. The monuments celebrated the national victories of the Napoleonic wars. Many of the London guides were dedicated to the king or celebrated the royal achievement in the transformation of the city. The books and monuments identified the Georgian Age with Classical Athens, but more particularly with Augustan Rome and Roman traditions of imperialism. The citizen republicanism which had fuelled the American and French revolutions was reshaped into a conservative Classicism and appropriated to serve the monarchy, imperialism and a new aristocratic order. That order identified itself with the public, and public benefit, and appropriated to itself and its socially exclusive stance the eternal verities of Classicism.

The anxieties of London living

At some point during the expansion of the city, it became clear that London was different. Size mattered. London literature of the eighteenth and nineteenth centuries emphasized social alienation and contrasted metropolitan life with an imagined rural or small-town world of stable social relations.[27] The city presented opportunities for the remaking of the individual, but those opportunities were balanced against the subjective experience of precariousness and social danger. The possibility of anonymity correlated with the potential trauma of coming unstuck from a social order and losing one's identity. Part of this insecurity was a sense of not knowing truly with whom one was engaging in the happenchance encounters in the great city.

Pierce Egan (1822: 22–3) asserted that in London one's neighbour was a great stranger. Grant wrote in *The Great Metropolis*:

> there is no such thing as neighbours in London, – in the usual meaning of the word. You may live for half a century in one house, without knowing the name of the person who lives next door: it is quite possible, indeed, you may not even know him by sight.
>
> *Grant 1836: I 10*

The anonymity of London allowed young Thomas de Quincey to hide from his guardians, drifting without home and knowing almost no one apart from the young prostitute, Ann, whose marginal and precarious situation was yet worse than his own (De Quincey 2013). It was the scale of London that most impressed de Quincey:

> It was a most heavenly day in May of this year (1800) when I first beheld and first entered this mighty wilderness, the city – no, not the city, but the nation of London. Often since then, at distances of two and three hundred miles or more from this colossal emporium of men, wealth, arts, and intellectual power, have I felt the sublime expression of her enormous magnitude . . . [A] suction is operating, night and day, summer and winter, and hurrying forever into one centre the infinite means needed for her infinite purposes, and the endless tributes to the skill or to the luxury of her endless population, crowds the imagination with a pomp to which there is nothing corresponding upon this planet, either amongst the things that have been or the things that are. Or, if any exception there is, it must be sought in ancient Rome.
>
> *De Quincey 1853: 204–5*

The city in its immensity and 'endless' population was also a desert. De Quincey felt during his approach to the city the falling away of identity. The sublimity of the experience of London turns everyone into another Atlantic wave or tree in a forest. Repeatedly, he focuses on the mental agitation caused by London, a sublime dread in which the individual is lost in the metropolis. London is Babylonian in its confusion, strange, foreign and other-worldly (De Quincey 1853; compare Mudie 1825).

In a period of statistical discovery, many of the guides used numbers to paint a picture of the city. The *Ambulator* (1782: ix) claimed the population to be 725,000–1,000,000 with a further 500,000 on the peripheries, though on no obvious basis. Feltham's *Picture of London* (1802) enumerated the streets, lanes and alleys (8,000), the squares (sixty) and the houses (160,000) before moving onto the warehouses. The population was given as 837,956. The annual consumption of bullocks (11,000), sheep and lambs (776,000), calves (210,000), hogs (210,000) and suckling pigs (60,000) attested to the monstrous appetite of the city while the 14,000 acres of vegetable and fruit production generated an economic hinterland. Feltham (1802: 14–22) counted 116 established churches, sixty-two funerary chapels, eleven Roman Catholic churches, seventeen churches and chapels for foreign protestants; six synagogues and 132 meeting houses for English non-Establishment protestants, before he moved on to the hospitals, asylums, almshouses, poorhouses, free schools, orphanages, parish schools and workhouses. *Leigh's New Picture of London* (Leigh 1830: 18, 30, 67–70) added to the enumeration an estimate of 30,000 prostitutes and 6,000 ale houses.

London was a spectacle. Panoramic views of the city became popular, allowing the visualization of the social and cultural topography of the city. The Coliseum, built on the edge of Regent's Park, displayed panoramic views of London as drawn in 1821 from the top of St Paul's (*Original Picture* 1826: xv, 161, 317; Elmes 1827: 23, 41, 71). Such an artistic representation turned the city into a visible object whose vast complexity could be understood, encompassed and consumed, all from the relative safety of Leicester Square or Regent's Park.

Textual guides proliferated. *The Ambulator or the Stranger's Companion in Tour Round London* went through editions in 1774, 1782, 1787, 1792, 1793, 1794, 1796, 1800, 1807, 1811, 1820 and 1825. *Leigh's New Picture of London* had editions in 1818, 1819, 1820, 1822, 1824, 1830, 1834 and 1839. Feltham's *The Picture of London* (1802) advertised itself as a guidebook to the city for persons who were not acquainted with the 'British Metropolis'. It claimed to be the first pocket-guide to the city. Under slightly different names, it was revised and republished annually at least as late as 1842. *A View of London* (1804) redeployed Feltham's text in a slightly different form.[28] David Hughson's *London* (1805) was rather less commercially successful but, like others, stressed the authority of the guide through personal experience. There were also heavy-weight descriptions of the city. James Malcolm's *London Redivivum* (1803–7) ran to four volumes. The two volume *The Great Metropolis* (Grant 1836; 1837) covered the architecture and society of the city. James Elmes's *Metropolitan Improvements* (1827) focused very heavily on the West End, but was also a guidebook of sorts, describing the city through the premise of walking tours. Robert Mudie's two volume *Babylon the Great* (1825) was weighted towards urban sociology (volume I) with a compendium of data in volume II. The large format volumes were impractical as tourist guides. They did, however, have a mass of information. Mudie replicated the panoramic scenography of the Coliseum.

> From St Paul's the wide horizon, crowded as it is with men and their dwellings, would form a panorama of industry and of life, more astonishing than could be gazed upon from any other point. In the streets immediately below one, the congregated multitude of men, of animals, and of machines, diminished as they are by the distance, appear like streams of living atoms reeling to and fro; and, as they are lost in the vapoury distances, rendered murky by the smoke of a million fires, the sublime but sad thought of the clashing and careering streams of life hurrying to and losing themselves in the impervious gloom of eternity, starts across the mind. Nor is the contemplation of the marvels of man's making, which that horizon displays, less wonderful than the multitudes and the movements of the men themselves. It seems as if the wand of an enchanter had been stretched out, or the fiat of a creating Divinity had gone forth over every foot of the land and of the waters. To-day one may discover a line of hovels; a month passes, and there is a rank of palaces. Now, the eye may haply light upon a few spots of that delicious green which is the native vesture of Old England.
>
> Mudie 1825: 4.

The guides reflected and responded to the anxieties generated by London. The fear was not so much of getting lost as being overwhelmed. The city's sublime scale presented issues of comprehension that statistics could not overcome.

Much of that anxiety related to issues of social recognition. In London, the mobility of the population and the seeming anonymity of the individual meant that any new person one met would have no evident reputation or social connections to vouch for their standing. The semiotics of status were also of limited help since fashionable costumes could be acquired by the less wealthy.

For provincials coming to London, the threat from crime was multiple. Without sufficient experience to recognize the fraudsters and tricksters and without necessary social connections, the provincial was at risk of exploitation and in need of a secure guide. Much of the literature purported to provide the visitor or newcomer with a measure of security. In the *Original Picture of London*, the editor commends the volume to its purchaser on the grounds, partly, that it was necessary for the safety of 'the *Stranger*', who might, among all the wonders of London, encounter 'the most depraved and vicious orders of society' and 'hypocrites, sharpers, and rogues of various orders'. Yet there is nothing in the text that might help an anxious stranger (*Original Picture* 1826: ix).

Guides to criminality emerged as a sub-genre to the city guidebook. *The London Guide and Stranger's Guide against Cheats, Swindlers and Pickpockets* of 1819 claimed to be a former criminal's insight into the world of London criminality (*London Guide* 1819). It is plotted from the perspective of a new arrival in London whose first encounter with the city came in the staging inn on the city's outskirts. There, the visitor had to watch out for the theft of their luggage, particularly at the hands of those posing as staff in the inn. Key to successfully negotiating entry into the city was to look and behave like a local which involved acting with a certain confidence, not being distracted by unfamiliar sights and sounds, and wearing a hat in a confident manner. Counterfeit currency was, supposedly, often passed in the inns. The *London Guide* discussed the techniques of pickpockets, whose art caused amusement even in the courts. Thieves dressed well so as not to arouse the suspicions of their victims. Women prostitutes supposedly picked pockets while forcing their embraces on potential clients. Violent assault also featured with the victims being tripped or knocked to the ground before being robbed, though this tended to be a problem in the quieter districts. Professional gamblers and card cheats abounded, even in West End establishments. Elaborate mechanisms were employed to lure the wealthy and naïve. Kidnap, false allegations, entrapment into labour and accusations of paternity were all employed to extract money. Considerable attention was given to prostitutes who ranged from courtesans seeking long-term lovers, street walkers, of whom there were supposedly 12,000 active on good days, to barmaids. Prostitutes supposedly gathered in the lobbies of theatres to seek assignations. Street prostitutes walked from the East End (Aldgate) to the highly fashionable St James's Street with all its clubs, via Lincoln's Inn, Covent Garden, Piccadilly and Oxford Street. The route brought the women from the relative poverty of the east to the wealth of the west.

An earlier fictionalized account (*Fortnights Ramble* 1795) painted a similar picture of social dangers. The hero is a wealthy young provincial sent to experience London. At every stage of his brief stay, he encountered criminals. An innkeeper attempted to lure an unaccompanied woman into prostitution. His pocket was picked in St Paul's. He was defrauded by street vendors. False bills of exchange were passed to him. He was defrauded at an auction. Even the distant family with whom he was supposedly to seek support intended to rob him. He was propositioned and assaulted by prostitutes, and he was rendered destitute and reliant on charity for his return fare after his fourteen days.

Edward Ward made a literary reputation through such accounts of criminality, starting with *The London Spy* (1703), which went through numerous editions and formats. The visitor's first encounter with the city is with gentlemen at an inn who share a meal. One of them is a maker of sword hilts and coins; another a barrel-maker. Wealth in London blurred traditional social boundaries. Sex and criminality were linked. Ward's *The Amorous Bugbear* (1725) is prefaced by a poem indicative of its contents which versified the social challenge of sexual anonymity.

> In former Days, our bold unguarded Youth
> Intrigu'd barefac'd, and show'd the Naked Truth,
> But now, new vitious Projects we devise,
> And make our wanton Courtships in Disguise,
> That neither Sex their Quality need own,
> But mutually indulge their Lusts unknown

The stranger to the city could be misled by someone's manner and fall into the power of criminals. Feltham (1802: 267) when describing the Sunday promenade in Hyde Park claimed that the duchess and her maid would be identically attired; the noble and the groom wore the same boots and had their hair cut in the same fashion. Respectable ladies, their hatmakers, and the courtesans all wore similar dresses.

Peter Egan's fictionalized account of life in London described the crowds in Hyde Park.

> It is in this Park ... that the PRINCE may be seen dressed as plain as the most humble individual in the kingdom; the *Tradesman* more stylish in his apparel than his LORDSHIP; and the *Shopman* with as fine clothes on his person as a DUKE. The COUNTESS not half so much 'bedizened' over as her own *Waiting-Maid*; the *Apprentice-Boy* as sprucely *set-off* as a young sprog of the Nobility; while the *Millner's Lass* in finery excels the DUCHESS. But the air of independence which each person seems to breathe renders the *tout ensemble* captivating.
>
> Egan 1822: 148–9

The anti-hero of Egan's account, Corinthian Tom, had the necessary knowledge to warn his country protégé, Jerry, that the beautiful young women he meets in the park were not, as appearances suggested, respectable ladies of fashion, but courtesans searching for a patron.

London was represented as a place of danger, particularly for young women who were subject to sexual predation. This is sometimes presented in comic terms, as in Hurstone's *The Piccadilly Ambulator* (1808), in which the sexual adventures of a thinly disguised nobleman were retold. Q.'s seductions led to one of his victims losing her lover, her reputation, her financial security and eventually her sanity. Another was alienated from her family but was able in the end to negotiate a respectable marriage. Others were able to manage the noble's lusts and manoeuvre their way to wealthy marriages.

The sex trade was a preoccupation of writings on London, often explored through a Georgian fascination with numbers. Robert Ainslie's (1836) sketch of the moral state of London, derived initially from a sermon, claimed that a single parish contained twenty-two brothels with about 176 prostitutes and that there were 80,000 prostitutes in the city, a number more than six times larger the figure given by *The London Guide* (1819). There were 2,700 cases of sexually transmitted disease in the under sixteens and Ainslie estimated those who became prostitutes would have had an average life expectancy of a further seven years. Clearly aware of the human cost of the sex industry, his cure was compulsory religious education, attributing the women's suffering to their moral weakness. It is unclear how Ainslie reached his numbers in the absence of any form of registration. One may doubt their accuracy and his classification of so many of the female population of the city. Yet, prostitution was very visible and Egan (1822: 22) talks of hundreds of child prostitutes and the social acceptability of their exploiters.

The literature of the period depicted London as a city divided by class. Defauconpret's (1824: 6–8) description, for instance, emphasized the three-class structure of society, noting that the upper order consisted of the nobles and merchants. *The Great Metropolis* divided London society into three component classes, each with distinct morals and behavioural patterns (Grant 1836: I 221–309). Alongside this discourse of class, the literature abounds with concern over social recognition.

Status was problematic in an absence of carefully policed class markers. Social anxiety was not merely a question of recognition but also of precariousness in the context of social fluidity. Fortunes could be made and lost. Poverty, criminality, addiction and sexual exploitation could lead to the disappearance of the respectable person into the wastes of the city. In an eighteenth-century understanding, the social self was particularly vulnerable. Hume's (1896), *A Treatise of Human Nature* (1st ed. 1739), argued that the self had no real substance and needed to be perceived repeatedly in performance to have continuity. Without an innate and intrinsic quality associated with class and in the context of social fluidity and a breakdown of traditions, particularly within the metropolis but also in the empire (Wilson 2003: 2), the preservation of identity required discipline to generate recognition and social security.

Such anxieties, in the literature at least, related almost wholly to the upper classes. The economic fluidities of the late eighteenth and early nineteenth centuries were significant in adjusting the social order. Some fortunes were made in the enrichment of the landed gentry who benefitted from the rise in rents and agricultural prices. Those holding urban land, especially in London, became very rich. Spectacular fortunes could also be made in trade and commerce. The writers of the period were keenly aware of the benefits to the national economy brought by commerce and of the contributions of the 'merchant princes' of London, a phrase that differentiated such wealth from the traditional political and moral stability of landed estates.

The resultant social mobility was surprising and unsettling for the more conservative members of the elite. People like Thomas Coram rose from being a sea captain to become one of the foremost philanthropists in London. Many of the key architects, such as Nash and Soane, were self-made men. This was the generation in which the Cadbury family of Birmingham rose to prominence (Davidoff and Hall 1987: 52–9). Indeed, even retail trades could generate fortunes with Feltham (1802: 32) retelling the story of a London pastry cook who left £100,000 to his heirs.

More spectacular were the fortunes to be made from exploiting the vices of the wealthy. William Crockford started as a London fishmonger with a talent for arithmetic. He became famous by running a private gambling club on St James's Street which entertained the most wealthy and powerful in London society. His club, decorated with much Classical ornamentation, was built in 1825 and cost £95,000, including the furnishings. The celebrated French cook, Monsieur Ude, renowned both for his cuisine and his ferocious temper, was supposedly paid £950 per year, perhaps fifty times more than an average respectable cook. By providing a luxurious experience for the wealthy, Crockford secured himself a reputation and made his club an exclusive place of entertainment for the rich. Many of these men may have been entertained, but they also left his club not quite so rich as when they entered. There were rumours of individuals losing £300,000 in a night and total transactions of £1 million in a single evening. Whether such figures were legendary or not, it gives a sense of the loose money from which the aristocracy could be relieved (Grant 1836: I 162–91).

Classicism and the Construction of Capital Cities

The Great Metropolis numbered the London upper classes as two or three thousand, compared with the 250,000 members of the middle classes. The latter were defined by an annual income of £250–300 per annum, which seems an absurdly low range (Grant 1836: I 170; I 273). The membership of clubs provides some a better guide to the size of the male upper order. The Carlton Club had 950 members, the Athenaeum 1,300, the Oxford and Cambridge Club 750, the United University Club 1,200, the Oriental Club, made up primarily of those who had made their fortunes in India, had 550 members, the Travellers' Club more than 700 members, the Junior United Service Club 1,500 members with 2,000 awaiting admission, and the Windham Club 600. Men might have been a member of more than one club and the club population was mobile, but even with on these partial figures, the male upper class in London was substantial.

The new wealth created a leisured class who advertised their status through conspicuous consumption. There seems to have been a general loosening of moral ties. Without material pressures and with significant disposable income, wealthy men found outlets in drink, sex and gambling. Adultery and seduction were, it seems, an accepted social norm among the upper classes (Grant 1836: I 230–1; Feltham 1802: 270). Seemingly less restrained by religious disciplines than their social equivalents a century earlier and certainly wealthier, London offered the rich gentleman opportunities for display and pleasure (Rendell 2002).

This new way of engaging with the city brought with it new terminology. The fashionable men and women were Corinthians. 'Corinthian' was architectural in derivation, seeing the figure of fashion as elaborately coiffured and decorated, and feminine in contrasting to the more manly and disciplined Doric columns. Professional gamblers were Greeks. Young women looking for husbands or supportive lovers were Cyprians. Female fashions were for Classical Greek-style dresses, or what they imagined these to be: flowing robes with low neck lines.

Peter Egan publicized this new urban culture in his *Life in London* (1822). His main characters were Corinthian Tom, his female equivalent, Corinthian Kate, and Tom's friend, the rustic son of the gentry, Jerry Hawthorn. Jerry's induction into London life is the primary plot device. Corinthian Tom's odyssey depended on his knowledge and connections and his smooth ability to traverse the city and its class topographies, from the clubs of the West End to Hyde Park to the drinking dens in the East. Tom was independently wealthy, hostile to conventional social ties and disrespectful of authority as displayed in his sometimes violent sprees through London.[29]

Egan was a highly successful sports journalist with his own newspaper and he exemplified the opportunities for social advancement. He began as a compositor before producing an account of the Prince Regent's affair with Mary Robinson and then turning to writing about boxing. *Life in London* was dedicated to the king, the author supposedly being emboldened by the king's own engagements with London (1822: v). *Life in London* was a hugely successful franchise with a journal of lightly fictionalized stories, the book and a play which ran at the Adelphi Theatre on the Strand for 300 performances (Grant 1836: I 72). There followed a vast range of theatrical versions and 'pirated' literary manifestations of Corinthian Tom and his companions (Egan 1830: 8–44). The adventures of Corinthian Tom and his friends were a celebration of London society. Despite anxieties over the dangers of the city, London provided the excitements and pleasures of encounter that are so characteristic of the modern urban experience.

Such encounters depended on mobility within the urban topography. Not only did the wealthy engage in adventures to the east of Regent Street, but the economy of elite pleasure attracted people westwards, whether it was to the shops of the West End or to provide the services necessary for the various elite institutions.

The sex industry had its own patterns of mobility, with the theatres being sites of social-sexual encounter (*London Guide* 1819: 114–36; Rendell 2002: 55–9). Egan was conscious of the costs of prostitution and the London lifestyle. He prefaced *Life in London* with a brief discussion of child prostitution (Egan: 1822: 22). In the successor volume, *Finish to the Adventures of Tom, Jerry, and Logic* (Egan 1830), bad ends were met. One of the lesser characters was committed to a debtors' prison. Logic died of a mysterious illness. Corinthian Kate, having been neglected by Tom, took a lover, was discovered and thrown out of the apartments where Tom was keeping her. She descended quickly into prostitution, from being a temporary mistress, to working the theatre, to working the streets, to taking poison. The story interlinks tales of disaster and culminates with a morose Tom meeting his death in a hunting accident. Jerry found peace in marriage and country living. Egan's riotous tale of urban immorality found moral resolutions; salvation came in a retreat to the countryside.

The class city of the early nineteenth century had less of the concern with social deprivation that we find later in the century. Robert Ainslie (1836) was worrying about the lack of Christian education in the poorer districts of the city, comparing residents to the 'heathens'. In London, 'the most vicious, depraved, and idle – the scum of the creation – have their abode, and exert their influence' (Ainslie 1836: 2), separated from the 'best portion of the population' who 'know but little' of their lives (v). For Ainslie, London's danger was the sexual corruption of the respectable. Attending the theatre was the first step towards poverty, sexually transmitted disease, loss of social standing, a failure of moral integrity and a life in the lowest brothels. Ainslie's was a fearsome rejection of the city of pleasure. His work was also a step along the way to the later Victorian conception of the poorer districts as an underworld. He saw the poor as an internal other whose moral standing required missionary zeal. Over these deserving impoverished, the rich and powerful would exercise natural and paternalistic authority. It never seems to have occurred to Ainslie that the problems faced by the poor were economic and political rather than moral.[30]

Grant (1836: I 293–309) similarly lamented the state of London's poor, focusing primarily on their morals. Alcohol, particularly gin, was seen as ruinous. Sexual promiscuity was rife. Prostitution was common with, supposedly, a third of girls and women under twenty involved. At the root of the problem was an absence of religion, which, if true, suggests hostility on the part of the poor to religious institutions. Similarly, there is no suggestion that economics, let alone predatory male sexuality, was the cause of prostitution. This blindness is despite a clear sense that gentlewomen might find themselves without other means of support. The situation was 'a matter of reproach to every Christian mind that while so much has been done for the heathen of Africa, scarcely anything has been done for the heathen of London' (Grant 1836: 1 308–9).

The imperial capital was, to use de Quincey's (1853: 204) phrase, sucking in the talents and the population of Britain as it sucked in the wealth of Empire. *The Great Metropolis* estimated that there were 130,000 Scots, 200,000 Irish and 30,000 French in London (Grant 1836: I 15–16). The wealthy and leisured aristocrats and the merchants of the city were joined by men and women of ambition who flocked to London. As the population of the city was in continuous transition and the economic structures of the city were shifting and developing, so the cultural values of the upper orders of society were always in flux. In time, the fashionable Corinthians and their Cyprians were to be replaced by the men of sombre disciplines and black coats (Gunn 2007; Harvey 1997).

The political achievement of the Georgian age was to bind together these diverse and ever-changing groups into a new elite. That new elite, perhaps through association with institutions such as the clubs, somehow managed to be both self-consciously new and traditional. Elmes (1827: iv) saw British imperial prosperity as arising from 'industry and a daring spirit of commercial enterprize' under the 'influence of or princely merchants' and the king's achievement was the integration of these new princes into the upper orders. Malcolm (1803–7: 11) compared the princely merchants of ancient Tyre with those of London, also suggesting influence and respectability. Babylon was a favoured historical comparandum, particularly useful given how little was known of Babylon. But the association captured a sense of diversity and trade and the multiplicity of activities by which people made their livings. Yet, the architectural forms of this new Babylon were Classical, and it was the fixed values of the Classical that provided the political and cultural symbolism to overcome the social and economic flux.

Chateaubriand (1849: III 335), always alert to the revolutionary potential of the great city, saw the British government as aristocratic, formed around rich landowners, men of industry and gentlemen farmers. These men spoke the language of liberty, order and propriety. There were social distinctions and hierarchies, and many boundaries remained: many of the texts were vehemently antisemitic, focusing ire particularly on Jewish bankers and moneylenders, presumably at home in this renewed Babylonian exile. 'Trade' families were excluded from the most conservative bastions of the establishment, such as Brook's club (Grant 1836: I 109–11; Arnold 2005: 16–17). There was also a measure of distaste for some of the aristocracy's behaviours and their sexual and financial recklessness. But the new wealthy penetrated the bastions of the old order. They could bring their families to the theatres and mix with the nobility, most notably at the King's Theatre, also known as the Italian Opera, in Haymarket. Even if not at Brooks's men of wealth and talent were accepted into the clubs. James Grant identified a culture of emulation among the merchants:

> The King's Theatre is the great place, among the metropolitan theatres, of fashionable resort. It is also very largely attended by merchants and others, who do not know a word of Italian. The reason is obvious: there is always a disposition among persons of wealth, however limited their education, and

humble their origin, to follow, in such matters, in the wake of the aristocratic portion of society.

Grant 1836: I 35

Topography blended the upper orders. In spite of the repeated claims of ignorance of one's neighbours, Mudie claimed that:

Among the ten thousands squares and streets, and lanes and courts, which lodge its varied inhabitants, it is impossible not to find one where your neighbours shall be your equals, – similar in employments, in habits, and in tastes, and marked by the same graces or by the same deformities.

Mudie 1825: 17

Nash's planning in West London focused explicitly on the generation of class neighbourhoods. In the *First Report of the Commissioners*, he displayed a rudimentary understanding of the processes of gentrification that would affect the economic and social trajectories of neighbourhoods adjacent to the Regent Street development (*First Report* 1812: 83–5). The enthusiasm of the Parliamentarians was driven by the financial benefits that they expected would accrue and the social benefits in the development of an exclusive, respectable neighbourhood.

This new public sphere belonged to the middle and upper classes. The architecture made this public visible and generated a sense of belonging, in part through the patterns of social interaction in the developing neighbourhoods. There was an educative process in developing the new citizen. This can be seen in the institutions of sociability that proliferated and were to become such a prominent feature of nineteenth-century civil society. These institutions educated the public in culture, behaviours and attitudes. This process is evident in the guidebooks to life in London, in fashions and most obviously in the explosion in the press. Guides to London devoted considerable attention to the daily, weekly and monthly journals. The whole of the second volume of *The Great Metropolis* meticulously listed the various journals published in the city, presumably because the scale of the press's production was a measure of the public sphere in the city (Grant 1837). The *Original Picture of London* listed eight morning newspapers, five evening papers, and forty-four weekly or monthly papers (*Original Picture* 1826: 347–50).

The architectural style of the new public sphere was Classical. Knowledge, refinement, discernment and citizenship values were the qualities required for ruling. A Classical education was seen as a better qualification for membership of the ruling classes than any technical skills. Fluency in Classicism was an act of self-definition that asserted a claim to belong in a public, elite culture. It also laid claim to a right to rule. This claim enhanced and was enhanced by the prestige of the Classical. By contrast, the absence of citizenship values and suitable intellectual qualities from the poorer part of the community was seen as evident in their morally corrupted behaviours. The unity of the upper orders was always partial and there were considerable tensions between the more morally conservative bourgeoisie and the landed wealthy, but Classical aesthetics and topographical distinction presented a unified upper order against the revolutionary threat posed by the poor.

That threat was felt to be real and pressing. The right of *habeas corpus* was suspended in 1818. The Peterloo Massacre was in 1819. In 1830, William IV thought it was too dangerous for him to venture to Mansion House for the Lord Mayor's Banquet (Arnold 2000: 71). And, as we have seen, Lord Liverpool and no doubt many others were haunted by the spectacle of France's revolution. The distinction between the upper and lower orders was freighted by cultural and moral justifications of the social inequalities and deprivation that marked London life. The upper orders were evidently aware of that deprivation but found ways of distancing themselves from the poor by stressing their immorality, irreligiosity, criminality, promiscuity and lack of civilized citizenship values. One might see the unification of the upper orders as a response to the fear of the mechanics. Yet, the evident benefits secured by the social and cultural distinction of the upper orders from the lower orders, were likely more important factors in drawing the elites together: those benefits figure much more in the literature than fear of proletarian revolutionaries. Those benefits included the concentration of the wealth and political resources of the new industrializing and imperial economy in the hands of the enlarged elite. This unification of the upper orders was profoundly political. The reshaping of London created the spaces for a newly defined public. It fostered a culture which looked to the political and cultural values of the Classical, appropriated its prestige and enhanced that prestige through its association with contemporary class hierarchies. The mechanics were excluded from this new public topographically and culturally, as they were excluded from political power and largely from the benefits of the new wealth. Marking the territory with Classical architectural forms reflected a broad cultural appropriation of the Classical by the London elite which differentiated that elite and provided cultural justification for their power.

From imperial Classicism to Christian nationalism

In 1834, John Billington perceived a political issue in the architectural focus on the houses of the rich.

> Public manners have a very decided influence in causing … striking disproportion in, and confusion of, the scale of propriety in the appearance of buildings. When the acquirement of power and the possession of riches afford men the means of obtaining luxuries, the simplicity of the style adopted in the habitations of their fellow citizens is rejected; they will no longer inhabit constructions which designate them as being mortals, but they raise for their dwellings, temples and other similar edifices. At Athens, the dwellings were simple, and the public edifices sumptuous. Rome also retained, for a long period, this same moderation in the residences of individual. Architecture suffers great injury from these customs and mistaken ideas of luxury.
>
> *Billington 1834: 292–3*

He offered a republican view in which the shared public sphere was the realm of the citizen and the nation and magnificence belonged properly to that sphere alone.

> If we consider the antique cities, where the arts took up their abode, how modest and unassuming appeared the residences! But how immense were their public edifices; how their temples, tribunals, &c., majestically distinguished themselves from the adjacent habitations! It was in them that the public pride and enjoyment was placed, being considered as the property of each citizen; and the fame and pleasure attached to their magnificence, was not individual, but national.
>
> Billington 1834: 294

Thomas Hope's architectural history paid due respect to Laugier in deriving Greek architecture from nature, but he also associated Greek excellence with political organization:

> That purely democratic organization of the Grecian states, which raised every citizen to a level with the rest, – if not in wealth, at least in rank and privileges, which, if any single individual had more influence, was more a leader of a party than others, made him more afraid lest an ostentatious display of his pre-eminence should awaken their jealousy or mortify their pride, – tended as much to keep private habitations low and unassuming, as it contributed to render public edifices vast and pompous ... But that very circumstance produced greater magnificence of public edifices. The citizen, unable to give vent to his pride in his private habitation, only sought the more to gratify it, in the constructions destined to the purposes of public magnificence or utility. These latter remained the less confounded with, soared more over the former. They attained in greater number that size of parts, that splendour of decoration, that has made them the wonder of all succeeding ages.
>
> Hope 1835: 48

Citizen government, which required a suppression of the elites, led directly to architectural excellence in the public sphere. Correspondingly, modern achievements were seen as subsequent to political and economic change:

> the truth is, that whatever new life and vigour and luxuriance literature and the fine arts acquired in Italy, so far from being the effect of foreign cultivation, was the spontaneous consequence of the new direction of men's minds to objects of beauty and pleasure, produced on the spot, by the abolition of the feudal shackles, the gradual return of liberty, industry, trade, ambition, information, public spirit, and whatever else had formerly, among the ancient Greeks, created a similar pre-eminence in taste and letters, over other contemporaneous nations.
>
> Hope 1835: 515

Classicism and the Construction of Capital Cities

Architectural excellence flowed from the end of feudalism. It was thus particular to the nation's stage of progression and its public economy. The intellectual move from earlier traditions was from an architectural idealism which saw Greek architecture as a transcendent good to such architectural excellence as an expression of certain clearly bourgeois social and economic values (liberty, industry, trade, public spirit). In its association with civilizational progress, architecture became an expression of national values which were firmly bourgeois. Hope (1835: 561) concluded his history with a call for a national architecture, which drew a distinction between British bourgeois identity and the values of other nations.

Much eighteenth-century Classicism had centred on aristocratic houses. These advertised their Palladian and Vitruvian origins and the expensively acquired refinements of their owners. The appropriation of this Classical style to mark the public sphere met a raft of political and cultural requirements. It helped define a new ruling coalition in London society and separate the bourgeois and upper orders from the lower classes. It established an association between this new order and imperial success. Trade and commerce found their place in the aesthetics of the new city. Although this may have been achieved in part by exaggerating the role of the trading and commercial classes in Classical Athens and Rome, it was based in a perception of those historical parallels as offering the best paradigms for a republican, imperialistic, public urban culture. The association encouraged architects to dress the city in Grecian columns as sculptors dressed the heroes of empire in Roman garb.

Yet, the association with the political systems of antiquity could not be controlled. Classicism brought with it the spectres of Athenian citizen democracy and the chaos of the fall of the Roman Republic. The seeming loosening of the moral fabric of society established parallels with the financial and sexual corruption of imperial Rome. The moral question loomed large in London and was not confined to the behaviour of the poor. It was embedded in Christian values and identity.

Although Gothic was often favoured for churches, a preference that went back to Laugier (1765: 115–17; see also Soane 2000: 118–23), there were extraordinary Classical churches built in this period. These include Henry Inwood's St Pancras parish church (1819–22) with its replica of the porch of the Caryatids from the Acropolis and St Matthew's, Brixton (1821–4) with its massive Doric portico.[31] Yet, such Classicism was to remain the exception for churches and Gothic architecture would come to represent Britain's national identity in its Christian form (Colley 1992: 11–54).

Classicism was the architectural expression of imperialism and was associated with a particular social and political elite and their vision of the nation. This limited public raised the question of the place of other social classes as well as that of regional elites. Other nationalistic and Christian versions of the English nation were possible and the suitability of Classicism as an expression of those values was open to question. Britain identified itself fundamentally as a Christian nation. Medievalism challenged Classicism. The heavy black cloths of Victorian fashion replaced the light and colourful modes of the Georgian era. The supposed certainties of a rural and aristocratic social hierarchy in which British values were imbued were preferred to the dangerous citizen and proletarian politics of the metropolis. Civic Classicism faded in the face of anti-urbanism and new visions of British nationalism and the urban community.

CHAPTER 2
ATHENS: THE COLONIZATION OF GREECE, 1830–1846

Introduction: 1821

In 1821, a wave of connected uprisings swept through the Balkans. This unrest can be attributed to a combination of resistance to the oppressive policies of the Ottomans, religious tensions between Christians and Muslims, and nascent nationalism, particularly among the Greek communities.

Despite being spread over a vast region and with diverse interests, backgrounds and relationships with the Ottoman rulers, the Greek communities were united by language and religion. Although there was a concentration of Greeks in the southern Balkans, Greeks were spread across extensive territories around the Aegean and Ionian seas and into the northern Balkans. Greeks lived alongside other Christian Orthodox populations and many Muslims. The emergence of an educated Phanariot elite (named after a residential district in Constantinople) had brought wealth and important political connections to at least some in this community. The Ottomans used Phanariotes as governors, diplomats and ministers. The rise of the Phanariotes reinforced an existing internationalism within the Greek diaspora. By the end of the eighteenth century, there were large Greek communities through the Balkans, the Levant, Russia, Italy and central Europe. The Greek diaspora maintained a network of cultural, religious and political connections and, from 1814, there were concerted efforts at organizing for Greek independence led by a secret society, *Filiki Etaireia*, that has been founded in Odessa.

In 1821, a co-ordinated attempt was made to sweep the Ottomans from the Balkans. Alexandros Ypsilanti and his brother Demetrios led an insurgency in Wallachia and Moldavia in late February 1821. The revolt, however, did not gather the expected support and divisions within the Phanariot community soon surfaced. A key ally, Capodistrias, who was minister in the Tsar's government, failed to deliver Russian support and found himself condemning the uprising. Michael Soutzos, who was the *hospodar* (governor) of Moldavia, and part of *Filiki Etaireia*, was forced out of office and then from Moldavia. The northern uprising failed. It did, however, force the Ottomans to concentrate forces towards the north, further away from the southern Balkan communities.

In the first months of 1821, the Greek population of Patras took to wearing weapons in the street. The Turks, fearful of a coming confrontation, retreated to the castle. The governor of the Peloponnese sought to head off trouble by summoning Christian leaders and local *primates* (leading men) to Tripolitsa, the centre of Ottoman political control. There they could be supervised and, if necessary, used as hostages. It was on the road to Tripolitsa that Bishop Germanos of Patras stopped and held a convocation. On 2 April 1821, the flag of Greece was raised. Germanos returned to the small town of Kalavryta high in the Peloponnesian mountains. The local Muslim population quickly surrendered. Patras revolted. The Turkish quarter was burnt and the fire spread through the city. The troops and the resident Muslim population responded and street-to-street fighting ensued (Gordon 1832: I 143–9).

On 6 April, a meeting of Greeks at Perachora led to Megara and the towns to the east of Corinth coming out in revolt. They marched on Corinth which was the major town in the region and the Turkish authorities retreated to Acrocorinth, the massive and near impregnable citadel that loomed over the Isthmos. In Messenia, the Bishop of Modon (Methoni) had been arrested and was being transported to Tripolitsa. He appealed to local peasants who killed his guards and then with a rag-tag army, he rushed to take Navarino, but the garrison was able to secure the citadel before they arrived (Gordon 1832: I 153). Koroni also closed its gates against the bishop. The major fortresses of the Peloponnese settled down to be besieged.

The British had been sheltering the Greek rebel Theodoros Kolokotronis in Zante. They had no more desire than any other of the great powers to destabilize the Balkans or to foster Greek independence. British political interest in Greece was minimal. Kolokotronis slipped away and sailed home to join other local potentates in the Mani. On 9 April, Petros Mavromichalis, the Bey of Mani, held an assembly at Kalamata accompanied by Kolokotronis. Mavromichalis had established a loose hegemony over the Mani under licence from the Ottoman authorities. This arrangement had maintained a fragile order and increased Mavromichalis' authority, but he threw his lot in with the rebellion.

Mavromichalis and Kolokotronis raised warrior bands and led them towards the rich agricultural lands of Messenia and Lakonia. Rural Muslim landowners fled before the advancing bandits. When news of the rising reached Mistras, the major town of Lakonia, the Muslim population, having neither hope of protection nor means of meaningful resistance, fled north to Tripolitsa (Gordon 1832: I 149–52).

Of the Aegean islands, Spetses joined the revolt by 9 April; Psara followed soon after while Hydra delayed until 16 April (Gordon 1832: I 163–70). The rich Greek merchants would have been aware that an extended war in the Aegean would be catastrophic for their businesses. The accession of the islands provided the Greeks with naval power sufficient to prevent the easy movement of Ottoman forces to the main theatres of war.

The war came slightly later to Attica. Christian Albanian peasants took to the hills west of Athens and a force from Megara headed to Menidi, just to the north of the city. The Ottoman population, mostly traders, were reluctant to take up arms, though the governmental forces stored weapons on the Acropolis and organized regular patrols along the city walls. But they relied on Greek townsmen for those patrols, suggesting that the authorities had failed to understand the extent of the revolt. On 6 May, the city was captured, but not before a garrison and at least some of the Muslim population had managed to retreat to the Acropolis (Gordon 1832: I 173–5).

The Greeks enjoyed spectacular success in the first months of the uprising. Much of the countryside came under the control of the Greek insurgents as did several of the major towns. Muslim garrisons controlled some of the urban centres and had been able to retreat to various citadels. Without cannon, fortified centres were easy to defend, but the speed of the revolt benefited the Greeks. The Ottoman authorities had not had time to lay in food, garrisons were small, and the populations in the towns were swelled by refugees. It is likely that the Greek insurgents hoped that Ottoman power in its European territories would be fatally weakened, and a new Greece would emerge after this short violent uprising. Instead, the events of spring 1821 set the scene for a vicious and long war.

I will not attempt to provide a narrative of that war in all its ebbs and flows across the Greek landscape. It is enough to stress the volatility of the period. The Greeks had initial ascendancy, then the Ottoman armies arrived. Greek victories generated some temporary stability and won the attention of the West. The sultan organized an Ottoman-Egyptian alliance which led to a large a deployment of Egyptian troops to Greece. This army brought Greece to the brink of defeat. Finally, an Anglo-French-Russian intervention imposed a settlement and secured independence for a small Greek state.

The conflict was marked by massacres at Navarino (Gordon 1832: I 230–1), Tripolitsa, where perhaps 8,000 inhabitants were killed (Finlay 1861: 267–9; eyewitness accounts in Raybaud 1824: 375–485 and Gordon 1832: I 233–47), Athens (Gordon 1832: I 347–50), Chios, with perhaps as many as 70,000 killed (Finlay 1861: I 306–20; Gordon 1832: I 356–69), Psara (Gordon 1832: II 130–8), and, most notoriously, Mesolongi (Finlay 1861: II 83–111; Gordon 1832: II 229–61). There were bitter battles through the streets of many towns and long sieges in Patras and Athens, which changed hands four times during the war (Gordon 1832: I 408–15, II 333–47, 375–402; Cochrane 1837: 79–83; Finlay 1861: II 115–54), a long sequence of sieges at Nauplio (Gordon 1832: I 329–31, I 346–7), the destruction of Galaxidi (Finlay 1861: I 272–3), and repeated burnings of Argos (Gordon 1832: II 195–225; Finlay 1861: II 62–79). The Souliotes, who lived near Preveza, were driven out (Gordon 1832: I 380–91). The revolutionaries displaced or murdered the Muslim rural population. Ibrahim Pasha's army ravaged the Peloponnese. Reshid Pasha was similarly brutal through northern Greece. In the islands, in addition to the heavy loss of life when the Ottomans stormed Chios and Psara, the trade on which the islands depended was destroyed.

Eight years of intense warfare brought immense destruction to Greece. At first, the Great Powers (Austria, France, Britain and Russia) were hostile to the uprising, fearing the war would escalate into a general European conflict and an extension of Russian influence over a fatally weakened Ottoman Empire. The Russians who potentially had more to gain from an Orthodox state in the Balkans and the disintegration of the Ottoman state in Europe were no more eager for an extended military campaign than their Western counterparts. All powers may also have felt that a rag-tag and ill-equipped band of farmers and shepherds led by an inexperienced and untrained political class would have no chance against the Ottoman military. The rebellion drew its friends from the Romantics and liberals of Europe, but there was no sympathy in the more conservative circles. Such indifference came under pressure from 1822. As Finlay writes:

> The success of the Greeks during the year 1822 established Greece as an independent state, and forced even those hostile to the Revolution to acknowledge that the war was no longer a struggle of the Porte with a few rebellious rayahs. The

importance of the Greek nation could no longer be denied, whatever might be the failings of the Greek government.

Finlay 1861: II 1–2

After the massacre of Mesolongi, public opinion mobilized behind the Greek cause. Finley again:

> The spectacle of a duel between a sovereign and the resuscitated Demos of Greece, was a spectacle that deservedly excited the attention of all civilised nations. Mohammedanism and Christianity, tyranny and liberty, despotism and law, were all deeply compromised in the result. The massacres at Chios and the defeat of Dramali were considered proofs that the sultan could not reconquer the Greeks, and Christendom would not allow him to exterminate a Christian people. Public opinion … began to growl a warning to Christian kings no longer to neglect the rights of Christian nations and statesmen began to feel that the sympathies of the people in Western Europe were at last fairly interested in the cause of Greece.
>
> *Finlay 1861: II 2*

By 1826–7, the embryonic Greek state was reliant on loans it had no hope of repaying and on donations from Philhellenic committees that were operating across most of Western Europe and North America. The military effort was supported by a small but growing cadre of foreign soldiers and military experts. Politically, the Greeks were divided to the point of internecine violence. Kolokotronis and Mavromichalis and their Maniotes were at loggerheads with other military groups and elements in the political leadership. The islanders were *de facto* independent, but even among themselves were not well co-ordinated. The likely outcome of a continuation of the war was a Greek defeat, but this was not an acceptable outcome for European public opinion.

The crucial diplomatic breakthrough came on 4 April 1826, when the Russians and British agreed a concordat to bring an end to the war and to jointly mediate on the formation of a Greek state (Gordon 1832: II 275; Finlay 1861: II 172). The British committed a fleet to the Eastern Mediterranean. The Treaty of London was agreed in July 1827, involving the Russians, French and British, and an armistice imposed (Finlay 1861: II 174–5). The sultan did not accept the treaty. Greek-held territories were tiny and about to become smaller since a new Egyptian fleet had set sail for the Peloponnese. On 27 October, that fleet was sunk at Navarino by British, French and Russian flotillas (Gordon 1832: II 424–32; Finlay 1861: II 179–84). In August 1828, a large French army landed near Koroni and on 5 October Ibrahim Pasha quit the Peloponnese bringing the war to a practical end (Finlay 1861: II 190–2).

In March 1829, the Great Powers drew their line on the map between Arta and Volos. In September 1829, the Ottomans agreed to the settlement. In the grand tradition of colonial impositions, the line did not correspond to any geopolitical division (Finlay 1861: II 222–3). Nevertheless, it called into being a small Greek state based around

Morea (the Peloponnese), Roumeli (Attica; Sterea Ellada (Central Greece) and Western Greece), and the Aegean Islands. As part of the agreement, the Great Powers offered sovereignty to Prince Leopold of Saxe-Coburg, who accepted the offer only to resign from it in May 1830 (Finlay 1861: II 224–9).

Greece was at that time under the presidency of Ioannis Capodistrias, the man who had failed to deliver Russian support in 1821. Schooled in Russian politics, his response to the fractious politics of Greece was authoritarian. The fragile freedom of the press was curtailed. Arbitrary imprisonment became common. After a political dispute, he sent a Russian fleet to sack Poros. He arrested prominent members of the Mavromichalis family and secured them in Nauplio. However, this tiger was not easily intimidated. The Mani revolted and on 9 October 1831 Capodistrias was assassinated on his way to church in Nauplio by two members of the Mavromichalis family (Finlay 1861: II 224–46; Cochrane 1837: 135–7). One can still see one of the bullets in the church wall. Greece was plunged into civil war. The war reinforced the Great Powers' view that Greece needed an external regal influence and on 26 June 1832, the national assembly, meeting at Pronoia just outside Nauplio, offered the sovereignty to Otto of Bavaria. Otto's father, Ludwig, accepted on his behalf (Finlay 1861: II 248–75).

The war exposed a fundamental lack of unity in Greek society. What had bound the resistance together, Christianity, language and a shared antipathy to Ottoman rule, was insufficient for a new Greek state to emerge smoothly from a patchwork of cultural traditions and economic and political interests. The Great Powers imposed a foreign leader who had no knowledge of and seemingly very little interest in Greece's diverse culture. The Bavarian-Greek state positioned itself as a modernizing influence. It understood the political and institutional fragmentation of Greece as resulting from a primitive, atavistic and premodern culture. That culture would inevitably fade before the triumph of an imposed modernity.

Some of the Greek population shared at least some of that ideological understanding. Greece under Otto was not a democratic state and so there is no obvious way to assess whether his government was truly popular. However, many local agents throughout Greece embraced the modernizing agenda, devising and implementing plans to develop education and build new cities. It is not difficult to believe that after years of repression and the brutality of the war many were eager to sweep away Ottoman traditions.

Athens was at the centre of this new Greek state. It symbolized the ambition of the Bavarian kings for a new Greek society. The choice of Athens as capital was symptomatic of the values of the regime. The city, ruined by the war, had little to recommend it except for the one advantage that overwhelmed all other considerations: the prestige of its Classical inheritance. Although the Classical heritage had played a negligible part in the efforts of Western sympathizers to rally support for the Greek cause (Rosen 1998: 72–3), certainly when compared with Christian fellowship, for the Bavarians, Greece was defined by its Classical inheritance.

In a state devastated by civil war and with a minimal and dysfunctional infrastructure, the Bavarians organized and funded the clearing of later accretions from Classical monuments, the reconstruction of Classical remains, archaeological parks and, eventually, a museum. The regime's ethos was thoroughly neoclassical. Ludwig of Bavaria was one of the more notable devotees of Greek revivalism and the rebuilding of Athens attracted several leading neoclassical architects. In its planning of the new Athens, the regime expressed its Enlightenment rationality. The ambition was to establish a Western civilizational hegemony in the Eastern Mediterranean for which a neoclassicized Athens was an evangelical site. Athens advertised the Bavarian regime as an Enlightened monarchy that would deliver modernity to the region. The Kingdom of Greece was to be but the first beneficiary of this new civilization.

The embracing of a Classical tradition and a neoclassical present involved a rejection of other pasts of Greece, notably the Byzantine Christian and folk traditions. The destruction of Athens encouraged the Bavarian authorities to believe, wrongly, that the Athens they inherited was empty ground on which an entirely new city could be constructed. The emergence of modern Athens was inevitably more complicated than the ordered fantasies of the regime. The rapid recovery and development of the city introduced a cultural hybridity into the neoclassical utopia that the Bavarians planned for their new capital.

In what follows, my aim is to link the urban development of Athens to the traditions of cultural identity within Greece and to European ideologies of Enlightenment and nationalism. The ideas that formed Greece were both local and exogenous. The war had been for freedom, but what that freedom meant was not agreed. The ideologies of Romanticism, Classicism and the Enlightenment intersected with local political structures. We might think of these ideologies as forming a network of related ideas that connected in the aftermath of the Greek revolution. An individual might have been affected by some or all of those ideas at different times and expressed their identity in different ways as circumstances seemed to require. The ideas operated with varying levels of intensity and political spread, from the internationalism of Classicism and Romanticism to the governmental networks by which the Bavarians attempted to create their modern state, to the local networks that had mobilized resistance, liberated Greece, and continued to defend Greek independence. Whereas the colonial mentality wished to group individuals into coherent ideological categories, the complexity of Greek intellectual and cultural life resisted simplistic divisions.

The next section considers the multiple pathways to the invention of the Greek nation, before the chapter shifts to a focus on Athens, from the first plans for the new city (and the removal of the old city) to the various attempts to implement the visions of the political leaders, architects and planners.

Imagining Greece in a time of revolution

National imaginaries are always contentious and frequently paradoxical and multiple. In the Greek instance, it was particularly so. Philhellenic sympathies were crucial to Greece's success in the war and these stressed Christian communitarianism, liberal Romanticism, and neoclassical Philhellenism. Yet, those exogenous views of Greece were frequently hostile to elements of Greek culture and society which European visitors regarded as traditional. Nevertheless, it was traditional social and cultural structures, particularly Orthodox Christianity and local military-political hierarchies, that had successfully mobilized Greek resistance. This tension shaped politics in the aftermath of the revolution.

Across many regions, nationalist ideologies had gained currency in the political and economic transformations at the end of the eighteenth century (Kedourie 1993: 1). Although exploiting symbolic and narrative elements that predate nationalism, sometimes by many centuries, the centrality of nations and nationalism to global geopolitics dates from *c*. 1800 (Smith 1986, 1991, 2000, 2004; Conversi 2007). Nationalism was frequently tied to an emergence of the public (Hobsbawm and Ranger 1992; Habermas 1991). The public sphere developed with larger, economically diverse cities and their changing patterns of sociability. New social patterns required the political articulation of a community which could not be face-to-face and hence required a symbolic representation. The emergence of such imaginary communities was connected to the spread of education, literacy, newspapers and journals, which were essential communicative systems in bourgeois cultures (Anderson 2006; Gellner 2008). These publics found their historical models in the Classical world, though their understandings of Classical history and culture often seems to us woefully inaccurate.

In South America, multiple national identities emerged in a short and intense revolutionary period in the first decades of the nineteenth century. There were revolutions in Bolivia (1802–25), Columbia (1810), Argentina (1810–18), Venezuela (1811), Paraguay (1811–42), Chile (1817), Ecuador (1820–2), Peru (1821), Brazil (1822) and Uruguay (1822–5). The revolutionary impetus arose from an intensification of colonial oppression against which local administrative and political classes reacted. Such bourgeois groups were supported by local administrative and economic networks and South American cultural exchanges (notably local print media).

Greece was an exceptional nation (Gourgouris 1996). There was intellectual and cultural nationalism within the Greek diaspora, but the southern Balkans lacked a potent bourgeoisie, developing public spaces, large urban centres, a significant popular press or a mechanism for the wide distribution of popular literature. Instead, there were powerful and divergent localized political and economic structures in the various regions of Greece and strong traditions of local leadership. It was on these local structures that the revolution depended.

The conditions that made possible the existence of (Modern) Greece were geopolitical. Stathis Gourgouris (1996: 5) sees Greece as being conceivable 'only in terms of its location within a wider range of historical formations' and as a distillation, 'of the interceding sociocultural relations between Europe and the Balkan or Eastern Mediterranean region'. Although emerging through the long war of liberation, Greece was an imposition of the Great Powers and depended on the political and ideological complexity of European imperialism and its self-definition against the East (*contra* Calhoun 2007: 161–3). For those imperial powers, nationhood was associated with the various characteristics of the West European state. The social practices of modernity were used to define and order the colonial world, differentiating between developed nations and nations in waiting (Stoler 1995; Mbembe 2001; Said 1980; 1993). That differentiation linked behavioural modes to politico-cultural standing. It embedded the societal norms of the imperial nations into the social and cultural expectations imposed on the colonized to qualify as a nation (Chaudhuri 2009; Chakrabarty 2002; Hall and Rose 2006). One characteristic of the developed nation, particularly of the early nineteenth-century, was the acceptance of Classical notions of citizenship (Pagden 2005; Alston 2010).

The Great Powers placed Greece in the category of nations in waiting, initially disqualified from full nationhood. Paradoxically, given the centrality of the Greek legacy to European identities, Classical Greek culture was seen only as demonstrating the potential of Greece to achieve national identity. In the colonial construction, contemporary Greeks were severed from the Classical heritage. Even though the Greek Enlightenment provided a bridge to Western European thought, it encouraged a colonial authoritarianism since Enlightenment values were held by a minority of the population, as seen with Capodistrias (Kitromilides 2013), rather than a citizen democracy. Despite a fundamental association between the ideologies of nationalism and the political rights of the people (Calhoun 2007), democracy was rejected as a possible regime for the new Greek state, as it had been opposed in Georgian Britian.

This ideological position was convenient for the Bavarian regime. The local Greeks were obliged by their political and military precariousness to accept their young Bavarian king. But such an acceptance did not obscure the ambivalences of the Greeks' interactions with the Bavarian discursive neoclassical construction of Greek identity. Multiple visions of the Greek nation co-existed some of which were inherently subversive of the Bavarian model. Gourgouris (1996: 16–17) talks of Greek national formation as a process of signification in which the amorphous dreams of Greek nationhood metamorphosized into concrete symbols of identity (particularly Athens itself). Such national narratives looked inwards at self-representation and outward at political recognition. Various ideas of the nation remained latent, capable of reanimation in support of or opposition to the Bavarians' hegemonic narratives.

Greek acquiescence in a colonial narrative that was foundational for the nation simultaneously alienated elements of the Greek community from that nation. Identity narratives were closely associated with the Greek language and Orthodox Christianity. The experience of genocidal conflict during a decade of war combined with local historical experiences of violence and resistance. Local identities and political structures were embedded in the narratives of the nation. The revolt was led, initially, by local bishops and regional military leaders, the *kapitani, klefti* and *palichari,* who relied on local power bases. The roles of the *kapitani* and the *klefti* were later romanticized as representations of Greek nationhood (Koliopoulos 1987; Kolokotrones 1969). These narratives functioned in default of any identification with a national, centralized state. The *megali idea* of Greek national identity was the unification of Orthodox Christian communities throughout the Balkans (see also pp. 90–2). This idea was suppressed in the formation of a limited territorial state but remained a powerful element in Greek politics for at least a century.

Further, Greek society developed rapidly after the revolution. It developed and adopted symbols of identity and imported elements of European bourgeois public culture. There was a sufficiently powerful press under Capodistrias that it was worth suppressing and newspapers were a vocal part of the intellectual scene of the new Greek state (Koutsopanagou and Droulia 2009) post-Capodistrias, spreading knowledge of contemporary events and providing for ideological debate.

Greek intellectual culture also drew heavily on currents in Western and Central Europe. Major intellectual figures such as Adamantios Korais and Rigas Velestinlis transmitted elements of the radicalism of the French Revolution to Greece. Greece was not isolated from the intellectual mainstream of Europe. This education was likely not limited to a small and isolated intellectual group: significant sectors of the Greek population were multilingual and highly mobile (Kitromilides 2010, 2013: 175–290). The multiplicity of Greek society generated a cultural hybridity that made a nonsense of simplistic views of 'the Modern Greek'.

In the remainder of this section, I outline various strands in the narratives of the nation: the Romantic discourse of Greece dissociated Greeks from their Classical heritage and Western European ideals of citizenship; a Greek Enlightenment tradition positioned Greece as a potential bastion of civilization against Ottoman oppression; a

Figure 2.1 Map of Greece.

Greek tradition of regional independence and resistance; the religious construction of Greece as the Orthodox Christian nation. These intersecting discourses influenced the development of Athens and reactions to that development over the next decades.

Romantic Greece

The Greek revolt was an attractive cause for Romantic liberals. It represented a struggle of Christians against Ottoman despotism. Greece was already a fantasy land in which dreams of freedom and oppression, culture and nature could be played out. Such dreams are associated with Byron, but Byron himself was likely inspired by William Haygarth's (1814) *Greece: A Poem,* which was a rural epic of the Greek struggle for freedom from the Turk, and Friedrich Hölderlin's (1797–9), influential epistolary novel of a philosophizing Greek freedom-fighter, Hyperion. Thomas Hope's 1819 episodic contemporary Greek Odyssey, *Anastasius,* was published contemporaneously with the latter parts of Byron's *Don Juan* (Cochran 2010). The popular Felicia Hemans (1821) published *Modern Greece*.[1] Her poem repeats tropes of anti-Islamic sentiment and mourns the loss of Classical Greek freedoms, picking up particularly on the 1803 mass suicide of Souliote women when trapped by an Ottoman army (Canto L). That episode was commemorated also in art (Janion 2015).[2] Similarly, Sydney Owenson (1809) found an ideal woman in an Athenian maid, Ida.

These stories established, with some complexity, an association of Greeks and the Greek landscape. Greeks are depicted are creatures of nature rather than culture. They display a primitive rurality which is opposed to the city. The Romantic sentiments of the Greek characters are often doomed or otherworldly. The moral values and political sentiments of the characters are not straightforward. Hope's Anastasius, for instance, seduces, robs, murders and betrays his way across the Levant, and seems mostly disengaged from motives higher than his own pleasure, until he is finally politicized through an encounter with a leading member of the Phanariot elite, Mavrocordatos. Anastasius' moral sensibilities drew criticism in reviews (Article V 1821; Kostova 2007). Hölderlin's Hyperion (1797–9) finds beauty in the Greek landscape. His political education comes through his romances with Alabanda (a noble, young freedom-fighter) and Diotima, both of whom die in the course of the novel. Diotima displays Classical Greek learning and an understanding of Athens, but she is not of the city. She is a creature of the countryside at home on precipitous cliffs or her wild Edenic garden. Hyperion ultimately finds his need for beauty and freedom thwarted in Greece and becomes an exile in Germany, with the implication that it is only there that he can find hope.

Sydney Owenson (1809) expressed the aim of her novel as 'to delineate the character of woman in the perfection of its natural state' (ix). This natural woman is to be found in Athens:

> where the genial influence of climate, the classic interest of scenery, and the sublimity of objects with which it abounds finely harmonize with that almost innate propensity to physical and moral beauty, that instinctive taste for the fair

ideal, and that lively and delicate susceptibility to ardent and tender impressions, which should distinguish the character of woman in its purest and highest state of excellence.

Owenson 1809: ix

Ida is an ideal of bourgeois womanhood, cultured, beautiful and focused on the care of her family. Almost every description of her is drawn through a comparison with Classical statuary, divinities or women from Greek history or myth. Her philosophy is transmitted to her not via books but by nature itself (Owenson 1809: I 12–24). Ida is equated to nature and Classical tradition. She is in opposition to the Ottoman authorities, the peasants who have lost all connection with their Classical heritage, her father, who had been corrupted, and the noisy discordant city of Athens. She is completely unconnected to Orthodox Christianity, a peculiarity that seems to have irritated Byron (Byron 1986: 93). Her lover, Osmyn, is an ideal heroic figure, educated in the Classics by a convenient monk. Their relationship is cemented while sheltering in a Classical temple from a fierce storm (Owenson 1809: II 77). The scene, recalling the story of Aeneas and Dido, is awash with sexual imagery without ever actually mentioning the removal of clothing. Eventually (Owenson 1809: IV), Ida flees Athens for London where she is threatened by a Lord B., a disguise so thin as to be near pointless, until Osmyn appears from Greece to marry her. Ida's mission is described as the betterment of Athenian life through the restoration of Classical practices, the discovery of archaeological fragments, and the introduction of English or French customs (Owenson 1809: II 45–6).

The most famous literary Philhellene was Byron. In 1811, he freely translated Rigas' patriotic hymn as 'Sons of the Greeks Arise', which turned on the Classical resistance to Persia. In 1812, he published the second canto of *Childe Harold's Pilgrimage* in which his hero ventures to Greece.[3] The Athens of stanzas 1–15 is a city of ruins, ignored by the Turks and the Greeks and despoiled by Elgin. Harold's journey through Greece touches on Greek classical monuments and remnants of Greek and Roman past (notably stanza 44).[4] Yet, the focus is on the wild landscape of Greece as, for example, in *The Bride of Abydos* (1813) and *The Siege of Corinth* (1816). The comic and scandalous *Don Juan* I and II came in 1819. At the end of Canto II, a shipwrecked and naked Juan was housed in a convenient cave by a Greek girl, Haidee. Their subsequent relations are described in III–V, published in 1821. Their primitive island of sexual freedom is Homeric, a fantasy ruined by the return of her pirate father. Byron's *Maid of Athens* (1810) encapsulates the Orientalism in Byron's Philhellenism. His 'Maid' was Teresa, daughter of the house of Makri, where he stayed in Athens, who was likely around twelve years old at the time of Byron's dalliance (Beaton 2013: 14–15).[5]

Perhaps the first novel of the new Greek nation was Panayiotis Soutsos' *Leandros* (1834). It has a thinly disguised female representative of Greekness, Classical in her beauty, and belonging to the countryside rather than city (Calotychos 2003: 111–18). The countryside represented a Greekness that stretched back through the ages, forming a palimpsest of Greek history and values, Classical and modern, that is embodied in the heroine and her chaste lover (Peckham 2001: 22–5). Soutsos' narrative was supportive of the Ottonian kingdom and yet the tragic ending of the story, with the couple only united in death and with their love never consummated, suggests that the achievement of national value was to be in a future which the characters cannot reach (Tziovas 2009: 211–24).

These poems and novels embedded moral characteristics in the rural environment. The wildness of the Greek landscape is rendered sublime and is contrasted to the city. Hyperion finds Athens a city of ruins though has hopes that Classicism might once more flourish. For Byron, Athens is a city multiply stripped of its heritage (Byron 1986: 95–6). Owenson's Athens is corrupted under the rule of the Turks and is a place of danger. If Greek rurality and Greek women inspired noble emotions, Greek cities and Greek men did not. This hostile evaluation shaped Western perceptions. As in other colonial literatures, women were seen as the bearers of national virtue and tradition (see, for example, Rendall 2006 and Chakrabarty 1992b). In the Greek case, these women had to be separated from contemporary society and located in Edenic gardens. These children of nature were absolute in their Classical beauty. Yet, their lives were precarious. Haidee and Diotima died, and Ida fled Athens. Greek womanhood found peace in England, Germany or death. They were not part of their own times but belong to a lost landscape of ruins. The vision is colonial.

Enlightenment Greece

William Leake (1835: 148; cf Hobhouse 1813: 574) found two major schools operating in Ioannina in 1809. The first taught a curriculum approved by the ecclesiastical authorities. The second was built by a Greek merchant, Pikrozoi, and was devoted to modern learning. Such institutions were a mechanism by which often radical European thought could pass into Greek culture. Soutsos, for instance, though born remote from the major centres of the Enlightenment, was influenced by contemporary French political thought, including the socialism of Henri de Saint-Simon. Greeks were part of the complex and intricate networks by which Enlightenment intellectual culture spread through Europe (Israel 2001, 2006).

Many of the leading figures of the Greek Enlightenment were from diaspora communities but their Greek-language texts circulated in Greek educational contexts and were influential across the various communities. The philosopher Evgenios Voulgaris (1716–1806) taught at Ioannina, Kozani and on Athos (from 1749) (Kitromilides 2013: 43–53). Iosipos Moisiodax's *Theory of Geography* (1781) brought a utilitarian, scientific geography to the Hellenophone world. Philippidis and Konstantas' *Modern Geography* (1988 [1791]) portrayed a lawless Balkan region under a despotic regime in contrast to a dream of an ordered, law-abiding and commercial new Greek state (Jusdanis 1991: 25; Kitromilides 1992, 2013: 98–116). The pamphlet Ἑλληνικὴ Νομαρχία (1806) was a virulently anti-clerical, nationalist and republican tract. Rather than drawing that republicanism from Classical models, the text looked to contemporary European paradigms (Kitromilides 2006). Adamantios Korais envisaged a modern, rational and scientific Greece. He sought to revive Greek as a scientific and philosophical language, purified from Byzantine and Turkish accretions (Kitromilides 2010, 2013: 175–89, 260–90; Gourgouris 1996: 90–121). Rigas Velestinlis connected the desire for political freedom with rationalism. His *New Political Constitution for the Inhabitants of Roumeli, Asia Minor, the Mediterranean Islands and Wallachia-Moldavia* (1797) was democratic and drew on the American Constitution and the French *Declaration of the Rights of Man* (Kitromilides 2013: 200–29).

The ideas of the Greek Enlightenment were in opposition to the current state of Greece and to those perceived to have authority on the ground, such as the ecclesiastical authorities. Politically, the Church's relationship with the Ottoman authorities was a source of tension. Patriarchs were inevitably subservient to the Sublime Porte since they required the acquiescence of the secular authorities to operate peacefully and the Ottomans held the Church responsible for the behaviour of Christian communities, as was brutally demonstrated in 1821.

Enlightenment thinkers were instrumental to the initial outbreak in the Northern Balkans (*contra* St Clair 2008: 94). Alexandros Mavrokordatos was at the centre of efforts to transform the rebellion of spring 1821 into a revolutionary state. He and his family had impeccable intellectual credentials: an elder Alexandros (1636–1709) was a significant author; Nikolaos (1670–1730) was a sponsor of learning and libraries; Constantinos (1711–63) abolished serfdom in his domains. Alexandros was with the Shelleys in Pisa when news of the revolution broke (Beaton 2013: 68–88).

Necessarily, the Greek Enlightenment carried with it the pervasive Enlightenment engagement with and elevation of the values and culture of Classical Greece. The Greek intellectual vision of a future Greece voiced a desire for a nation that would overcome differences of ethnicity, language and religion to form a republic that would stretch through the Balkans and across the Aegean (Kitromilides 2003). Enlightenment liberalism was fundamental to the attempts to form the Greek state. Alexandros Mavrokordatos was likely the main author of the first major constitution of the Greek state, the Epidavros Constitution of 1822. The constitution enshrined liberal values: freedom of worship (Clause 2.2), equality before the law (2.3), security of property, person and honour (2.7), and a complex system of representative government (3).[6] The constitution made Orthodoxy the religion of the Greek state and Greece a Christian country, with consequent issues for any Muslim population. It had some peculiarities, such as a system of annual rotation of certain magistracies which seems Classically inspired. The constitutionalists consulted the philosophical elite of Europe and attracted the critical support of Jeremy Bentham (Rosen 1992: 78–102). The constitution reflected a confidence that the remarkable Greek victories of 1821 would pave the way to the establishment of a liberal modern state in the southern Balkans (Gordon 1832: I 324).

Such ambitions did not survive the catastrophic events of the war (Gourgouris 1996: 49–53). The radicalism of a Korais or a Velestinlis called for the inculcation of modern values. Yet, the violence empowered factional non-state actors. The heroes of the revolution were the *kapitani*, *palichari* and *klefti*. For the Great Powers, these quasi-Homeric heroes were not suited to the leadership of a modern state and an Enlightened Greece could only be delivered from the outside, especially after the assassination of

Capodistrias. Thus, the democratic civic republicanism of Mavrokordatos mutated into a colonial authoritarianism committed to the imposition of modernity on the supposedly natural Greeks (Kitromilides 2006). Homeric heroes might wander the mountains and deliver Greece its independence, but Classical Greece belonged to the Enlightenment nations. The Bavarian regime appropriated Classical Athens to assert its legitimacy to a European audience and justify the extraordinary and paradoxical result of the Greek war of independence: a Bavarian prince.

The Greece of the kapitani

The differences between the various Greek groups were a theme of the many travellers' accounts (Angelomatis-Tsougarakis 1990: 1–24). They commented on the red caps worn by the sailors of Spetses, on the costumes of the *palikari* and the ornate dress of the bandit-leaders of Roumeli (see, *exempli gratia*, von Klenze 1838: 89–99; About 1883: 36–7, whose visit was in 1852; Cochrane, 1837: 1–10; Thiersch 1833: 218–34). The descriptions marked out the various peoples as being part of worlds separate from the West and from each other. They reflected sensible differences in economic, social and cultural organization in the various regions of Greece. Like Gaul before Caesar's invasion, Greece could be divided into three parts: the islanders, the Moreotes and the Rumeliotes. As with Caesar's geography, these were terms of convenience that masked further localized social and political groupings.

These narratives of regional identity potentially undermined any sense of political and cultural unity. Hobhouse's account of his journey through the region with Byron in 1809–10 is in the minority in seeing the Greeks as a uniform people. He described a complex situation in the region from Preveza and Arta to Ioannina. '*Romaios*' was used as a religious designation and applied to two groups that Hobhouse saw as distinct, the Albanians who lived mostly in the countryside, and the Greeks, who lived in the cities, notably Ioannina. These Greeks were, in Hobhouse's view, identical to the Greeks he encountered in Morea (1813: 70) and he associated these men with their Classical forebears.

> It cannot appear at all surprising, that in their habits of life the modern Greeks should very much resemble the picture that has been transmitted to us of the ancient illustrious inhabitants of their country. Living on the fruits of the same soil, and under the same climate, apparently not changed since the earliest ages, it would be strange if their physical constitutions, and in some measure their tempers, were not very similar to those of the great people whom we call their ancestors; and, in fact, I take their bodily appearance, their dress, their diet, and, as I said before, their tempers, to differ but little from those of the ancient Greeks.... Their faces are just such as served for models to the ancient sculptors, and their young men in particular, are of that perfect beauty, which we should perhaps consider too soft and effeminate in that age in our more northern climate.
>
> *Hobhouse 1813: 495*

He was less impressed by the women, whose faces, body-shapes and heights offered him a ready explanation for the Ancient Greek male's fondness for prostitutes (Hobhouse 1813: 496–7). Nevertheless, Hobhouse was convinced that the Greeks were ready for self-government and would prosper under such conditions.

Others were less sanguine about Greek potential. William Leake (1835: 145) did not see the Greeks as meeting his colonialist requirements for a nation in large part because of the subordination of women. At the height of the war, he saw no prospect of a unified Greek nation coming into being. His solution was a federated state which mirrored the multiple *poleis* of the Classical world (Leake 1826: 139). Leake was a Classical revivalist:

> There is no nation, as far as history has left us the means of judging, that has so little changed in the long course of ages as the Greeks. It may be sufficient, without adverting to the less certain indications of manners or physical aspect, to remark, that the Greeks still employ the same character in writing which was used in the remotest age of their history; that their language has received only such corruptions as cannot fail, for the greater part, to fall into disuse, as literary education and a familiarity with their ancient writers shall be diffused among them.
>
> *Leake 1826: 1*

In Leake's view (1826: 132–3), the leaders who had emerged during the war were little more than bandits. The clergy were unenlightened. The Christian landowners were 'tainted' by Ottoman practices. It was to the commercial classes in the small cities, the most cosmopolitan and bourgeois elements, whom he looked for leadership. That leadership could be detected in a desire to follow the modes of the West:

> Already some strong indications of improvement may be remarked in every class of the people. Among the more civilized who are now attempting to govern the nation, may be perceived an anxiety to merit the good opinion, as well as to profit by the advice, superior knowledge, and political experience of those who are more enlightened than themselves.
>
> *Leake 1826: 142*

Palma di Cesnola (1826: 48–51) also considered the idea of a federated republic but concluded that the 'English model' of Enlightened constitutional monarchy would be the best solution, easing Greece towards modernity by degrees.

Edgar Quinet visited Greece in 1829. Landing at Navarino, he discovered Homeric Greece. He was taken by the beauty of the landscape in Laconia and Messenia (Quinet 1830: 25–54). When he stumbled onto a Greek family living outside Sparta, he found a nearby inscription that mentioned a Menelaus and was transported into Homeric reveries (153–4). His journey in the company of the *pallichari* (sic) drew him to compare the new warriors of those of old (166–7). He was not blind to the terrible destruction of the war. In Messenia he had encountered starving women harvesting herbs from the hillsides (43). Yet, he was predisposed to see the Greek revolution as an epic adventure, a resurgence of folk culture that recalled the *Iliad*, Robin Hood and El Cid (142). In all that glory, he was confronted with the fetid smell and the unburied and mutilated remains of the dead (140). At Mistras and Tripolitsa, he encountered townscapes in ruin, denuded of their populations and mass 'graves' where the uncovered bodies of humans and animals were left to decay in the sun (166–86).

Urban Classical Greece was lost. Periclean Athens was a landscape of ruins (Quinet 1830: 330–55). Other urban centres were either scenes of death or pestilence (266). Yet, Quinet was optimistic that Greece was set on a new path of development that would lead to her modernization. The old powers of Greek society were in decay. The monks and priests, whom he held in contempt, were seen as steeped in superstition. He was offended by monks who failed to offer hospitality (69) and amused by an episcopal pageant (115). The days of the *palichari* were, in his view, over. Quinet expected them to disappear in a modern constitutional Greece (201, 209–10).

Similar views were offered by Samuel Howe (1828) in his history of the Greek revolution. For Howe, the Greeks of the islands and cities had been corrupted by Turkish influence. The commercialism of the islanders rendered them deceitful, but the Greeks of the mountains and especially the 'kleftes' were the true inheritors of the Classical tradition. Classicism was inscribed in the language and bodies of the mountain Greeks who were the true lovers of liberty. Yet, he asserted that 'Greeks are children in the art of Government' (Howe 1828: xvii–xx, 141, 221).

Edward Blaquière (1824, 1826), a fervently anti-Islamic writer for whom the war was for religion and civilization, argued that Greece's long oppression by Muslims was not such as to devalue the potential of the Greeks and that after the French revolution Greeks had emerged as a people eager for Enlightenment:

> The events of the French revolution which put the whole of Europe into motion, were ..., highly favourable to the people of Greece, by greatly increasing their commercial relation, and bringing them into frequent contact with the more civilized nations of the west. The beneficial effects of communication were soon evinced in a variety of ways: a new spirit of inquiry was awakened; education made rapid progress among all classes; numerous schools were founded at various points of the Continent and Archipelago, in which able professors instructed the youth in modern science and the literature of their ancestors. The enthusiasm manifested by all classes of the Greek people, to improve since the above period, has been a just source of admiration to travellers, while it proves them to be worthy of that freedom for which they are now struggling: – never did any people betray a greater ardour in the pursuit of knowledge than did the Greeks of thirty years ago, and never were the benign effects more happily illustrated than in the wonderful change which has taken place among them within that short period.
>
> *Blaquière 1824: 17*

That Enlightenment paradigm was caught up with class differentials. He lavished considerable praise on the Phanariotes, but the Maniotes were robbers, the traditional

Greek leaders and the bishops corrupt, and Bishop Germanos of Patras was singled out as vain, ambitious, selfish and intriguing (Blaquière 1824: 103, 118–19).

Lytton Bulwer, who can be characterized as an Establishment intellectual, visited Greece, briefly, in autumn 1824. His overwhelming hostility to Islam transmuted into his political views: Islamic rule offended 'natural' principles to excite 'our … risibility and detestation' (Bulwer 1826: 4–5). Without ever explaining his political logic, Bulwer linked Christianity and liberty and Islam and tyranny. Yet, he was also disparaging of contemporary Greeks. 'In parts', Greece was excellent, but the whole was barbarous (Bulwer 1826: 7). He was sadly disappointed in the attractiveness of Greek women, who gossiped and spent time in the bath houses. He did, however, make an exception for the women of Skios:

Their large black eyes have an expression of melancholy voluptuousness, drowsy seriousness of lust, which suits well their luxuriant locks and rich complexions.

Bulwer 1826: 117

In common with several of his masculine European contemporaries, Bulwer found that gazing on Greek women was sufficient to make complex political assessments of the readiness of Greece for self-rule (compare Garston 1842: 88–9). Bulwer disparaged Orthodox religion as old-fashioned and primitive (1826: 116–17). The 'Captains' and their followers were not heroic, but mercenaries (9, 12, 58, 286–7). Little trace of Classical morality survived in Greek society. The Greek leadership was vain and ambitious and needed to be repressed, but only after the war had been won (98). He supported Mavrokordatos (102–3) but noted that he lacked local support. Bulwer's solution was an executive imposed and presumably manned by the European powers (297–9) and with a large enough army to overawe the Captains. The struggle for Greece was not, in the last instance, for the Greeks. They were players in a proxy war between freedom and tyranny, Christianity and Islam, West and East.

Frédéric Thiersch, who was closely connected to the Ottonian regime, also took a hostile view of the traditional powers in Greek society. For Thiersch, who was a Professor of Classics in Munich, the Church represented the medievalism of contemporary Greeks. Although he acknowledged the importance of the Church in rallying the Greeks to the revolutionary cause, in his view, the new state ought to be established on 'reciprocity of interests and laws and mutual trust, which alone, can be regarded as a durable foundation in the volcanic soil of the Orient' (Thiersch 1833: 194). The future of Greece lay in the emergence of a strong central state, the curbing of the influence of the Church, uniting disparate interest groups in a new political settlement (194–5), a modern bureaucracy, contractual relations, and commercialism (180–99, 195). His view was close to that of Capodistrias (Woodhouse 1973: 353–409). Critical reviews of Thiersch's account focused on his favourable treatment of Capodistrias rather than on the modernization project itself (Examen critique 1835).

The colonial mentality is seen throughout George Cochrane's (1837) colourful account of his time in Greece. He interspersed his eye-witness account of the last years of the war, when he accompanied his uncle Lord Cochrane, with ethnographic descriptions. His first encounter with the sailors of Hydra focuses on their red caps, their wild, long hair and their moustaches. He was drawn to compare them with the Ancient Britons, only marginally more civilized since they wore cloth rather than skins (Cochrane 1837: I 8–12). Cochrane's frank astonishment caused Orlando, his guide in matters Greek, to intervene:

> I perceive, my friend, that you are quite astonished at the rude and savage appearance of my countrymen; but I hope that you will not think the worse of them for their outsides. Recollect … that these men have been the principal obstacle to the Turk in the whole war; and they have immortalized their island by their feats of valour. These men … although under so unfavourable an appearance, have wives and children at home, upon whom they lavish as much tenderness as you in more civilized climes. Their hearts are, I assure you, sensible to benevolent and lively impressions; and they have proved that they are brave.
>
> *Cochrane 1837: I 10*

Orlando balanced domestic virtue and manly bravery as markers of civilization against primitive dress. Cochrane, who sometimes seems an astonishingly naïve reporter, was fixated on externals: his impressions of an encounter with Kolokotronis and his companions focused on their picturesque costumes and their personal weapons (Cochrane 1837: I 33–4). He also exemplified the Byronic urge for sexual adventure in the colonial encounter. He saw Greece through women, starting with the silent, fifteen-year-old daughter of Admiral Tombazi, who is described as 'picturesque' (Cochrane 1837: I 29–30). The girl was scenery. His behaviour towards her caused disquiet in the salon of the admiral. His later meeting with Orlando's wife and daughters is described in similar terms (Cochrane 1837: I 89–92).

When Cochrane met Karaiskakis, a hero of the revolution, his attention was diverted by Karaiskakis' lover. She was supposedly free from marital conventions yet maintained feminine modesty. Cochrane (1837: I 42–5) renders her child-like in her supposed attraction to his uncle on account of the gold lace of his uniform. He was a man of high status who looked on women and judged. Those women were assessed against a series of interlinked criteria: physical beauty; a perceived connection to the supposed blonde, blue-eyed, white-skinned women of Greek antiquity, and their oriental manner (Cochrane 1837: I 64–5, 93–4).

Cochrane returned to Greece in 1834. His reports centre on the elaborate society events given by the various dignitaries, including a musical evening held by the Countess Armansperg in Nauplio, a ball she gave to celebrate the arrival of Otto in Athens, another given by the British ambassador (at which solid English food was served), the celebrations for the arrival of Otto's father, King Ludwig I of Bavaria, and a royal ball to celebrate the laying of the foundation stone of the new palace (Cochrane 1837: I 141–2, 152–6, 160–3, 222–5, 307–8). These balls brought him into contact with Greek ladies and allowed him to trace what he saw as the emergence of women from oriental manners. The adoption of 'European' customs surprised him and excited his approval. He notes that at the British ambassadorial ball (I 163) all his dancing partners spoke fluent French. He also provided a guide to changing etiquette. The Greek ladies had put aside their simple cotton dresses in favour of Parisian fashions (I 308). He concluded that Athens had 'emerged from barbarism to incipient civilization', signified by fine dancing, the speaking of French, the presence of 'high society' and female conversation (I 156).

Cochrane frequently noted the presence of the old Greek war leaders at the various events, perhaps surprised that the *kapitani* would mix in such circles. He appears, like many colonialists, not to have considered the locals' capacity for shifting through cultural codes. Nor does it appear to have crossed his mind that many of the dancing ladies of Athens had learnt French as part of the necessary education of the European *haute bourgeoisie*. That women dressed simply during war and later adopted fashionable Parisian dresses (Cochrane 1837: I 304) was not interpreted as a sign of improved economic circumstances, but of civilization brought to Athens by the European powers. For him, the balls mattered because they reflected a recognizable class structure that replicated the values that he associated with civilization.

Nevertheless, while other outsiders assumed that the *kapitani* would disappear, Cochrane (1837: II 5–10) was conscious of their continuing power. When a rebellion broke out near Mesolongi, it was the *kapitani* and their *palichari*, once more on the payroll of the Greek state, who were despatched to deal with the problem.

Political leadership in Roumeli was embedded in a long tradition of localized armed groups. These were called *armatoli* and were commanded by *kapitani* when licensed by the various authorities, and *kleftis* when on the run from those authorities. Such bands came into operation in a difficult economic environment with weak state-level control that necessitated local systems of protection (Koliopoulos 1987, 1989). Before 1821, the Ottomans had employed a form of clientelism which relied on local strong men. This process created a patchwork of local agents which although inherently unstable (Hobsbawm 1969; Tilly 2003; Walston 1988), became embedded in the political culture of the Roumeli and the Mani (Reid 2000: 119–74). In the Mani, the Mavromichalis were one of several leading families and their fragile hegemony stemmed from their recognition as Beys by the Ottomans.

Banditry was often a family business. Kolokotronis was the third generation of his family to be a bandit leader (Kolokotrones 1969). Several generations of the Karaiskakis family were *armatoli*. The successful Greek bandit was not a lone wolf but was closely embedded within the structures of the patriarchal family, the locality, and with links to state power (Gallant 1989; compare Blok 1972, 1974; Hobsbawm 1969; Lewin 1979). The longevity of individual bandits depended on their compatibility with other power brokers and their ability to build strong local allegiances. Under the Ottomans, state subsidies brought the *kapitani* a measure of security and stability. The war provided opportunities, particularly in raiding cities and estates, and promised a greater independence for the *kapitani*. It also disrupted agriculture and trade networks, diverted manpower from productive activities, destroyed equipment, killed livestock and degraded the economic infrastructure. The war itself drove more people into dependency on the *kapitani*.

The *armatoli* maintained as complex a relationship to the Greek state as they had had with the Ottoman authorities. Although they could claim, with some reason, to represent the Greek cause, their motivations were shaped largely by local concerns, and their primary political requirement was to secure sufficient resources to maintain their followers.

During the war, leaders in the Roumeli especially needed to decide whether their security was better provided for by the Greeks or Ottomans. Gogos Bakolas raised the people of Arta against the Porte, but Arta was on the front-line and exposed to Ottoman reprisals (Reid 2000: 121). He was under pressure and suspected of treachery at the catastrophic defeat at Peta in 1822, where the sudden retreat of his forces exposed the Greek lines and led to many of their troops being surrounded (Gordon 1832: I 380–91; Leake 1826: 79; Howe 1828: 87–92 with an eye-witness account). Another Roumeli leader, Odysseus, who held Athens in the middle years of the war, acquired his territory without obvious support from other Greek leaders and showed little regard for the 'official' Greek government. Odysseus was eventually supplanted by a rival *kapitanos*, Gouras, who unceremoniously threw his rival off the top of the Acropolis (Gordon 1832: II 184–7). Gouras was in turn eclipsed by Karaiskakis, who was from a prominent dynasty of *armatoli*, and consequently well connected.

The *kapitani* had benefited from looting in the earlier stages of the war, but later required subsidies to maintain their troops in the field. Greek governmental money, obtained primarily from loans or gifts from Philhellenic groups, was transferred to the *kapitani*, an act deprecated by at least some of the Europeans who thought that the loans could be used to establish a national army (Bulwer 1826: 12; Palma di Cesnola 1826: 1–7, 17–18). Still more idealistic were those who thought that the Greeks should fight without monetary support and that the loans were unnecessary (Palma di Cesnola 1826: 22–3, reports such views). But the *kapitani* provided the only viable land forces and those troops were loyal to their local leaders (Gordon 1832: II 176–80). The result was mutual dependence.

With the end of the war, the military-political equation changed. The threat from the Ottomans was reduced and French and then Bavarian troops provided the regency with forces independent of the *kapitani*. Consequently, one of the first acts of the Ottonian regency was to stop paying the *armatoli*. As we have seen, Europeans assumed that the *palichari* would fade away. Yet, banditry was embedded within the economy and culture of the region and the *klefti* either could not make a living in villages devastated during the war or did not care to. Some crossed the frontier to seek employment with the Ottomans. Other supported themselves from banditry (Koliopoulos 1987: 77). Kapitanos Vasos ran a small fiefdom around Menidi in what is now suburban north Athens. From there, he threatened local Albanian villages and fed off the routes south from Oropos. Even the main roads from Athens to Corinth and Piraeus were considered dangerous: Wordsworth (1836: 254–5) in 1832–3 found himself threatened by bandits in northern Attica and was advised by his local guides to only travel to the Piraeus in a strong party (compare Miller 1926: 7).

Some leaders successfully made the transition into national figures. As heroes of the revolution, they carried emotional and political resonances in the new state. In coming together, they represented an idea of Greece, an idea embedded in local power networks, in villages and mountains, but not in the city. Yet, an independent violent local leadership was not easily integrated into a modern nation. The Maniotes resisted Greek governmental efforts to limit their independence, leading to the death of Capodistrias (Woodhouse 1973; Finlay 1861: II 194–221). In 1836, in the absence of Otto who was finding himself a wife, many of the Rumeliotes revolted. There was an associated tax boycott. Resistance to the bureaucratic mechanisms of the modern state was led by *klephtic* leaders. The regency, under Count Armansperg, was obliged to turn to other *kapitani*, Tzavelas, Grivas, Vasos, Gouras and others. The fragmentation of the *kleftic* groups gave the Ottonian state an advantage, but the state also needed the irregulars (Petropoulos 1968: 262–3; Cochrane 1837: II 5–10). Consequently, the Bavarian-Greek state was obliged to restore the flows of money that allowed the leadership to maintain local power bases.

Frédéric Thiersch (1833: 218) described the Roumeli as an area that maintained the chivalrous spirit of the medieval period, 'a mix of bravoura and brigandage, hospitality and violence, ignorance and presumption . . .' in which there was an enjoyment of 'savage liberty'. This savage liberty was part of the national imaginary and the romance of the *klepht* became integral to the myths of nationalistic identity throughout the nineteenth century, a romance that emphasized the local rather than the national and counterpoised the *klephtic* tradition to the disciplines of the modern state (Sant Cassia 1993).

The Orthodox nation

Religion was central to the local formation of identity and the war was as much one of religion as of the nation. In the Peloponnese, the Bishops of Patras, Modon and Elos were at the forefront of campaigning. On the news of the revolt reaching Constantinople, the Ottomans hung the body of the Patriarch George V from his palace gates. It was Easter Sunday, 21 April 1821 (Beaton 2013: 72–9). Both sides perpetrated massacres justified by religious differences (St Clair 2008: 1–12). The massacre at Tripolitsa was preceded by news of ethnic slaughters in Constantinople and Smyrna (Raybaud 1824: 419–20 and Gordon 1832: I 237 for contrasting accounts). Promises of safe passage were regularly broken. There were mass murders at Mesolongi, Chios, Psara and elsewhere (Finlay 1861: I 272–3, 306–20; II 2, II 83–111; Gordon 1832: I 172, 347–69; II: 130–8, 229–61).

Much of the Moslem heritage of Southern Greece was destroyed. Islamic Tripolitsa was burnt. Even the tombs were destroyed. Frédéric Thiersch (1833: 199) found Muslim landowners, merchants and soldiers at Nauplio who awaited the arrival of their Bavarian king. Thiersch's acquaintances were optimists. The continued Muslim presence was an important sign that the new state would have room for all, regardless of religion (Gordon 1832: I 324). Most European travellers made almost no mention of a living Moslem tradition in the regal period. A lithograph of Nauplio from 1828 (held in the Benaki Museum) shows distinctive pencil thin minarets, none of which are visible in a Rottmann watercolour of 1835. Wolf's 1837 depiction of the arrival of Otto and Amalia in Athens shows minarets in the old city (Biris 2005: 68).[7] Three years later, Ferdinand Stademann's panorama of the city of 1840/41 shows mosques or the remains of mosques, but no minarets (Stademann 1841). The Greek nation had little space for religious diversity.

On 23 July/4 August 1833, a synod proclaimed formal independence of the Orthodox Church in Greece from the Church in Constantinople.[8] It was configured as a national Church with Otto as its temporal head and had a permanent synod appointed directly by Otto (Strong 1842: 348–56). This association of Church and state reinforced the imagined community of the nation as Orthodox and anti-Islamic. Yet, Otto never found Athens worth an Orthodox liturgy.

When the Great Powers drew a line on the map in March 1829 between Volos and Arta, they were making a judgement which was diplomatic and military but not cultural or religious. The Greek Revolution had had little traction to the north of the line, but if Greece was imagined as a religious community, many Greeks remained north of the border. Ioannis Kolettis gave expression to what has become known as the *megali idea* (the big idea) (Clogg 1988). In a speech of 1844, he said that:

> The Kingdom of Greece is not Greece. It constitutes only one part, the smallest and feeblest. The name Hellenes describes not only those who live in this kingdom, but also those who live in Jannina, in Thessaloniki, in Serres, in Adrianople, in Constantinople, in Trebizond, in Crete, in Samos and in any territory associated with Hellenic history and the Hellenic race. [...] There are two prime cores of Hellenism: Athens, the capital of the Hellenic Kingdom, and the City (Constantinople), the vision and hope of all Hellenes.
>
> *Kolettis 2007 [1844]*

This was not the articulation of a nationalistic megalomania, but a fundamental imagining of the Greek nation that was more obviously embedded within Greek political culture than any form of Classical revivalism. Thiersch claimed that:

> If you ask a man of the lower class of the people what is the capital of Greece, he would answer you that it is Constantinople. You add 'your revolution, when will it end?' His answer will be, 'When the Greek cross is lifted over Hagia Sophia!'
>
> *Thiersch 1833: 198–9*

The Classics professor found lower-class Greeks peculiar in their nationalistic sentiments and unrealistic in their geo-political ambition. But their view was shared by at least some of the Greek political class. It was an issue that came to a head with the choosing of the new capital. For many, the state formed at the end of the war of liberation was merely a stage in the historical progression of the Greek nation towards the unification of the Christian Balkans. In a letter of March 13/15 1833, Kolettis, who was clearly losing the debate, argued for a pause, and that it was self-evident that Constantinople was the historical and future home of the Greek nation (Papadopoulou-Sumeonidou 1996: Document 1.5). Many of his contemporaries seem to have agreed (Bastéa 2000: 7; 118).

The return to Athens was the historical destiny of the Greek people only for Classicists and the doyens of the Enlightenment.

These four interlinked and competing strands in Greek identity politicized cultural life. The Bavarians' attempt to establish a monopoly of legitimate violence emphasized a particular imagining of the nation. The wearing of traditional accoutrements of violence could be interpreted as a gesture of opposition (Tilly 2003: 86–9) and adherence to ideas that could be grouped under the slogan of the *megali idea*. The romanticization of the *kleft* had the potential to entrench an 'ideology of difference' (for Italian comparanda, see Franchetti and Sonnino 1974 and Moss 1979). Such a dichotomy gives added significance to the portrait of Ioannis Kolettis painted by Dominique Papety in 1848 in which the former ambassador to Paris and founder of the 'French party' in Greece chose to be depicted in the velvet coat and the *koboloi*, the sash, which marked him as a Greek of the mountains.[9] Similarly, Drakos's painting of his successor as prime minister, Kitsos Tzavelas (in the National Historical Museum), shows him as a Rumeliot warrior, complete with dagger.[10] Tzavelas had been an important *kapitanos* in Western Greece as had his father and grandfather before him.

From a colonialist position, these various visions of Greece should have been incompatible, but in the maelstrom of competing ideas, individuals could move between different conceptions of the nation. Even Otto was in readiness to sail on Constantinople following the death of Mahmud II in 1839 (Bastéa 2000: 118). After 1843, the Greek government pursued, mostly in clandestine fashion, an extension of Greek influence across the border through *armatoli* and the 1854 revolt of Epirus encouraged the *megali idea*. Rather than fading away, the Greek national romance of the *kleft* gathered pace (Rose 1897; Koliopoulos 1989) even as the association of Greek identity with religion was fading in favour of the linking of language and identity in the emerging nations of the northern Balkans (Wilkinson 1951; Peckham 2000).

These different ideological strands could co-exist in part because of the distance between ideology and practice. Some might imagine a unified Orthodox state, but political and military realities dictated the terms of the settlement. In the practical world of politics, the competing visions of the Greek nation needed to co-exist. As the Ottonians needed the *palichari* so the *kapitani* welcomed the security of the Greek kingdom. The various parties were united in their antipathy to Ottoman rule, but the new state was not embedded in any pre-existing social and political structures. It had no obvious local constituency. And yet, all had an interest in its survival.

It was predictable that the Great Powers would opt for a colonial solution to Greece. Leake (1826: 1; 133–9) had argued for a federated Republic, presumably on the model of the USA, influenced by his understanding of Classical Greek history. George Finlay (1861: I 20–37, 41) took a similar view. He thought that the regency and Ottonian attempt to impose a strong central state was a mistake since it ignored the primary loyalties of the Greeks to their localities and the surprisingly efficient and functional local institutions. But such inventiveness ran counter to a European fondness for more centralized governance of which Capodistrias, schooled in a Russian authoritarian tradition, was representative. After his assassination in 1831, the Great Powers secured Otto of Bavaria,

Classicism and the Construction of Capital Cities

and the national assembly invited him to take office on 26 June 1832 (Finlay 1861: II: 275). Otto had just turned seventeen. A regency was established under the Bavarians von Armansperg and von Maurer and funded with British and Bavarian money. The Bavarians were more liberal than Capodistrias and were modernizers of the Enlightenment tradition, but their approach was colonial.

Classicism was an element in these political debates, but a small element. Stanhope (1825), for example, begins with a preface (not authored by Stanhope), which recalls the ancient glories of Greece, but reads the uprising in Greece as an Enlightenment revolution. Leading figures such as Blaquière (1824; 1826) and Palma di Cesnola (1826) hardly mentioned the Classical past in making the case for a free Greece. The issues they worked through were religious. Classicism belonged to the West and was alienated from Greece as surely as were the 'Elgin Marbles'. Although always with the potential for reappropriation, the Classical returned to Greece as the colonial.

The nation's capital: Designing Athens

There were a number of options for the nation's capital. In addition to Athens, Nauplio, Aigina, Argos, Corinth, Megara, Syros and Tripolis were suggested (Miller 1926: 2). The various local powers realized the benefits of securing the capital, its administrative functions and the court. On May 12/24 1832, even before the elevation of Otto and during a near civil war, the government commissioned two young architects, Eduard Schaubert and Stamatios Kleanthis, to plan a new Athens. This city was, according to Kleanthis, to be 'equal with the ancient fame and glory of the city and worthy of the century in which we live'.[11]

Kleanthis was a Greek born in Kozani. He had fought at the battle of Dragatsani and subsequently went into exile. He went to Berlin to study architecture with Schinkel and afterwards set out to Italy, accompanied by Schaubert, his friend and fellow architect. They carried letters of introduction from Schinkel to General von Heideck. Heideck was a Philhellene and a professional soldier who had fought in the war of independence and had held military command under Capodistrias. He was a keen painter and maintained an artistic circle. He was well placed to sponsor the development of architecture in Greece, especially after he was appointed to the Regency Council. He provided Schaubert and Kleanthis with additional letters of introduction and sent then to Capodistrias. Capodistrias sent them on to Athens in 1831 and they were already in place when the post-Capodistrian government commissioned an urban plan in the following May (Papageorgiou-Venetas 2010a; Bastéa 2000: 70).

The choice of capital was still being debated. In March 1833, Kolettis wrote in favour of Megara even though he thought 'the capital of the kingdom of Greece must be Constantinople'. Constantinople was the capital of the Byzantine emperors and at the forefront of 'our civilization' and 'of spreading light, in the consolidation of laws' (Papadopoulou-Sumeonidou 1996: document 1.5). Kolettis neatly blended an Enlightenment perspective and traditional Greek concerns. A report of May 1833 commented on the healthiness of Athens when compared with Corinth, the rich agriculture on the plain of Athens, particularly the olive groves, the availability of water and other natural resources, the communication routes, the port, and the monuments which made the city one of the most important in the world. The report also commented on population, seeing 8,000–10,000 as a viable population for the nation's capital (Papadopoulou-Sumeonidou 1996: document 1.1). At about the same time, Spyridon Trikoupis was writing in favour of a city at the Isthmos, though pointing also to the large market town on Syros (Papadopoulou-Sumeonidou 1996: document 1.2). Mavrokordatos also favoured a capital on the Isthmos, emphasizing the good communications, the potential for development along the coast toward Loutraki, and the relative cheapness of land (Papadopoulou-Sumeonidou 1996: document 1.4). On 27 May 1833, the newspaper *Athena* argued against Athens and for a commercial centre (Bastéa 2000: 7–8).

The boundaries of the new Greek state effectively put the Isthmos at its centre. It had excellent naval facilities and controlled land routes between Morea and Roumeli. Corinth was an established commercial centre, though it had been battered in the war. Yet, one suspects that the reasons for not choosing Athens were a mirror of the reasons Athens was chosen. Choosing Athens classicized the notion of the Greek state and weakened the *megali idea*.

It looks like an argument that was already lost. Sending Kleanthis and Schaubert to Athens signalled Capodistrias's intent. For neoclassicists, including Ludwig of Bavaria, the attraction of Athens was immense. For the European cultural elite, no other city in Greece, or possibly anywhere, could compete with its cultural and emotional attachments (Angelomatis-Tsougarakis 1990; Samiou 2009). In July 1833, it was decided that the capital would move from Nauplio to Athens on 1 January 1834 (von Klenze 1838: 21).

In 1829, when Edgar Quinet sailed from Nauplio to Piraeus with a view to visiting Athens, he found the harbour deserted and only with great difficulty managed to secure transport into the city. When he reached Athens:

> its misery surpassed our expectations. On the reverse of the mountain, where the town is raised up a little on the side, and in a semi-circle that it traces at its base, some houses in broken ground are rolled across yellow mounds, where the eye cannot recognise any form ... the rooves are dismantled, the walls open, leaving the impression of recent destruction ...
>
> *Quinet 1830: 335–6*

Bodies lay by the roadside, partially covered, and everywhere was the smell of death. Ever the enthusiast, Quinet (1830: 335–55) attempted to copy an inscription but was stoned and beat a retreat.

When Christopher Wordsworth visited in 1832, the city was still in a terrible state:

> The town of Athens is now lying in ruins. The streets are almost deserted: nearly all the houses are without roofs. The churches are reduced to bare walls and heaps of stones and mortar. There is but one church in which the service is performed. A

few new wooden houses, one or two more solid structures, and the two lines of planked sheds which form the bazar are all the inhabited dwelling that Athens can now boast. In this state of *modern* desolation, the grandeur of the ancient buildings which still survive here is more striking: their preservation is more wonderful… The least ruined objects here, are some of the Ruins themselves.

Wordsworth 1836: 51

Wordsworth was a prize-winning poet (*Complete Collection* 1859: 138–53) and a desolate Athens brought out his Romantic disposition.

Our abode is the nearest building to the Temple of Theseus. Formerly its site was in the heart of the city: it is now of the extreme verge of the modern town, to the west of it. There are few other buildings near it. At a little distance to the south a peasant is engaged in plowing the earth with a team of two oxen: the soil along which he is driving his furrows, was once part of the Agora of Athens … There would be rural sights such as Aristophanes describes of husbandmen issuing out into the fields, with their iron implements of agriculture shining in the sun, at the conclusion of a long war: perhaps a festal procession might just be losing itself in a distant grove. All this has now disappeared, and there is nothing of the kind in its place. Now from this point, here and there a solitary Albanian peasant is seen following his mule laden with wood along the road into the town; and the most cheerful sight in the plain before us, is that of the thick wood of olives growing on the site of the Academy toward the left – which looks now like a silver sea rippling in the autumnal breeze.

Wordsworth 1836: 53

It was not the destruction of the Ottoman city that affected Wordsworth, but the spectre of its remote Classical predecessor. Indeed, Wordsworth seems blind to recent history, preferring the romance of a fallen Classical civilization to which he and his readers were already emotionally and culturally attuned.

Wordsworth was seeing the Ottoman city in its last days and filled it with Orientalist tropes:

The Muezzin still mounts the scaffold in the bazar here to call the Mussulman to prayer at the stated hours; a few Turks still doze in the archways of the Acropolis, or recline smoking their pipes, and leaning with their backs against the rusty cannon which are planted in the battlements of its walls; the Athenian peasant, as he drives his laden mule from Hymettus through the eastern gate of the town, still flings his small bundle of thyme and brushwood, from the load which he brings on his mule's back, as a tribute to the Mussulman toll-gatherer, who sits at the entrance to the town; and a few days ago the cannon of the Acropolis fired the signal of the conclusion of the Turkish Ramazam – the last which will ever be celebrated in Athens.

Wordsworth 1836: 247

Yet, for all their literary flourishes, the travellers' tales are easy to believe. The population before the war may have been as high as 12,000 (Biris and Kardamisi-Adami 2001: 72). In 1824, it was reckoned at 9,040 (Gordon 1832: II 188). When the Bavarians entered the city on 1 April 1833, there were perhaps as few as 300 houses in the city (Miller 1926: 3–5). Estimates suggest a population of about 6,000 (Russack 1942: 28), though at around twenty people per house their reliability can be questioned. Whatever the precise truth, the housing stock was severely damaged, and the population was likely living in overcrowded and squalid conditions.

By 1834, George Cochrane was able to find a hotel, but was still disgruntled:

The view of the Acropolis is exceedingly impressive, and engenders an exalted idea of the magnificence of the city; but on reaching it, what a melancholy contrast presented itself! It was ... scarcely possible to conceive of a more disgusting filthy place. At every step my baggage horses sank half way to their knees in mud, the odours arising from which must have been pestilential.

Cochrane 1837: 146

By that year, Kleanthis and Schaubert had been long at work. Their first task was to map the city. There were earlier topographical sketches (Mallouchou-Tufano 1994), but the first recognizable map was made by Fauvel in 1787 (Korres 2010b). That map shows a walled city sited beneath the Acropolis. Close to the Acropolis, the multiple streets and alleys show no sign of regular planning, but further away, the streets appear broader and more regular and fan out from a central point. Some of the main buildings of the city appear, notably mosques and churches. A map of Athens in 1820 listed 158 churches and monasteries in the city (Malouchou 2010; Papageorgiou-Venetas 2010b). The Bessan map of 1826 shows a recognizably similar street system though some areas of the old city were either unmapped or had been abandoned (Korres 2010a; Papageorgiou-Venetas 2001: 23).

Kleanthis and Schaubert produced a detailed large-scale map of the city in 1831–2 (Papageorgiou-Venetas 2010a). The map detailed the irregularity of Athens. In a memorandum of 1832, Kleanthis and Schaubert (1994) described the streets as crooked and narrow. They identified 115 small churches, of which around thirty were functional, four mosques and two bath houses. The majority of residences were described as 'huts', though twenty-five qualified as houses. Although less extreme than the contemporary literary accounts, they depict a city that had ceased to function.

Their first plan for the new city, which is little more than a sketch, was probably devised in 1831 with further versions in 1832. These first plans were recognizably similar to the plan submitted in 1833 (Biris 2005: 26–30; Papageorgiou-Venetas 2001: 45–8). Athens is a city with a strong natural topography, built between the Acropolis and Lykabettos hills, and framed by the larger mountains of Hymettos, Pendeli and Egaleo. The old city wrapped itself round the Acropolis hill, sliding down to Monastiraki and the Roman and Ancient *agorai*. Kleanthis and Schaubert acknowledged the centrality of the Acropolis, but otherwise imposed an artificial topography on the city.

Classicism and the Construction of Capital Cities

Figure 2.2 The Fauvel plan of Athens (1787).

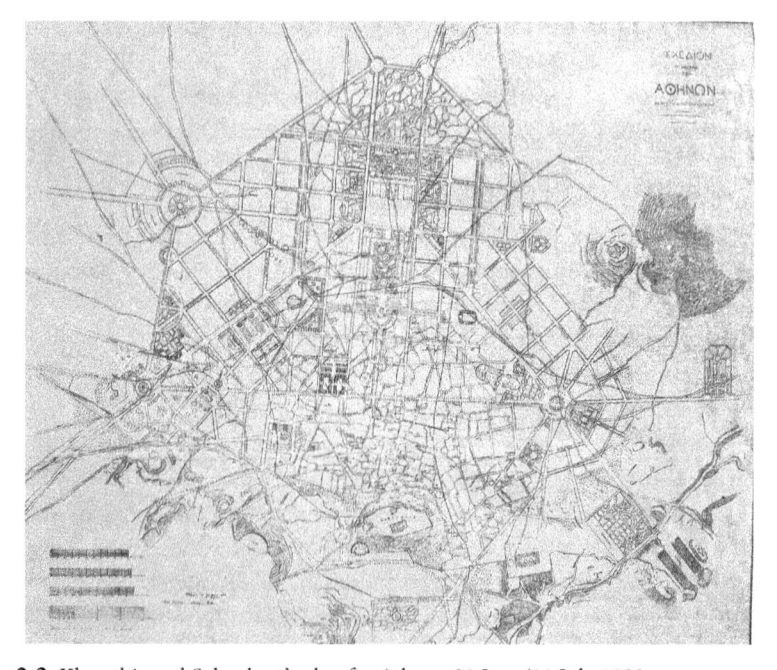

Figure 2.3 Kleanthis and Schaubert's plan for Athens, 29 June/11 July 1833.

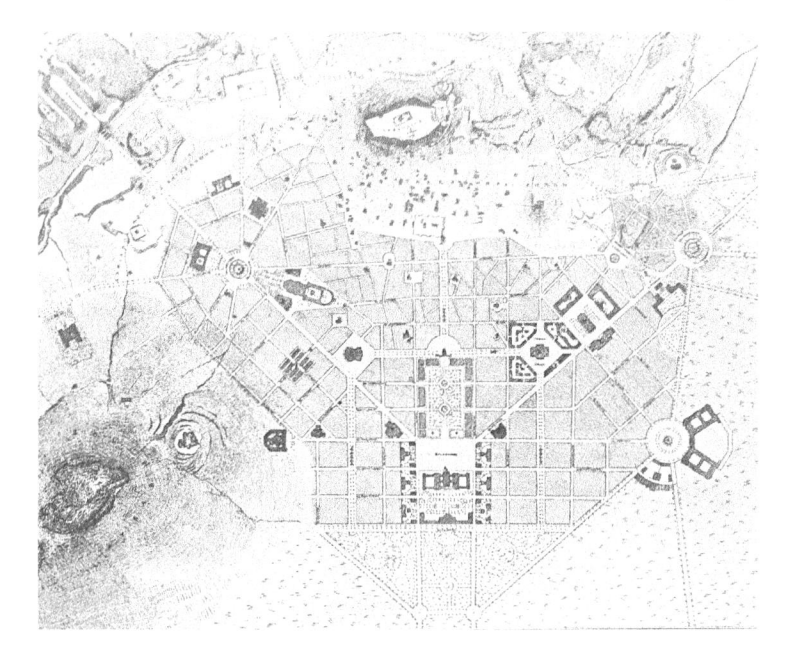

Figure 2.4 Kleanthis and Schaubert's plan for Athens, late 1833.

Their plan was remarkable in its ambition. In its June/July iteration, they planned for a complex geometry with a large central strip which blended into a triangular form with a flanking district centred on a large circular piazza. This plan was progressively simplified but remained recognizable in its later iterations.

The frame for the plan was composed of a triangle of avenues formed by the Odos Peiraios, the Odos Stadiou, and the Odos Hermou. Peiraios and Stadiou met to form a 90 degree angle at the proposed site of the palace. This later became Plateia Omonoia (Concord Square). The other angles formed Plateia Mouson (Square of the Muses), which became Syntagma (Constitution Square) and Plateia Kekrops (now the Technopolis Park). The triangle was split exactly in the middle by Athinas, a road running from Monastiraki (Library of Hadrian) to Omonoia at 90 degrees to Hermou. The road connected the palace to the Roman agora, where some of the more impressive surviving Classical remains were visible. It created a vista between the proposed palace and the Acropolis. About half way to Omonoia, a road (modern Euripidou) running parallel to Ermou cut across from Stadiou to Peiraios. It joined the roads at two small squares, now Eleftherias and Klauthmonos. This road and Athinas were to be lined with trees, creating shaded boulevards that further emphasized the centrality of routes through the city (Biris 2005: 26–30).

The old city was to be swept away. The new city was to accommodate about 40,000 people, at least three times the population of the Ottoman city before the war, in about 4,000 houses, each of which was to have a courtyard or garden. Kleanthis and Schaubert envisaged an improved condition of domestic life in new Athens.

The plan included extensive formal gardens in which the palace was set. These were complimented by smaller gardens set along Athinas, which led into the markets. There was a plan for a botanical garden in the south-east (near the Temple of Olympian Zeus). Facilities were functionally divided. The economic quarter was along the Piraeus road with the post office, the customs house, the police and courthouse. It was thought that the houses would be occupied by merchants. The eastern flank of the city, towards Lykabettos, became the governmental quarter with the finance ministry, the war ministry, the mint, the armoury and small foundry. Stadiou was to be a social area with a large church, a theatre, the bourse, and the casino. The more unpleasant urban functions were located away from the city: the hospital, the slaughterhouse, the graveyard and the oil mills. Water was to come from the Ilissos, off Hymettos, and from the Hadrianic aqueduct that brought water from Kifissia (Kleanthis and Schaubert 1994).

The plan laid out what was to become the basic morphology of the modern city. It was constructed around a series of interlocked triangles formed by long straight roads. These established lines of access, points of communication and long vistas. Such connectivity allowed the city to be displayed and walked in an ordered fashion (not wandered). It placed emphasis on the visual, which was dominated by the royal palace and associated gardens at the city's heart, and the Acropolis as a counterpoint to that centre.

The plan was aesthetically and politically conservative. Friedrich Weinbrenner's Karlsruhe and Gilly's Berlin had both envisaged their ideal viewer as a citizen-wanderer who strolled through locales and encountered monuments. Gilly's masterpiece, the Friedrichsdenkmal, was a Classical temple designed to be walked around rather than seen from afar (Neumeyer 1994: 44). By contrast, the traditional Baroque urban form emphasized vistas to monumental conclusions. This was seen as monarchic and authoritarian (Brownlee 1986: 3–22; Bergdoll 2000: 134–5). It is difficult to imagine that Kleanthis and Schaubert were unaware of the political associations of their plan. Papageorgiou-Venetas (2011b) connects the style to the eighteenth-century regal cities such as Versailles (see also Tsiomis 2017: 154–9). Kaftanzoglou (1839) complained that the plan was more suited to regal gardens. There was an evident contrast between old Athens as a network of districts and communities and new Athens with its unifying plan (Russack 1942: 29; Bastéa 2000: 51–3; 126).

In the ruins of Athens and among the *armatoli*, Kleanthis and Schaubert may have thought that they were dealing, in effect, with an empty city. In such circumstances, the only source of authority, order and improvement was the king. Athens was imagined primarily as the king's city. Indeed, Leo von Klenze (1838: 432) proposed that it be called Ottonopolis.

The city was imagined as a place of government, commerce and culture, with each of the three elements given their own sectors. The architects were planning for a future city which encompassed merchants, traders, bureaucrats and military officers. This bourgeoisie required social spaces. In a city in ruins, a theatre and a casino were seen as priorities. Indeed, the theatre was one of the first major buildings to be begun in 1835. Though building was stopped soon after, the desire for a theatre remained through the 1830s (Roubien 2017: 17; Biris 2005: 73–4). Gardens were also necessary for the promenade of the respectable. Apart from the bazaar area, it was not a city for the small craftsmen and traders who had likely made up a considerable proportion of the city before 1821. The city appears as a regal bourgeois community transposed into the Greek landscape.

In its geometric design, new Athens was in keeping with efforts to rebuild elsewhere in Greece (Hastaoglou-Martinidis 1995; Hastaoglou-Martinidis, Kafkoula and Papamichos 1993). Capodistrias had received nine plans for new cities and Otto forty (Bastéa 2000: 17; 43; Biris and Kardamisi-Adami 2001: 58). All envisaged a grid plan (Dorovinis (1980). At Mistras, for example, a new plan was required to resolve issues with the water supply and the related consequences for health (Quinet 1830: 128–33; Hastaoglou-Martinidis, Kafkoula and Papamichos 1993), but shifting the whole city to Sparti manifested a desire to break from the recent past and connected with the Classical era. The picturesque lanes of Mistras and its multiple Byzantine churches were sacrificed (reasonably enough) for rectilinear design, clean water, a school and a hospital.

The Kleanthis-Schaubert plan regarded the old city as open land. Von Quast (1834: 29–31) compared their plans to those for New York, Washington and Philadelphia where the cities were to be cut into almost virgin territory. There was no recognition of a pre-existing urban framework and although some of the land towards the north was indeed 'green field', much of the new city was to be constructed in the ruins of the old. This disregard extended to ecclesiastical structures. There were 115 churches on the Kleanthis-Schaubert map, reduced from the pre-war totals of perhaps 130 or even 160 (Papageorgiou-Venetas, 2008a: 73). Perhaps fewer than forty-five survived into the Ottonian period (Papageorgiou-Venetas 2010c). There was no sense that this Christian architectural heritage was of any value. It was to take a further generation before the medieval remains of old Athens were considered worthy of attention. By then, most had gone (McNeal 1991).

The Classical antiquities were treated very differently. Shifting the city northwards left many of the key archaeological areas on its fringes. Although there was no available money, this allowed space for an archaeological park, which Kleanthis and Schaubert (1994) envisaged as stretching from the Monument of Lysikrates, past the Tower of the Winds and the Gymnasium of Hadrian, through the old agora and to the southern slopes of the Acropolis. The boundaries of this large archaeological zone were contentious in a city with such a rich archaeological heritage (Papageorgiou-Venetas, 2011a). The planned park assumed that there would be no revitalization or expansion of the old city, and thereby created considerable tension with the residents of that area (Papageorgiou-Venetas 1994: 6-8; Tsiomis 2017: 169–72).

There were other possibilities and Lysandros Kaftanzoglou, a young Greek architect from Thessaloniki and a Classical revivalist, proposed a strict grid plan and to move the new city further away from any important archaeological remains. The grid was formed around garden squares on the model of London, to encourage sociability and provide green spaces (Kaftanzoglou 1994).

The Acropolis was the point around which Kleanthis and Schaubert aligned their vistas. The palace was connected visually to the Acropolis by the avenue of Athinas (Roubien 2013). There was, however, no attempt to incorporate the Acropolis as a living part of the city. The Acropolis was purely a point of reference, an aesthetic and cultural symbol, but removed from the new city (Hall 1997: 100–17).

The Kleanthis-Schaubert plan was for a city of the Enlightenment. Nineteenth-century architects were aware of the ancient Greek origins of urban design (von Klenze

1838: 287) but in this period, urban planning was the imposition of modern rationality on a potentially chaotic city. It was a way of establishing an ordered urban society, as we can see in the plan's functional division of the city into zones and in the exclusion of 'unhealthy' elements (the sick and the dead). Such cities were part of the building of a rationalist nation (Durand 2000: 84; Hastaoglou-Martinidis, Kafkoula and Papamichos 1993). The architects envisaged nothing less than a Greek Renaissance (Roubien 2017: 19) to emerge through the destruction of the old ways and in a visual relationship to the preeminent symbol of Classical antiquity.

Such ambition is captured in von Quast's (1834) book on the new Athens. Von Quast wrote without feeling the need to visit the city. His source for old Athens was Pausanias, the intervening 1,700 years conveniently forgotten. His envisaged new Athens was to be visually and culturally aligned to the old, associating itself with Themistokles, Kimon and Perikles, and the cultural achievements of Classical Greece. Its purpose was to achieve cultural and political transformation in the East (von Quast 1834: 3–32).

The Kleanthis-Schaubert plan was never completed. The regency sought the advice of Leo von Klenze, possibly the leading neoclassical architect of his day whom Ludwig of Bavaria had already employed for his Glyptothek in Munich (Nerdinger 2000; *Griechichischer Traum* 1986: 37–57). Von Klenze was already on his way to Greece when a letter from Count von Armansperg, the regent, found him on Corfu. The letter laid out the project in terms irresistible to a fervent neoclassicist:

> It is my conviction that you would not be able to regard with indifference the glory which would forever be attached and which must seal a renown already assured through the creation of a plan for the city of Athens, a city to which is attached so many glorious memories.
>
> *von Klenze 1838: 20*

Von Klenze's first act on accepting the invitation was to write to Kleanthis and Schaubert. Although it seems that he was the lead architect, the three men worked closely together and their proposal of 1834 retained most of the morphological characteristics of the earlier Kleanthis-Schaubert plan (von Klenze 1838: 285). Nevertheless, the ambition to remove much of the old town was dropped. Rather than being a central thoroughfare, Euripidou became a border between the old and the new cities (von Klenze 1838: 464). The 1834 version lessened the monumentality of the city. There were fewer, smaller squares. The gardens were reduced and there was more residential space.

Over the course of a year, fulfilling the Kleanthis-Schaubert plan had become a daunting task. Kolettis, as minister of the interior, attempted to clear the streets, concentrating on the ruined buildings on the slopes of the Acropolis. He helped the architects in laying out new roads and squares and expropriating properties (von Klenze 1838: 400). But, despite the energy and rapidity with which the regime turned to the task, the city had escaped their control.

The war had not just displaced the poor, but also the rich and powerful. People were returning to Athens and reclaiming their properties. For the major families of the Greek diaspora, Athens was to provide a congenial home. Being close to the centre of power

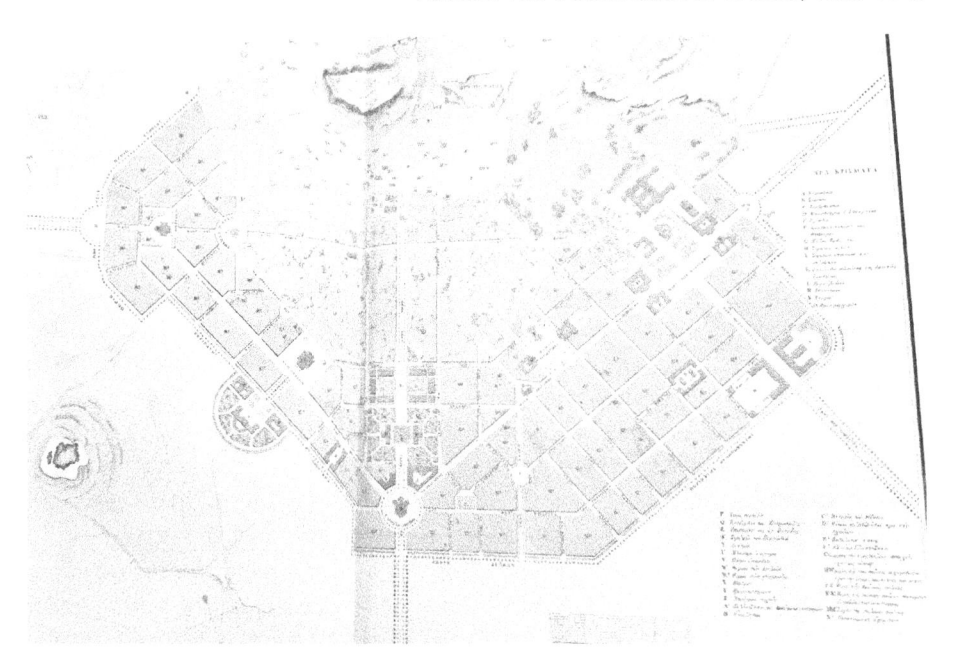

Figure 2.5 Detail from the von Klenze plan of Athens.

had been a central strategy of the Phanariot community in Constantinople and it was a reasonable assumption that proximity to Otto's court would bring them political and financial benefits. Newcomers were buying homes. These included Kleanthis and Schaubert themselves, who reconstructed a house in the Rizokastro district, General Makrigiannis, Admiral Malcolm, Michael Soutzos (a Phanariot leader), and the prominent Chiote banker, Konstantoulos (Biris 2005: 22, 31).

Athens was rebuilding itself, perhaps in a somewhat chaotic fashion. When Richard Burgess visited Athens in the summer of 1834, he observed that the

> desolation caused by the siege of 1827 is yet, for the most part unrepaired; whole streets lie prostrate in the dust, and beaten paths are made over the heaps of rubbish which point out the site of the Turkish bath, or the Serai of an Aga: but, at a distance from the ruined habitations, and on the higher ground nearest the Acropolis, which is destined, I conceive to become the most eligible part of Athens, you see large houses, reared here and there, indicating the return of wealth and peace, if not of authority.
>
> Burgess 1835: 275

George Finlay (1836: 66–73) noted a tension between the people's desire to rebuild their houses and the government's desire to plan the new city. The Regency hesitated with the result that the new avenues were described, as 'an abortive essay' and seen as a failure of the regime. In fact, the avenues were realized in the face of powerful vested interests, including the minister for war, but slowly.

Another factor was cost. After von Klenze presented the plan in September 1834, he was awarded money to buy the required land and to clear it, though not, it seems, to construct any new buildings. The grant was 1,367,000 drachmas (von Klenze 1838: 391, 421–6). The tax return for 1834 was 11,820,000 drachmas (Strong 1842: 206–15). If we add to this figure the money being spent on the Acropolis (see below), just over 12 per cent of the national tax income was being committed to the reshaping of Athens in a country beset by banditry, significant economic problems and a degraded infrastructure. Even so, this might not have been enough. Strong (1842: 40) suggests that a poor house was worth about 2,500 drachmas and that there were 4,000 or so such houses in Athens, a significant rise on the 300 thought to be occupied at the Bavarian entry in 1833. The funds available would have purchased a few more than 500 houses. Kaftanzoglou (1839) noted that an initial willingness of householders to give up their property to the government for minimal recompense evaporated as the value of land increased. Any budget for the rebuilding of the city needed to account for labour and administrative costs. The total cost for the planned rebuild might have been as much as 12,000,000 drachmas (Papageorgiou-Venetas 2008b: 43).

Even though we must presume that there was a considerable number of former agriculturalists and soldiers displaced by the conflict and in need of work, migrant labour from Odessa, Trieste and Marseilles was attracted to the city. As early as 1834, there was a building boom and the market in land was sufficiently sophisticated to allow for speculation (von Klenze 1838: 403). If, in 1833, the city of ruins had seemed a desert, by 1834 the city was, if not thriving, certainly reviving. The Kleanthis-Schaubert plan could only have been achieved by mass appropriation and by 1834 this would have entailed considerable and perhaps unimaginable costs. A less ambitious course was to accept the realities of a rapidly changing situation.

The September 1834 plan (Sechs Lithographien n.d.) rearranged the public buildings of the city. The palace was removed from Omonoia and the square that replaced it, Plateia Othonos (Otho's Square), was given a primarily monumental function. It was to feature a large equestrian statue of the King. Odos Nikes (Victory Road) ran towards the centre of the city. Formal gardens were laid out down the route of Athinas, towards the Acropolis, at the centre of which was a large pool, possibly a Romanizing architectural flourish. There were, however, associated functional elements: a school and a gymnasium linked the monumental centre with education, that touchstone of Enlightenment value. A small market area was also located nearby. Von Klenze planned a governmental complex to the east of the city, consisting of the palace itself, stables, carriage houses, ministerial buildings and a senate house. Gardens were located behind the palace, stretching into the archaeological zone. The western monumental complex (Syntagma) was scaled down, becoming Plateia Platonos.

Von Klenze's city was still ambitious. This was a city which a few years earlier had been devoid of almost all non-religious civic facilities. Now, it was proposed to build a new governmental centre and to equip the city with the institutions required to meet high cultural ambitions. The planned buildings included a treasury, the mint, a cavalry barracks, an infantry barracks, a Catholic church (presumably for the Bavarians), the post office, the city hall, markets, the bishop's seat and synod, bath houses (for men and women), a bazaar, public gardens, a theatre, a university, academies of art and science, and a national library, fountains and a hospital (located at a distance from the city proper). Von Klenze named the streets after the gods, battles and Classical literary and political figures. Figures of more recent history were not honoured, with the exception of Otto who in addition to his square was to be honoured by the naming of the city Ottonopolis (von Klenze 1838: 432, 472–3; Tab II).

Foreign observers offered an extreme narrative of the city. Athens was seen as a city of ruins in ruins. The city was not understood in the context of the recent vicious and prolonged fighting. Wordsworth wrapped Athens in the poetics of civilizational fall and Orientalist desolation that was supposed to capture the essential characteristics of contemporary Athens. Western responses were blind to the importance of the city in the late Ottoman period: it had been a significant regional centre and not just a village clinging to the ruins of the Acropolis. During the conflict, many of its wealthier citizens had relocated to the island of Aigina but they returned at the end of the war.

By the time of Otto's first visit to the city in 1833, there was a functioning religious and civic administration to celebrate his arrival. He was received at the Piraeus and then more formally at the Theseion on his entry into the city. Cochrane describes a gathering of old soldiers, regency officials and 5,000 Athenians (Cochrane 1837: 150). By contrast, Peter von Hess's painting of the event has Otto and his smart and ordered escort being greeted by a jumble of women and children, *palichari*, priests, Greek men in various costumes and even some Turkish spectators lounging at the back of the scene. This very small crowd reflected the contemporary Orientalist image of the urban community. The old city is neatly obscured by the temple, but there is a fine view of the Acropolis. The painting presents a meeting of three cultures, one modern and disciplined, another picturesque and Oriental, and a third celebrated and of the past.[12] Later in the year, the Athenian population celebrated again when the Acropolis was given up by the Turks (Miliarkis 1884).

The 1833 and 1834 plans seem unconscious of the Athens which was already there. This willed ignorance reflected the political and cultural values of the new regime and its general view of the post-Classical history of Greece. Despite the preservation of some of the churches in the von Klenze plan, no value was placed on the Orthodox city nor on local commercial sectors nor Ottoman-period civic organization. Muslim traditions were to disappear. Ottonopolis was to be the centrepiece of the Enlightenment project that was the Greek state. It was created in opposition to those strands of the national imaginary embedded in the social structures of the Greek regions. Rebuilding Athens was an ideological assertion of the primacy of the monarchy against the values of localities. It opposed Enlightenment modernity to the traditions that had sustained the Greek revolution. It imagined a modern Greece divested of many of its pasts and traditional cultures.

The Ottonian Acropolis

The decision to relocate the capital to Athens raised the issue of the residence of the king (Papageorgiou-Venetas 2011b). There was no suitable existing building, though Otto was found a twelve-room house with a large ball room in 1834–5 (Cochrane 1837: 150–1). That was, however, a temporary solution. Kleanthis and Schaubert had identified a location for the palace, at the fulcrum of the city, but appear not to have gone so far as to produce an architectural plan. In May 1833, yet another architect arrived from Bavaria, Johann Gutensohn. His trip did not, however, resolve the issue and a decision was taken to consult Schinkel, probably the leading architect of the day (Kühn 1979; Biris 2005: 25).

Schinkel submitted ambitious plans in 1834. He proposed turning the whole of the Acropolis into a royal palace. He justified this plan through historical associations. The Acropolis was 'a brilliant highpoint in human history whose radiance would illuminate the path of higher thought for all time'. Such feelings might be thought to be in some tension with locating a large modern palace on the archaeological site, even if Schinkel's plan incorporated the Temple of Minerva, as he called the Parthenon. The association of palace and Acropolis was an act of cultural appropriation and *homage* to the Classical past. He was displaying the Ottonian palace as being in continuity with the Parthenon in the illumination of this 'path of higher thought' (Schinkel 1840: 1, with quotations as given in Carter 1979). His plan was to repurpose the Acropolis and enhance its symbolic value as a display of Enlightenment civilization.

Schinkel used a neoclassical eclecticism that deployed Greek and Roman architectural elements without any of the academic concerns that affected contemporary Greek revivalism (Hope 1835: 69–77). The planned imposition of the palace was an implicit claim to have possession of the best of both Classical and neoclassical traditions and to be free in their reuse. Schinkel's plan and elevation show a small circular temple-like structure that recalled Rome's Pantheon. A hippodrome sat alongside the temple leading into what appears to have been intended as a reception room that provided entry into the elaborate complex that formed the palace proper. A long colonnade flanked the palace and presented an element of Classical uniformity to the city below. These elements

Figure 2.6 Schinkel's palace on the Acropolis (Schinkel 1840).

recalled the grand villa architecture of the second century CE, which had its most influential textual representation in Pliny's (*Epistles* 2.17) description of his Laurentine villa, and which was archaeologically visible in Hadrian's villa at Tivoli. The Tivoli villa was an archetype of the Romantic ruin (De La Ruffiniere du Prey 1994; Adembri 2000; Pinto 2012). Schinkel also found space on the Acropolis for small formal and informal gardens. The whole was completed by a colossal statue of Athena Promachos (Carter 1979).

Schinkel evidently saw no disparity between the communitarian grandeur of the Parthenon and the private villa architecture of Rome. His vision for the palace was not just an appropriation of the Parthenon, but a privatization of a space that had represented the Athenians' communal identity over centuries. The gardens, the multiple spaces and the complexities of the built topography reflect this privatized form. It was a country house. The palace laid claim to the closest of identifications of the regime with the Classical past, but in the freedom with which that Classical past was treated, it became a plaything in the regime's remaking of the city. The Acropolis was an ever-present site of memory and a symbol of the civic community of Athens and the traditions of Greece. Schinkel's palace remade the Acropolis into a symbol of European civilization and the power of the regime. The parallel with Elgin's depredations is evident.

The envisioned relationship between the palace and the contemporary city was one of separation and domination. Schinkel thought there was a need for a secure and defensible site, and this made the Acropolis an obvious location. The statue of Athena Promachos placed the Classical goddess over the Christian city. The possibilities of dominance are also captured by von Klenze's 1846 painting reconstructing Classical Athens. He imagined a small group of citizens meeting in the shadow of the Acropolis over which the war-like Athena herself looms.[13] As Athenian democracy was under the controlling eye of the deity, so Schinkel's Athens was under the autocratic Classical dominance of the Bavarian regime.

In the context of contemporary cities and monarchies, the defensive location of the palace was startling. Despite the various revolutionary movements of the period, royal palaces in Western Europe had lost almost all military accoutrements. Schinkel's plan was emphatically colonialist: it represented a set of political relations in which the Bavarian state was severed from its Greek population, but intimately linked to a Classical tradition which, as a modern European regime, it represented and owned (Leontis 1995). That tradition provided hope for progress and Enlightenment for the nation and region.

It is obvious why it did not get built. The plan faced significant technical difficulties, not least of which was getting enough water to the top of the hill. It would have been vastly expensive to realize. Schinkel significantly misjudged the Bavarians' attitude towards the antiquities and the Classical past more generally. The political relations it envisaged were inimical to the regime. The Acropolis Palace would have transformed the spatial and cultural logic of Athens. It would have associated the regime more closely with the Classical past and metamorphosized the Acropolis from a place of ruination and absence, of aesthetic idealism, of imagination and the sublime, into the central location of state power. One might imagine regimes for which this association would have had an appeal, perhaps an ultra-nationalistic state eager to espouse its world-historical significance (Hamilakis 2007; Herzfeld 1987: 50–3). Von Klenze's brief commentary (1838: 484–6) on the plan criticized it as being suitable for a *Volksführer*, a tyrant or a popular leader. The plan feels now like cultural vandalism in part because of the offence it causes to the transcendent spatial values of the Acropolis; Schinkel evidently did not experience such qualms (Leontis 1995: 40–66).

The Bavarian attitude to the site focused on the restoration of the antique elements. Ludwig Ross, the archaeologist in charge of the Acropolis, had arrived in Piraeus in 1832 (Miller 1926: 4). He was immediately engaged on the Acropolis. Kleanthis, Schaubert and Ross were given 72,000 drachmas for clearing and restoration. In September 1834, on his second visit to the city, the king was guided round the Acropolis (von Klenze 1838: 303–8; Stademann 1841: 3). Otto ceremonially administered the re-erection of a column on a reconstructed column base. In what must have been a rather strange event for the observing crowds, von Klenze gave a passionate and poetic speech of welcome, recalling the days of Perikles and Themistokles. A translation was handed out to the crowd (von Klenze 1838: 383–7). Classicism had returned, but in German. Von Klenze's also presented his new plan for the city (von Klenze 1838: 308, 391).

The Acropolis had a powerful significance for European culture, representing a pinnacle of architectural and cultural achievement (Kondaratos 1994). When Ludwig I came to visit his son's capital, his first act was to visit the Acropolis (Cochrane 1837: 222; Papageorgiou-Venetas 1996). For von Klenze, as for so many others, the Acropolis was of central symbolic importance (Leontis 1995: 40–66). As a preamble to his account of Otto's visit to the Acropolis, von Klenze (1838: 309–83) inserted into his account of his time in Greece an eighty-page disquisition on the development of art to which the Acropolis is the architectural culmination. In his view, the Parthenon was to be appreciated not because of its place in the historical and cultural development of Athens, though that was recognized in his appraisal of the site in his speech to Otto, but for an aesthetic excellence which transcended history.

The regime's investment in the Classical Acropolis was at the expense of other histories (Middleton 2004: 25–39. For the Byzantine Parthenon, see Kaldellis 2009). They cleared fortifications from the site. The mosque mostly disappeared sometime after 1835 with the last remains being cleared by 1842.[14] The 'Turkish' houses also went. These had featured in Smirke's 1802 drawing of the Parthenon from the west and Stuart and Revett's drawing of 1765 (Mallouchou-Tufano 1994; Breton 1862: 67–87). The site was turned into a single-period monument in which Classical Athenian architecture was to be uncontested by later features. The Parthenon was an aesthetic triumph, not a historical monument and consequently was restored to an ahistorical state in which architecture is the focus. It became, as McNeal (1991) puts it, a monument to the intellectual tyranny of neoclassicism.

Whereas every modern leader who visits Athens is obliged to pay homage to the Acropolis as the symbol of Western democracy, there was no suggestion that the restoration of Athens would involve a reinvention of democracy. Leo von Klenze's speech to Otto on the Acropolis referenced that Classical political tradition. He claimed that the restoration of the Acropolis was an end of barbarism and the resumption of a work of civilization interrupted for 2,000 years (presumably he was thinking of the Roman conquest of Athens as the break point). The significant contrast was not between constitutional forms, between an authoritarian regime and a citizen-led government, but between the cultured and the barbarian. For von Klenze, Otto stood on holy rock, following precisely in the footsteps of Themistokles, Aristeides, Kimon and Perikles (Papageorgiou-Venetas 2000: 17; von Klenze 1838: 383–7). But he appears unaware of any irony in linking the untrammelled monarchy of Otto (at least in theory) with the democratic leaders of the fifth century BCE. Instead, the Greeks represented civilized culture as opposed to barbarism of the post-Classical world.

It was 'good government' which would enable the development of Greece and the resumption of the work of civilization (Rosen 1998). The association between cultural achievement and citizen power featured in discussions of how Greeks had been corrupted by their enslavement, but the restoration of Greece was associated exclusively with a return to cultural and aesthetic excellence and particular bourgeois values, as exemplified by the semi-fictional women of Greece (for example, Howe 1928: x). But that acquisition of excellence and proper values would take time. Rosen (1998: 72–3) shows that the British press gave no credence to the immediate prospect of Greek government in Greece. Good government was embedded in Enlightenment cultural values that required learning and education. In default of those values, good government had to be imposed, and Greece was committed to the category of a nation-in-waiting. The Bavarian project was thus colonial and justified by the regime's adherence to a high bourgeois culture familiar from the West and differentiated from local customs. This high culture included theatre, balls and Parisian dresses and the veneration of Classical aesthetics. The regime's care of the Classical past was thus also a claim to rule.

Von Klenze construed 2,000 years of Athenian history as a gap. His ideological confidence is notable. The predominant view of history was progressive, being the march of Western values. It was also a sleight of hand since it deprived areas outside the progressive zone of the West of their history (compare Mill's (1817) dismissal of Indian culture; Alston 2010). The omission of 2,000 years from Greek history consigned various versions of the nation to oblivion. Such lost pasts were to haunt Greece's march to modernity (Herzfeld 1987; Peckham 2001: 62–75). Predictably, Byzantine history and folk traditions became foci of nationalistic resistance to European understandings of Greece (Hamilakis 2007: 57–123; Plantzos 2014). In 1834, for the Bavarian regime, folk traditions were invisible or irrelevant. They were to be forgotten in the neoclassicism of new Athens.

The Ottonian ceremony on the Acropolis was meant as a point of connection between the regime and the Classical Greek past. It was also meant to involve the Greek population: this past was shared but that sharing was asymmetrical. As Elgin had appropriated the statuary, so the history and aesthetic value of the site became a European cultural artefact of which the regime was now the guardian. Greek participation in that European heritage allowed the Greeks access to the site, but only through the lens of modernity. Greek national identity was being constructed on a promise of a future in which Greece might realize and reappropriate its Classical past (Jusdanis 1991) in a present in which that Classical past was a colonial form. Greek identity, Classicism and colonialism were lines of thought in an elaborate process identity formation, not so much as opposed forces as different threads in a tapestry yet to be woven (Calotychos 2003: 50–1).

The Acropolis was intensely overloaded with symbolic significance in Western culture. Generations of European visitors had a strong emotional response to being on the Acropolis (Leontis 1995: 40–66). The Acropolis as re-created was an otherly space, a 'heterotopia' (Foucault 1984). Its heterotopic quality emerged from its transcendence of the normal spatial principles by which we understand our place in the world. The reaction of a Freud or a Flaubert was one of disorientation (Freud 1932–6; DuBois 2008: 7–11; Leontis 1995: 48–50; Armstrong 2006: 1–4). There was both a sense of unreality in the presence of such a culturally loaded monument and a heightened reality since the experience was mediated through a response to the monument as an epitome of Western culture. The Bavarian Acropolis was extracted from the everyday of the city below and extracted its cultured visitors from their everyday. Contemporary Athens often disappeared from views of the Acropolis (for example, *Description of the View* 1842). The Acropolis was a symbol of absolute aesthetic value and a space of home-coming for the transnational European Philhellene. It has remained a European site, useful in Greek assertions of a European identity, but problematic as a location of nationalism (Yalouri 2001; Hamilakis 2007: 169–204).

Heterotopic and 'normal' spaces are adjuncts. The adjacency of the Acropolis became commentary on the Greek city below, generating and symbolizing the relationship between 'the Greeks' and 'the Modern Greeks' and between the Acropolis and the Neustadt of Ottonopolis. Otto belonged in the new city, not in the rarefied air of the Acropolis. The neoclassical city was not Classical. The protection and management of that sacred space was a justification for the regime, an appropriation, and a commitment to Enlightenment universalism.

The palaces of Ottonian Athens

The Schinkel plan for the royal palace was a consequence of the rejection of the suggested location for the palace in the Kleanthis-Schaubert plan. Von Klenze's plan relocated the palace from the fulcrum of the city to its fringe, off the Piraeus road. His proposal advanced sufficiently that he made drawings of the palace. The elevations show an ambitious but less grandiose palace than that proposed by Schinkel. It was to be constructed on a large platform elevated over the surrounding countryside and accessed by ramps and stairs. It comprised a rectangle of six three-storey towers, which were linked by flanking open colonnades or long corridor buildings. These formed an open central court which could be accessed and viewed from outside. One of the central towers functioned as a grand entrance, complete with facing columns and a triangular pediment that echoed the Parthenon (Sechs Lithographien n.d.: pl. 1–3). The access ramp was to be adorned with neo-Classical sculptures, including a figure of Justice. It was to be equipped with richly decorated reception areas. The drawings suggest a fashionable early-nineteenth-century country house.

Athens: The Colonization of Greece, 1830–1846

Figure 2.7 Von Klenze's design for the Royal Palace (Sechs Lithographien).

The design was different from that of Schinkel both in its politics and in its stylistic associations. Von Klenze wanted a distinctively Greek style. He claims that such a style could only emerge from a fusion of southern Classical traditions and contemporary North European styles. Such a fusion would, he hoped, generate a revival in Greek (national) architecture. Whereas in the northern cities, important buildings were conjoined by avenues and streets, von Klenze's southern style worked with the natural terrain. Although the buildings themselves should show symmetry and order, the combination was designed to be more like a garden on the contemporary English model (von Klenze 1838: 476–87)

This city as garden was very different from the planned French formal urban gardens or a Versailles. Von Klenze valued the picturesque (Hamdorf 1986) and the German for 'picturesque', '*malerisch*', appears throughout his account of his Greek sojourn as a sign of approbation. He was a keen painter, creating contemporary Romantic landscapes, such as the *Landscape with the Castle of Massa di Carrara* (1827), the *Salvatorkirche und Walhalla* (1839) and reconstructions of historical landscapes, such as his *The Acropolis at Athens* (1846).[15] Von Klenze imagined the Athenian palace as rural rather than urban, with peasants wandering by, unmade pathways and artistically deployed trees that gradually blend the wildness of the countryside into the relative formality of the gardens and architecture (Tsiomis 2017: 75). This was in keeping with the fashions for *rus in urbe* that we see in the development of London and in Schinkel's extraordinary designs for an isolated royal retreat at Orianda in the Crimea (Schinkel 1848). Inevitably, the palace was aligned to the Acropolis, but in the emphasis on the picturesque landscape and on the 'southern quality' of the new architecture of Greece there was a lack of integration of the palace with the urban frameworks (Tsiomis 2017: 201–2). The palace was envisaged as suburban, connected visually with the ancient, contemporary and future cities, but on the boundary between Enlightenment city and Romantic (Greek) rurality. The openness of the design is striking with multiple approaches and points of access. The open vistas reflected a form of regal politics radically different from that of Schinkel's Acropolis dweller.

The rural landscape signified permanence and what was left when civilization was lost. It was this Greece that had emerged heroically in the nineteenth century (Güthenke 2008). Contemporary travellers read Homeric heroes when they encountered the *kapitani* and the *palichari*, dissolving centuries of history in literary association (Leake 1835: 145; About 1883: 49, 153–4, 165; Quinet 1830: 80, 142, 153–4). Von Klenze (1838: 486) sought architectural forms that resonated with this rural landscape. His Romanticism in engagement with the Greek landscape was a historically transcendent Hellenism. Consequently, the King needed to be integrated with the land (Güthenke 2008). We might think of the palace as Odyssean, a place of kingly rule and entertainment, of domestic power and beneficence, but not of the city.

The palace was not built. The site fell from favour after an outbreak of malaria in 1835. The eventual palace was designed by Friedrich von Gärtner (Hederer 1976). Von Gärtner came to Athens with King Ludwig in December 1835. He had studied in Paris under Durand and worked also with von Klenze. He was responsible for various of Ludwig's buildings including the Ludwigskirche, the National Library and University Square. He worked through a restrained neoclassicism, though he allowed more ornamentation within buildings than on the outside.

Ludwig of Bavaria seems to have personally chosen the site, going for the third angle of the grand plan, what is now Syntagma. The first elevations suggest a setting in a low garden, with the hill of Lykabettos and the Hymettos mountain rising behind. The contrast being played on is between the restrained palace and the rugged majesty of the Attic landscape (Biris 2005: 65–7; Bastéa 2000: 151–6). Indeed, the palace appears to have been chosen primarily for it positioning on the rise of the hill, capturing the mountains, the developing city, and the Acropolis, with which it was aligned (Cochrane 1837: 303–6). Edgar Garston, who visited in 1840, thought the palace 'beautifully situated', though the building itself was not promising.

> I have not seen the plans, but for the present it looks as if rather intended for a barrack than for a royal palace, and threatens to have little in accordance, as regards architectural beauty, with what remains of the works of the ancient Athenians: the architect is Bavarian.
>
> *Garston 1842: 228*

Ludwig approved the site and the design and paid for the palace, which was begun in January 1836 and completed in 1843. It had none of the architectural variety or the invention of the earlier plans (Russack 1942: 73–4). The building is a heavy, block-like, large cuboid with limited external neoclassical ornamentation (Papageorgiou-Venetas 1970: 10). The impression is of solidity and permanence, perhaps even utility, but with nothing of the engagement with the landscape that inspired Schinkel and von Klenze.

Figure 2.8 The Royal Palace, Athens.

Nor does it have the variation of line and forms, the architectural differentiation of particular zones, or the incorporation of gardens that would make a palace of pleasure. The interiors had Pompeian echoes, but the exterior was dull (Papageorgiou-Venetas 1992). Von Gärtner's other buildings in Greece, notably the mint and the military hospital, conformed to this block form (Biris and Kardamisi-Adami 2001: 87–8). Papageorgiou-Venetas (2011b) attributes the style to the financial constraints afflicting the regime. But it was also a turning away from the cultural ambition of von Klenze and his desired Greek architectural renaissance. This palace was a piece of the North dropped onto a Greek landscape.

That was how it was interpreted by contemporaries. Wordsworth (1836: 275–81) appended a letter from Charles Holte Bracebridge to his memoir to reflect the situation in Athens in late 1835. The letter noted that the decision had been made on the von Gärtner plan and that speculators were immensely annoyed by the shifting of the site for the palace. Bracebridge commented that 'the plan ... is handsome and commodious, without being extravagant...', and observed that it faced the Acropolis and was connected to the city by gardens and a square. His commentary on the new Athenian style claims that it 'is rather modern German than anything else: neither the picturesque (and in this climate agreeable) Turkish house nor the Italian colonnade is seen: happily the English red brick is also absent' (Wordsworth 1836: 280–1).

Unease about the palace and its design was reflected in the faint praise with which the building was received, even in plan, from normally pro-Ottonian writers. Travellers were surprised by the size of a palace in a city and nation in ruins after the war (Bastéa 2000: 151–6). Otto and Amalia had been living in a relatively modest neoclassical house close to where the university was to be built. The palace suggested that the king's new priority was establishing his own residence as a permanent and visible mark on the landscape. Leake (1851: 9–10), who was a friend of the revolution but hostile to the Bavarian settlement, complained that the Greeks had exchanged Ottoman for German despotism and that Otto had 'built a palace for a sovereign of paupers'. Any notion of democratic freedom or even of a monarch attuned to his people's needs was lost in the style, luxury and scale of the palace. Even the contrast between the austere exterior and the luxurious interior suggested a king without commitment to the public.

The von Gärtner design turned to the aesthetics of Germany and North Europe. The palace made almost no reference to local architectural traditions. It lacked the balconies, the light-wells, the internal courts, the gardens, the variations in levels and the permeability that were characteristic of Roman palatial architecture. It had nothing of the shaded balconies and large open reception rooms of Ottoman architecture. Such designs provided for spaces that were habitable in the heat of a Mediterranean summer. Von Gärtner's closed walls and the near unbroken façades seem peculiarly out of place. In Ferdinand Stademann's (1841) panoramic views of Athens and in the early sketches and photographs, the palace is separate, at one step removed from the city, and it was to remain on the edge of Athens as the nineteenth-century city developed.

In 1836, Otto married Amalia, daughter of the Duke of Oldenburg, and they returned to Greece in February 1837. Amalia immediately began to campaign for a garden. Land was designated on the southern side of the palace, and she began planting in 1839 (Biris 2005: 67). The garden was both large and expensive, supposedly taking up 5 per cent of the king's income. It provided much needed shade and air in the summer and although it was closed off when Amalia promenaded, it was opened to the public at other times. The design was English picturesque, in contrast to the regularities of French baroque. It owed nothing to the traditional Greek landscape or to the dry desolation of Attica that had delighted earlier travellers. The laying out of the garden uncovered the remains of a large Roman villa. Amalia had it dug out and the remains redeployed for miscellaneous picturesque features.

The gardens completed the arrangement for the palace and fulfilled a narrative arc. It had begun as an absolutist monument to an Enlightenment king. In Schinkel's hands, it was an aesthetic fusion of ancient and modern and a return to the Acropolis for the *Volksführer*. The von Klenze plan was more Romantic, though equally ambitious. The union of Otto and his people would be achieved by establishing a relationship between the king and the countryside. The picturesque spoke to the land and to the Homeric and continuous character of the Greeks. Its siting offered a conjunction between the Classical past, the landscape, and the Ottonian, Western future. That was evidently a fantasy, and probably a very expensive one (Biris 2005: 65–7). The eventual palace signified the solid presence of the regime. It spoke of a Germanic modernity. The queen's gardens similarly brought northern Europe to Athens, an island of the north in the city of the south. The palace was to be looked from rather than looked at. From their palace, Ludwig, Otto and Amalia could gaze on the Attic mountains, view the sea across the gentle slopes, and, of course, contemplate the Acropolis. But it is a building that presented an estranged front to the city (Biris 2005: 78–82).

The various palaces were symbols of the colonial project. The justification for the Bavarian regime was that it would bring the Enlightenment to Greece. The legitimacy of the regime as advertised to the rest of Europe and probably to itself, rested on the differentiation of the new rulers from the old Ottoman authorities and from the traditions of contemporary Greece. If the Greeks became 'modern', then the justification for the regime would dissipate. But if the Greeks remained unruly, troublesome children, they needed European tutors.

Separation from its people was the colonial regime's *raison d'être*. And yet, such separation enabled a rhetoric of opposition. Edward Morris (1843) published a travelogue of his trip round the East in 1843. He was not impressed by his encounters with Greek people. Like many male travellers of the period, he was attracted to the physiques of Greek men (Morris 1843: 6). But he filled his account with Orientalist tropes, noting the languidness of the cities, and the repression and seclusion of women (37), and the dishonesty of men. The heroes of the war were seen as having retreated to their mountain fastnesses, separate and independent from the new Greece. While Athens itself is filled with 'idlers' thronging the cafés as fleas thronged the hotels (18). He reports the unpopularity of the regime:

> King Otho has nothing national about him but the Greek costume. His head and heart are Bavarian, and he governs Greece but as an appendage of Bavaria. Most of the high offices are filled by Bavarians, and they are invariably found in the offices of profit ... His reign has been an hindrance to the development of the national resources. He has consumed not only the principal of the loan advanced by the great powers, but has never yet paid the interest on it. The country has been in a progressive state of impoverishment, and while its revenues are daily diminishing, King Otho is erecting himself a splendid palace of Pentelican marble, which is to rival the glories of the Parthenon! With the exception of a public road from Athens into Boeotia, out of the metropolis there are no signs of the existence of a government ... The king is a vain silly young man, intoxicated with the idea of holding a sceptre, and ambitious not to restore a fallen and yet fine race of people to the dignity and renown of their glorious ancestry, but simply to play a part among the other despots of Europe.
>
> *Morris 1843: 19*

The palace became the symbol of the regime's failure. It reflected the core problems in the colonial formation of a Greek modernity sometimes described as 'belated' or 'incomplete' (Jusdanis 1991: xiii). The colonial project required both the modernization of Greece and the portrayal of Greeks as separate from that modernity. It forced many elements of Greek society into a mode of resistance that drew strength from traditional, local and regional cultural and political resources. Those social and cultural elements had delivered the victories of the Greek revolution and were increasingly mythologized in the formation of Greek political identity.

Making bourgeois Athens: Reclaiming the Classical

This dichotomic understanding of Greek society and the colonial regime was undermined by the various economic and cultural transformations in the aftermath of the war. The colonial view was anyhow an almost parodic Orientalist misunderstanding of the complexity of Greek society. With peace, trade networks recovered and extended. Connections to the Western Mediterranean were enhanced. Schools, the university and cultural and learned institutions opened. The press expanded. The wealthy and educated were attracted to the opportunities of Athens. A bourgeois Athenian society emerged, exhibiting many of the markers of such societies elsewhere in Europe. Although some of the foreign visitors seemed to have been horrified by the seeming backwardness of Athens, one suspects that they harboured unrealistic expectations for a poor country recovering from the devastation of war.

The moral and cultural values of the rising Athenian bourgeoisie found grounding in a perception of traditional society and gender roles. The availability of the Classical heritage for the nationalist imaginary encouraged a deeper engagement with and reclamation of the Classical tradition. Classicism did not completely cease to be colonialist in Athens. But in language, art and architecture, the Greek bourgeoisie asserted its national identity through the adoption of Classical forms and dismissed Bavarian monopolistic claims to represent modernity and their appropriation of the Classical heritage. In 1843, a Parliamentary regime was forced upon the reluctant Otto.

The speed of recovery can be traced through the available population statistics. Hobhouse (1813: 303) estimated a population of 8,000–10,000 in 1808–9. The population was perhaps about 12,000 in 1821 (Biris and Kardamisi-Adami 2001: 72). The Ephors (councillors) of the city registered 9,040 residents in 1824 (Gordon 1832: II 188). During the war, the population had likely fallen to below 6,000 by 1831 (Badema-Phountoulake

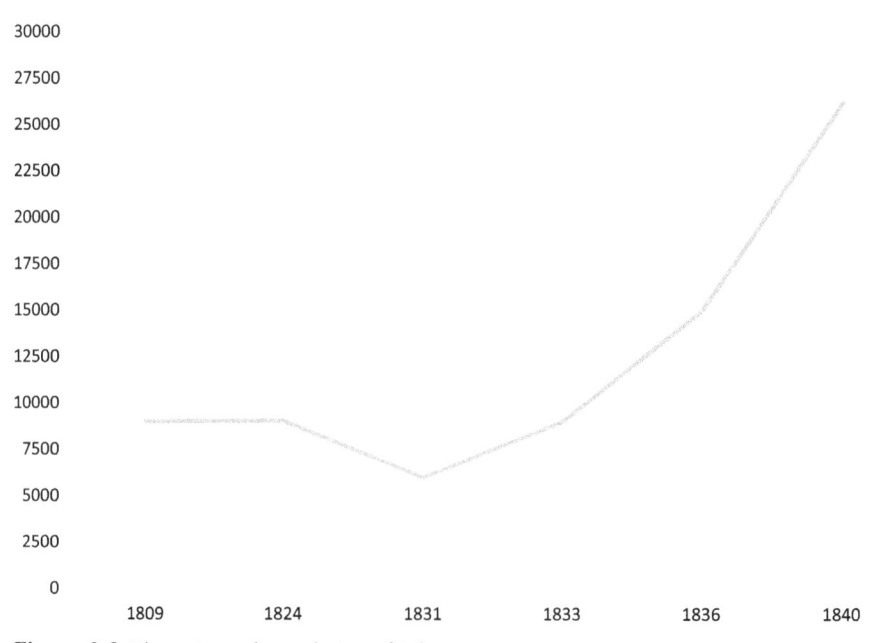

Figure 2.9 The estimated population of Athens: 1809–40.

2001: 87–8) and a report from the Regency administration from 11/20 May 1833 gave a wide estimate of 8,000–10,000 (Papadopoulou-Sumeonidou 1996: Document 1.1). In 1832, Kleanthis and Schaubert (1994) aspired to a city of about 40,000 in 4,000 houses, but Bracebridge in 1836 thought the population had not reached 15,000 (Wordsworth 1836: 280). By 1840, according to Frederick Strong (1842: 37), the population had risen to 26,237 of whom 6,404 were men, 4,862 women, 6,318 boys and 3,713 girls and 4,940 soldiers and foreign residents.[16]

From the effective end of the war, the population of Athens increased by about 340 per cent in nine years to perhaps three times more than the pre-war population. Some of the people were likely returning, but many were new residents, seeking to take advantage of the opportunities in the nation's capital. Strong's (1842: 37) figures suggest a young population, though the sex ratio suggests that more men than women and girls were coming to the city. Peace and the new economic opportunities encouraged people to establish families. In 1840, there were 171 marriages, 1,319 births and 863 deaths, a natural increase in the urban population of just over 2 per cent per annum.

Of that Athenian population, around 153 were in 'professions', 287 if we include priests, with a further eighty-three large landowners. Small traders made up 1,450 people (presumably men) while agriculturalists were 897 and 'mechanics' 3,610. Of the 4,560 houses in 1840, 88 per cent were valued at 2,500 drachmas or below. Seven per cent were valued at more than 15,000 drachmas of which ten houses were valued at more than 30,000 (Strong 1842: 40). The majority of the population were living in low-standard housing with a small middling and upper order occupying housing of a higher standard.

The number of prominent families in the city remained small through the 1830s. Stademann (1841: pl. 7–10) was able to identify the more important houses and families in his topographic panorama. He picked out houses belonging to Constantin Schinas, Prince Kantakouzenos, von Armansperg, Kobell, de Herbst, Comte Bocciari, General Heideck, the Casalis, the king and Kleanthis. Kostas Biris (2005: 30–1, 46–7) listed just over twenty prominent families and individuals who established houses in Athens in the 1830s. Some were foreigners, others Phanariotes or Moldavians relocating into the new Greek state, and others prominent political figures. The rich and powerful were making their way to the capital. Garston (1842: 27) admired spacious and well-built mansions which had replaced the blackened ruins he had seen in his first visit to the city.

Two of the finest houses of the period were designed by Kleanthis in the early 1840s for the Duchess of Plaisance, Sophie de Marbourg. The duchess, who was estranged from her husband, strongly supported Greek independence. She had left Nauplio and Greece after a disagreement with Capodistrias but returned to make her home in Athens. The Villa Ilissia was her central Athens residence; it is now the Byzantine Museum. It had some Classical elements in the décor but is most similar to the traditional mansion structure that can be seen in the Mansion Benizelou in Plaka and, indeed, at the Kleanthis and Schaubert house below the Acropolis. The core feature is a second storey closed balcony which provided the main social space for the house and blended into the reception rooms on the same floor. Her country house was Rododafnes Castle at Penteli, also designed by Kleanthis. Manos Biris and Maro Kardamisi-Adami (2001: 92) describe

Figure 2.10 Villa Ilissia.

the house as picturesque and within a Classical tradition. Yet stylistically the two flanking towers with a connecting portico formed by Gothic-style arches above which is an open balcony seems rather more Byzantine or Ottoman than Classical (Scully 1963).

Kleanthis did build houses in a more conventional neoclassical style, such as the 1835 house for Ambrosius Rallis on Dragatzani which was later to house the British legation, the 1832 house for Admiral Malcolm, and the 1846 house of the Countess Jane Theotoki (Biris 2005: 24, 98). As a busy house builder, Kleanthis reused architectural elements in various of his domestic structures. His 1841 palaia polykatoikia had an Italianate style, demonstrating his diversity and, indeed, a lack of an ideological commitment to a particular stylistic repertoire (Biris 2005: 94).

Theatre was one of the main institutions of respectable sociability in the early nineteenth century. The first theatre in Athens was the Skontozopoulos Theatre, which opened as early as 1835 as a temporary structure (Roubien 2017: 17). The Boukoura Theatre followed in 1839 and opened with Donizetti's *Lucia di Lammermoor* in January 1840. The theatre only held just over 113 and had a simple design. The production was a success and a scandal. The opera attracted a considerable range of patrons, some of whom became devotees of the female lead (Xepapadakou 2022). Edgar Garston (1842: 28) visited the opera house and admired the beauty of Queen Amalia and the daughter of Count Bozzaris, showing that, as elsewhere in Europe, theatrical evenings were not necessarily focused on the stage.[17]

There were two clubs (casinos), one called the Green Tree which was patronized by the military and a 'Greek' casino with a reading room, billiards, library and bar (Strong 1842: 38). Morris (1843: 18) complained of the idlers thronging the cafés, which were becoming a prominent feature of Athenian society (About 1883: 41). Hotels were being developed: Cochrane (1838: 281) had found himself miserably served at the Hotel de France in 1834. By 1840 Garston (1842: 27) was comfortably housed in the Hotel Royal, though Stademann (1841: pl. 9) thought the Casali Hotel the only decent establishment in the city and Morris (1843: 18) was unimpressed by the Hotel de Londres. Strong (1842: 37) listed the Hotels de Londres, de l'Europe, des Etrangers and de Russie.

In a memorandum of 16 June 1834 (*Greek Government* 1834), the government laid down their cultural and educational requirements for the city. They included a central public library, a public museum for antiquities, a numismatic cabinet, a natural history cabinet, a cabinet of mathematical and physics instruments, a chemistry laboratory, an anatomy theatre, an academy of surgical materials, a collection of models, a collection of paintings, a collection of copper engravings, a collection of astronomical observation equipment, and a collection of technical equipment. Many of these institutions took time, but the memorandum attests to the ambition of the regime to provide modern cultural and scientific institutions.

The other staple of the rising bourgeois city was the press (Koutsopanagou and Droulia 2009: 1–31). The Greek-language press began with the revolution. Local newspapers were published from 1821 in Galaxidi, Kalamata and Mesolongi. More papers were set up in 1822 and 1824, and the first English-language Greek newspaper was published in 1824. At least six newspapers were founded in 1831 and another three by 1837. The first women's paper was published in 1838. Many of these papers had relatively short careers and the early press had to encounter Capodistrias. In Athens in 1842, there were fifteen newspapers, fifty-two in 1883 and 131 by 1890 (Jusdanis 1991: 104).

The Bavarian regime was committed to education. By 1840, there were 252 regular schools in Greece. The first high school was founded on Aigina by Capodistrias in 1833 and Otto opened the Nauplio Gymnasium in 1834. The Athens Gymnasium opened in 1835 (Strong 1842: 369–72). John and Frances Hill who had come to Athens as missionaries, established a popular and prominent girls' school in 1831, which seems an extraordinary achievement given the state of Athens at the time. Although retaining his missionary role and concerned to educate his wealthy young ladies in English-language culture, Hill was careful of the religious sensibilities of the Orthodox authorities and of the families who had entrusted their daughters to him (Garston 1842: 99–103; Morris 1843: 27). Girls from the Hills' school welcomed Otto to the Acropolis in 1834 (Miliarkis 1884). The Arsakeio girls' school was founded in 1836 and initially met in a private house. Designs for a grand building ran into difficulties with contrasting plans offered by Kleanthis and Lysandros Kaftanzoglou. Kaftanzoglou's design was preferred. It now houses the Council of State and is a dull neoclassical block the main aesthetic feature of which is six columns embedded in the façade of the second storey. Kleanthis proposed a much grander neoclassical building with a large three-storey entrance and Classicizing pavilions emerging from the wings of the building. The competition dissolved into a stinging polemic between Kleanthis and Kaftanzoglou over the Greekness of neoclassicism (Karydis 2022).

A university was part of the early plans for Athens. It was constituted on 31 December 1836/12 January 1837 and was initially based in the house of Kleanthis and Schaubert. There were seven professors, all German. It initially had fifty-two students registered. By 1840–1 it had 159 students, ninety of whom were Greek. Work began on a new university building in 1839 with the foundation stone being laid on 21 June/3 July. The building was designed by Christian Hansen and opened in 1841 (Miller 1926: 20–1; Strong 1842: 376–83). Its central feature is an Ionic portico that provides a shaded entry point and social space before the lecture theatres. The architectural reference is clearly to the Acropolis (Karydis 2022).

Hansen had come to Athens in the immediate aftermath of the war (Schwarz 2003). He was first recruited to work with Ludwig Ross on the survey of the Acropolis (Badema-Phountoulake 2001: 35–7) and deployed his engineering and architectural skills in the partial clearance of the site and the reconstruction of the Classical remains. Together with Ross and Schaubert, he published a key study of the Temple of Nike (Ross, Hansen and Schaubert 1839). This deep knowledge of Classical Greek architecture is evident in his design for the university.

From the middle of the century, Christian worked together with his brother, Theophil, and Ernst Ziller. These three, together with Lysandros Kaftantzoglou, were responsible for many of the notable neoclassical buildings of nineteenth-century Athens, including completion of the 'trilogy' of the University, the Akademias and the National Library. These displayed a disciplined and academic Classicism, with the latter two using temple forms. Christian Hansen designed the mint and the eye hospital, neither of which were particular monumental, and various churches. Theophil Hansen was responsible for the Athens observatory and the Zappeion, a Classically-fronted conference hall on the edge of the botanical gardens. Theophil was to achieve more fame for his work in Vienna (Bastl, Hirhager, and Schober 2013; Panetsos and Cassimatis 2014).

Kaftanzoglou was a fervent Classical revivalist. In March 1839, he was arguing against the city plan for Athens on the grounds that it would interfere with the archaeology (Kaftanzoglou 1839). He had considerable influence as the Director of the Polytechnio in Athens, which taught fine and applied art, including architecture. He was also a polemicist.

Figure 2.11 The Academy, Athens.

He argued for the purity of the Greek architectural and cultural tradition. He was prominent in the Greek archaeological committee and in that role was able to force through the clearing of the Frankish Tower from the Acropolis. Kaftanzoglou identified the Greek nation with Greek Classicism (Fatsea 2000: 214–46)

Kaftanzoglou's Classical revivalism was paralleled in the language debate in nineteenth-century Greece. Late-eighteenth-century Greek intellectuals had concerned themselves with the development of a language suitable for Enlightenment intellectual and social discourse. The problem was the perceived inadequacy of contemporary (demotic) spoken Greek and religious (koine) Greek for a literary and political renaissance. Debate focused on whether to deploy an archaic Classical form or a cleansed (*katharevousa*) form from which loan words (primarily Turkish) were to be removed. A form of *katharevousa* was employed in official and literary publications by the 1830s but as an intermediate step towards the eventual ambition of the restoration of Classical Greek. Consequently, Classical Greek became the language of the school system.

By the 1880s, demotic had become a literary language with many prominent supporters, but educated Greeks felt obliged to switch codes. Novelists might narrate in *katharevousa* but render naturalistic dialogue in demotic; speeches might be made in *katharevousa* but debated in demotic. *Katharevousa* was sufficiently archaic to require a specific training for native Greek-speakers. It resonated with Classical revivalism and was adopted by the mid-twentieth-century military junta as a central element in their nationalistic Classical revivalism. The fall of the generals led to the adoption of demotic as the official language in 1976 (Mackridge 2010; Jusdanis 1991: 41–6).

The artifice of *katharevousa* had broad sociological and cultural implications. It denigrated folk traditions, songs and other cultural expression in demotic in favour of Classicism. It reinforced an association of Classicism and nationalism. As Michael Herzfeld argues:

> *katharevousa* and several other neo-Classical codes (notably in architecture) did not represent a passive acceptance of foreign neo-Classicism; on the contrary, it was an attempt to take internal and external control in a game where the definition of Greek culture was still largely in foreign hands ... Greek neo-Classicism was thus an attempt at *reclamation*.
>
> *Herzfeld 1987: 53*

Classicism intersected with the various fault lines in Greek society. In its association with bourgeois society, it looked towards Western Europe and its cultural values. Those values were affirmed by that European tradition, signifying the bourgeoisie's progressive and modern values. Classicism was not a unifying symbolic language precisely because of the contentious formation of national ideologies.

The tensions in the Greek nation were played out topographically, from the sublime pinnacle of the Acropolis through the neoclassicism of the capital to the villages and mountain communities of the Mani and Roumeli and onwards to the great idea of a 'return' to Constantinople (Leontis 1995). These spectral topographies intersected with the materiality of power. Athens was chosen as the capital in large part because of the political dependency of the fragile Greek state on the Great Powers. It developed in a complex entanglement of class and nation in which the rapid rise of a Greek bourgeois culture shaped the built environment. Classicism was interwoven into political symbolism as the aesthetic of the mythic origins of the nation, of a colonial imposition, and of an emergent Europe-facing bourgeoisie. The aesthetic was political and contentious.

Nevertheless, these ideological and aesthetic divisions were extremely permeable. The colonial eye may have demanded clarity of ideology and aesthetics, but Greeks were at ease with code switching. Many Greeks exhibited a *diglossa*, an ability to switch between linguistic and cultural levels, to be both the *palichari* and the sophisticated, cultured diplomats, to follow local traditions and wear the latest French fashions. Understanding the city as pure symbol fails in the face of the complexity of socio-economic interactions of urban life. That multiplicity and complexity overwhelm the simplicity of any unified aesthetic-political vision. The colonial vision for Athens broke down in the face of the rapid and successful revitalization of the city. That social transformation allowed for the emergence of a nationalistic, bourgeois Classicism. Colonial Classicism remained an element in the Greek engagement with the Classical past, in part because it situated Greece and her middle classes within a European intellectual and civilizational framework. But Classicism was reappropriated from the Bavarian regime and retained as one of several aesthetic codes by which the nation could be represented.

CHAPTER 3
ROME: CITY OF UNITY, 1870–1911

Introduction

Rome became the intended capital of Italy in late 1861 (Ugolini 2011) when the city was still under Papal control. The rule of the Popes had been challenged in 1849 when, as part of a wave of revolutionary movements across Europe, the Repubblica romana was formed and the Papal authorities expelled. The Repubblica had employed the symbols of the Classical Republic (Giardina and Vauchez 2000: 117–22), but in 1850 the Papal states were restored, indirectly by the Austro-Hungarian defeat of the Piedmontese and more directly by French military intervention. Louis Napoleon had been elected President of France in part through the support of *ultramontane* Catholics and they demanded that France answer Pius IX's call for help. Despite the street-fighting skills of the inhabitants of Trastevere, Pius's army of Neapolitan, French and Papal troops had overwhelming superiority. Nevertheless, Papal control remained fragile, unpopular in Italy, and uneasily dependent on French military support.

When the wars of 1860–1 unified most of Italy, Rome stood out against the *risorgimento*. Garibaldi's attempts on the city were not supported by King Vittorio Emanuele, who needed French support in his struggles with Austro-Hungary. Consequently, Italy was founded as a nation state without Rome. The nation needed a capital. Turin was the capital of the Sardinian state and became the capital of the new Italy in 1861. In 1865, the capital was moved to Florence. There were other options, such as Milan and Naples, but it was Rome that had an imaginative hold on Italian nationalists. Leading figures, such as Garibaldi, Mazzini and Sella were committed to Rome as the future capital of Italy.

The war of 1866 saw a further extension of Italy with the annexation of Venetia. Yet, despite Garibaldi's efforts and a revolt against the Pope led by the Cairoli brothers in September 1867, Papal and French forces successfully maintained the Pope's temporal power. On 9 December 1867, the Italian parliament affirmed its ambition to have Rome as its capital. Quintino Sella (1887: 183–93) argued that the return to Rome was a necessary condition for the preservation of Italian unity and that this was a unanimous view.

In 1870, with the outbreak of the Franco-Prussian war, France recalled her soldiers from Rome. French defeat left the Pope without significant diplomatic or military resources. Although Vittorio Emanuele opened diplomatic negotiations for a peaceful annexation of Rome, Pius IX was not minded to accept the inevitable. On 20 September 1870, Italian forces breached the walls of Rome. Resistance was more than token but lasted only three hours. Indeed, the photographer of the assault found the scene sufficiently lacking in drama that it had to be restaged and primitive techniques of photomontage were employed to make more visible the Italian fallen (Kirk 2011). As soon as the wall and barricades were breached, the fighting stopped. The soldiers pressed into the city and were met by the diplomatic corps and cheering crowds. The troops gathered in piazza Termini, before one section was sent to piazza Colonna and another to the Campidoglio. With the capture of these two piazzas, secular Rome was brought under Italian control.

Piazza Colonna was the scene of popular celebration. The *tricolore* was everywhere. Children were dressed up and carried on the shoulders of the troops. Wine, liquor, sugar and biscuits appeared. In the Campidoglio, the papal forces were disarmed (Bersezio 1872: 475–84; De Amicis 1870: 44–62; Pesci 1895: 106–42). The Pope retreated to the Vatican and declared himself a prisoner. There was no meaningful attempt to extend Italian military power into Città Leonina (St Peter's and associated buildings). Yet the Pope made no evident attempt to stop the victorious troops visiting the basilica. The military unification of Italy was complete.

On 23 September an advisory council for Rome was appointed by General Cadorna. A plebiscite was organized to ratify the unification Rome and Italy. The results were sent to Vittorio Emanuele on 7 October. Eleven days later, Quintino Sella arrived in the city (Pesci 1895: 202, 223; Pesci 1907: 65). By 13 November a city council with sixty members was appointed and by 30 November a commission of engineers and architects was established to plan for civic improvements (Calza 1911: 4–7). On 24 January 1871, the deputies debated the translation of the capital. The government moved to Rome on 3 February 1871. On 2 July, the King made his ceremonial entry into the city and was met by cheering crowds (Pesci 1907: 65).

It was never enough for Rome to be a modest capital; it came freighted with grandiose civilizational claims. The new nation was to embrace modernity and to reject the poverty and underdevelopment of the past. The political offer of the regime lay in delivering a progressive national modernity that would rectify the comparative underdevelopment of Italy. Yet, there were many direct beneficiaries of the *status quo* including landowners, office-holders, politicians and clergy. The Italian state faced fragmentation as a result of fissures between elements 'modern' and 'traditional', urban and rural, northern and southern (on which see Gramsci 1957, 1971). Rome could be seen as having fallen out of the progressive stream of modernity: the eternal city immovably in the past. But like all nationalist regimes, the liberal Italian state looked to that past for its identity and legitimacy. Italy's claim to be a great nation was inevitably reliant on the legacies of Classical and Papal Romes. Italy needed the third version of Rome, *la terza Roma*, to represent those pasts and to be the city of the future. Rome was to be the showcase of the Italian nation and the canvas on which the regime would encapsulate glorious traditions. Rome was the symbol through which to transform the nation into a modern state and unite a fragmented people.

In what follows, I trace the tensions in the development of Rome. I begin with an exploration of the developing ideology of *la terza Roma* in differentiation from the sepulchral city of the nineteenth-century Papacy. In the next section, I examine the challenges of the 1870s. Rome was rapidly transformed into the administrative and political capital of the nation. A new Rome grew up alongside the old city. This new

Rome was bourgeois and modernizing. It had little use for Classicism, adopting and adapting the predominant architectural styles of nineteenth-century Italy. The legacy and prestige of Classical Rome was deeply felt and underpinned the nationalism manifest in the notion of *la terza Roma*, but in its first generation, *la terza Roma* predominantly looked to the future and for a civilizational role for Italy at the centre of a new scientific age. Stylistically, this city was developed largely through the deployment of a Renaissance style, mostly eschewing monumentalism in favour of restrained bourgeois forms. Classicism returned to the fore with the national monument to Vittorio Emanuele II, il Vittoriano.

The myth of Classical Rome runs through all nineteenth-century responses to the city. Yet, the relationship to the Classical past manifested in different ways in different periods. For visitors to the Papal city, the dominant mode was a Romantic response to a civilizational fall. To the extent to which they saw the modern city, it was as a sepulchre for lost Classical glory. For the revolutionaries of the *risorgimento*, Classical Rome represented a promise of liberty and civilizational excellence to which their new Italy could aspire. The liberal governments' tense relations with the Papacy encouraged multiple symbolic differentiations of their Rome from that of the Popes. If Classical Rome was an inspiration, *la terza Roma* was to be a new city of innovation and practicality. It could not be a museum. The progressive city broke with traditions of Classical and Papal urbanism in favour of a bourgeois city culture.

Rome was a city honoured as the font of Western civilization and a direct line was drawn from Classical Rome to the contemporary wealth and power of the West. That Classical inheritance was imbibed by the European bourgeoisie. Their Classical educations laid claim to civilizational superiority and gave the bourgeoisie their place in history and culture and a justification for their class-based national and imperial power.

Visitors to the city were placed in a complex situation. The city of their dreams was imperial Rome in all its grandeur and monumentalism. The city they visited was neither economically nor culturally advanced. Non-Italian visitors were notably impervious to the contemporary city. As Giardina and Vauchez (2000: 169) put it, visitors expressed a high degree of autonomy. Contemporary Rome was seen as a city of the dead, twice excluded from history since it was neither part of the modern world nor living in its Classical past. Rome in ruins was the scenic backdrop for an encounter with the bourgeois self, which was the ultimate repository of Classical culture. Rome generated a morbid anxiety that bourgeois and Western culture was already dead or, at best, precariously perched on the precipice of civilizational collapse.

By contrast, Italian nationalists imagined a future Italian capital that was technocratic. Rome was a mythic space in which the nationalistic dream of *la terza Roma* could emerge. Mazzini's ambition was for a modern city that would inspire the nationalist movement and replicate the centrality of Renaissance and Classical Romes to their chronologically delimited civilizations. Since contemporary Rome was emphatically not modern in the view of contemporaries, *la terza Roma* would emerge in its difference from the contemporary papal city. The civilizational rhetoric mirrored the immediate political rhetoric in which the progressive Italian nation existed in opposition to Papal

Rome's medievalism. There was an implicit tension between a nationalistic mythic revival that drew on the imperial traditions of Rome and a progressive technocracy that sought a city of bourgeois modernity and respectability. This tension can be seen in a polarity between the 'organic' architectural styles of *cinquecentismo* and the 'rhetorical egoism' of monumental structures. The polarity reflected differing views of the nature of Italy and Rome and the future of the Italian nation.

Post-1870, the Italian state had the opportunity to bring a new Rome into being. It invested in new civic infrastructure, new roads, new quarters and new state administrative buildings. A modern city required ease of circulation and 'hygiene'. This modernity was identified with science, rationality and the bourgeoisie. Much of the development focused on the provision of adequate housing and urban structures for this new bourgeoisie. Rome became a socially zoned city with quarters for the working classes in Trastevere and Testaccio and large bourgeois suburbs surrounding the old city. It was a city of movement, defined more by the flows of its citizens through the city on a multiplicity of private odysseys than any central assembly, authority or monumental location. This polyfocal modern city existed alongside the Classical ruins. Architecturally, the city looked to its immediate traditions rather than to Classicism, eschewing grand monumental projects in favour of a quieter industrious middle-class capitalism that rapidly appropriated, or tried to, the historical prestige of the city. Classicism was present in the cultural world of the bourgeoisie but subordinated to modernity.

Rome's morphology and the relationship of the city to the past changed with the monument to Vittorio Emanuele II. Il Vittoriano foregrounded the Classical past in the mythography of the Italian nation. The monument provided Rome with a central point, though the decisive formation of its centrality came only in the fascist remodelling of piazza Venezia. If the cityscape of the *risorgimento* city was only loosely connected to the Classical past, the ultranationalist il Vittoriano offered an imperial vision of Italy's future.

La città morta to *la terza Roma*

Hippolyte Taine was particularly depressed by Rome (Brice 1998: 13).

> One advances and trace of life disappears. One believes oneself to be in an abandoned city and in the dead skeleton of a suddenly destroyed people. One passes under the arcades of palazzo Colonna, the long silent walls of its gardens and one hears nothing and one sees nothing that is human; alone at the end of a winding street in the indistinct darkness of a porch which seems like a basement window a dying street light flickers with its circle of yellow light. The closed houses, the high walls stretch in their inhospitable row like a line of a dangerous rocks on the side of a hill and on leaving their shadow, great spaces open up suddenly, blanched by the moonlight to seem like a deserted sandy beach.
>
> *Taine 1866: I 32*

Taine would seem to be visiting a gothic novel. His gloom is unrelenting: 'You ask how one amuses oneself in Rome. To amuse oneself does not have the same sense as in Paris. Here, when one is not in the country, one must study' (Taine 1866: I 131). Rome in the evening is a 'spectacle mortuaire'.

> The Piazza Barberini ... is a stone tomb where some forgotten torches burn. The poor little lights seem to be swallowed in the dismal shroud of shadow and the fountain whispers indistinctly in the silence with the swish of a ghost. One cannot render this aspect of Rome at night. The day is of death, but the night is all the horror and the grandeur of the tomb.
>
> *Taine 1866: I 155*

His thoughts returned repeatedly to death. Even as he explored the countryside via the northern gate of Porta del Popolo, he was struck by its desertion. The Tiber was viscous and an evil serpent. There were no trees, houses or cultivation. He found the ruins of the villa of Julius II, with a great staircase leading nowhere, and lamented for the land of Michelangelo and Raphael. In a great Roman cemetery, he reflected on the recruits from all the nations, France, Spain, Africa, Germany and Asia whose bones were beneath the ground (Taine 1866: I 429–33). Death was global in Rome. Taine (1866: I 445) saw the urban poor as trapped within the Middle Ages and ignored by a papacy which had never attempted to bring civilization or modernity.

In a brief stay from November 1786 to February 1787, Goethe (1870: I 120–75) was similarly moved. Rome was the city of which he had dreamed from his youth and come to know from his books. After a week's residence, he was inspired to reflect on history and destiny. Rome had undergone profound change and yet the sun and hills were the same. He could see columns and walls and detect traces of the Ancient Romans in the people of the contemporary city. Yet, the topographical and genetic continuities merely emphasized the absences. Rome was a palimpsest of a city, but true magnificence had gone: 'What the Barbarians had left, the architects of new Rome have destroyed' (Goethe 1870: I 125). What was worth seeing were the traces of antiquity, which were best enjoyed in moonlit walks alone.

Chateaubriand (1827: 166–202) also found solitude in Rome. His impression on arrival (27 June 1803) was of a deserted city. Mass at St Peter's was superb, but the church deserted (29 June). On 3 July he mused that the second Rome had fallen in turn, 'all is finished'. On a visit to Tivoli, he found himself studying Latin epitaphs of children: 'After 2,000 years, I come, me, barbarian of the Gauls, amongst the ruins of Rome' (Chateaubriand 1827: 173). The literary focus is Chateaubriand, the latter-day Gaul in a place that is out of time. Chateaubriand somehow represented the Classical tradition in himself. He was a product of its culture. In his wandering through Rome, he experienced a death of society and culture. All that was of value was reduced to the isolated, educated self. His primary discovery in the Temple of Vesta was solitude. When he took a moonlit walk in Rome, he met a young woman begging. He gave her money not out of sympathy for her plight, but because she had the appearance of a Madonna. She was an object of art and beauty who inspired in Chateaubriand an aesthetic response which in turn inspired his charity. He did not see a contemporary socio-economic tragedy. The city was bathed in pale solitude, the streets without inhabitants. Rome, ancient, medieval and contemporary, had disappeared. What remained was Chateaubriand and the drama of his spiritual encounter with death, time, art and himself.

In a letter from Rome to Thomas Love Peacock of mid-December 1818, Shelley first laments the Italianate behaviour of Lord Byron whose sexual corruption had found its decadent Italian home. Then he turned to the Colosseum:

> It has come to be overgrown with wild olives and myrtles and figs and threaded through with paths and flowers and grass. The Forum is a kind of desart [sic] full of heaps of stones and pits and though so near the habitations of men, is the most desolate place you can conceive ... Behold the wrecks of what a great nation once dedicated to the abstractions of the mind. Rome is a city as it were of the dead, or rather of those who cannot die, and who survive the puny generations which inhabit and pass over the spot which they have made sacred to eternity. In Rome, at least in the first enthusiasm of your recognitions of antient time, you see nothing of the Italians. The nature of the city assists the delusion, for its vast and antique walls describe a circumference of sixteen miles, and thus the population is thinly scattered over this space nearly as great as London. Wide wild fields are enclosed within it, and there are grassy lanes and copses which overhang the Tiber. The gardens of the modern palaces are like wild woods of cedar and cypress and pine, and the neglected walks are overgrown with weeds. The English burying place is a green slope near the walls, under the pyramidal tomb of Cestius, and is I think the most beautiful and solemn cemetery I ever beheld.
>
> *Shelley 1964: letter 488*

For Shelley, Rome is a place for philosophizing on death and civilization and where nature has reclaimed culture.

Foreign travellers had found the Romantic in Rome since Piranesi's transformation of the ruin into the aesthetic representation of time and civilizational decline (Pinto 2012: 10). Their accounts suggest a desire for a city which had inhabited their youthful dreams. In the absence of antique Rome, they covered contemporary Rome with a veil of silence, finding solitude in the ruins and in their contemplation of death and transience. It was a place outside time in which they could encounter their individuality in contemplation of the end of the world. They were unable to see the contemporary city.

Similar tropes filtered into the post-1870 representations of Rome. Vittorio Bersezio's account stressed some of the same archaic and undeveloped elements of the city such as the desert of piazza Termini (1872: 11). He claimed to prefer the Corso to the Rue de Rivoli, that most famous of Paris's modern commercial streets, for its picturesque qualities. But the hotels, cafés and trattorie lacked elegance, and the food outlets spread fatty smells. Bersezio (1872: 15) was amazed by the cattle at pasture in the city, recalling Claude Lorrain's *Capriccio with ruins of the Roman Forum* (1634) from two-and-a-half centuries earlier. For Bersezio, Rome of 1870 was a city of carelessness, dirt and abandonment (1872: 308).

Rome: City of Unity, 1870–1911

Bersezio repeatedly orientalized Papal Rome. It was the city of 365 churches (1872: 365) that made no provision for the poor. It displayed 'almost Asiatic pomp', and an oppression of liberty that recalled oriental baseness (394). It was a city of slavery which lacked a bourgeois intelligentsia (454). Rome was the backward city to be civilized through the importation of new civic values. Although there was an evident tension with the nationalistic spiritual identification of all Romes as one Rome (6), the future city could not be Republican or Imperial Rome, nor the Rome of the Popes, but the Rome of a peaceful, prosperous and free people (7).

In the etchings that illustrate the book (by Manteuil), we are shown the picturesque poverty of a Roman cobbler. His face is heavy and distorted. His stall is no more than a table. He has almost no stock, only three boots are visible. He is sheltered by a plank which is somehow suspended between two Classical columns of a portico over which a cloth has been carelessly flung. Behind, a shady figure lurks beneath hat and cloak. We see poverty and degeneration among the Classical ruins. As telling is the view of St Peter's from the Tiber in which we are transported to a pastoral scene complete with shepherd and goat.

Yet, there are signs of gentility, particularly in the depictions of the piazza del Popolo and the gardens of Pincio. One of Manteuil's engravings shows small groups of bourgeois promenaders beneath the terrace on the Pincio hill. The piazza del Popolo was a highlight of late Papal urban development. It had been redesigned by Giuseppe Valadier in the early 1790s (Debenedetti 1985; Ciampi 1870: 31–3). Valadier had tied the piazza to the Pincio and so to a network of villa gardens including those of the Villa Borghese that stretched out towards the Esquiline hill. Much as they do today, these provided a city park for the Romans and opportunities for families to take their *passeggiata*. Giovanni

Figure 3.1 'A Roman Cobbler' (Bersezio 1872).

Classicism and the Construction of Capital Cities

Volpato depicted young middle-class Romans socializing on the Pincio *c.* 1800. Gustav Palm painted the gardens in 1844.[1] Ippolito Caffi in *c.* 1850 and Felix Benoist in 1870 painted families relaxing at the Villa Borghese.

The Corso was a social space. It had been used for horse races through the city and for the carnival. Valadier had built a theatre at the piazza Venezia in 1807. In an etching of 1850, Luigi Rossini (1850) depicts a busy street with groups of well-dressed men conducting their business. Ippolito Caffi painted the carnival of 1845 and a procession along the Corso. By the early nineteenth century, a network of piazzas, roads and gardens had developed to the north-east of Rome which provided for elegant society (Cassetto 2005: 76–90). As in so many other European urban centres, these were spaces for the new middle classes to interact and socialize, equivalent to the spaces which the aristocracy would have had privately within their *palazzi*.

Roman social life focused on piazza Colonna (Bersezio 1872: 24). Emile Zola (1896: 159–60) describes it as the most vibrant piazza in the city. The triumphant march of the Italian troops on 20 September 1870 found celebrating crowds in the piazza Colonna (De Amicis 1870: 45–7). Arturo Calza (1911: 11) called it the true centre of Rome. René Bazin (1894: 126–7) watched the *passeggiata* of the Romans along the Corso, admiring the women in their bright dresses, as they made their way to the piazza Colonna for an evening of social interaction, though Bazin was generally unimpressed with the Corso (a mediocre street) and saw the evening gathering in the piazza as evidence of the tenacious loyalty of the Romans to the old ways.

Despite this evidence that Rome was far from a sepulchre, the prospect of a revived Rome, *la terza Roma*, became a promise of renaissance for the nation and for Rome. Giuseppe Mazzini (1805–72), the intellectual forefather of Italian nationalism transformed the vague and cosmopolitan notion of a renewal of European civilization in *la terza Roma* into a nationalistic slogan (Fournier-Finocchiaro 2012). Mazzini's *terza Roma* emerged in the revolutionary context of 1848–9 and the *Repubblica romana*. His idea drew on the Classical Roman Republic and French revolutionary ideas. In his autobiographical notes, he was rhapsodic, connecting a promise of civilizational renewal to the future city.

> Rome was the dream of my young years, the mother-idea in the conception of the mind, the religion of the spirit; and I entered, in the evening, on foot, on the first of March, anxious and almost adoring. For me, Rome was, and is despite the shame of today, the Temple of Humanity. From Rome there will come the religious transformation that will give, for the third time, moral unity to Europe.
>
> *Mazzini 1864: VII 185*

His encounter with the city was a transcendent experience.

> I started, crossing the Porta del Popolo, with an almost electric shock, of a flush of new life. I will never see Rome again, but I will remember it when dying, between a thought of God and of a dearest person.
>
> *Mazzini 1864: VII 185*

He imagined that his bones would rise up with that same electrical shock when the flag of the Republic was raised on the Campidoglio and the Vatican. Mazzini's vision of a new Italy was mystical and his nationalism religious (Fournier-Finocchiaro and Frétigné 2018; Gentile 1996: 4; 2007: 37–9; Berezin 1997: 43–4). Rome as 'the Temple of Humanity' and the source of a European renewal spoke to grand ambitions.

For Cavour, Prime Minister of Italy, Rome was the only city that could become the focal point of a great Italian state in the traditions of the Caesars (Arthurs 2010: 119). Quintino Sella, Finance Minister, enthused in a triumphant speech to the electors of Masserano on 13 November 1870:

> Rome: Magical word that moves profoundly every patriot … Who of us has not from his first youth dreamt of Italy with Rome as her capital?
>
> *Sella 1885: 36*

Educated in the liberal Classical tradition, Rome was central to Sella's sense of self as well as his understanding of nation. He embraced Rome's civilizational significance and, like Mazzini, saw Rome as an idea that moved the world.

It was an idea that Sella held to. In a debate on the transfer of the seat of government to Rome, held on 24 January 1871, Sella (1887: 207–10) argued that Rome was far from just a political idea. It was a philosophical notion. As in so many of these debates, the precise meaning is elusive but the distinction between the political and philosophical would seem to point to a difference between the issues of the moment and the essential truths of Italy or even of modern civilization. Moving the capital to Rome was, according to Sella, essential to Italy, to the unity of the state, and to religion. Rome operated politically and ideologically as a counterpoint to the centrifugal tendencies embedded in the regional differences in Italy and the everyday political divisions of the state. It performed the symbolic work of uniting the Italian people with a Roman past that was common and civilizational. For Sella (1887: 183–9), Rome was central to the programme of national foundation to which all true Italians were committed. In a speech of 24 January 1881, Sella (1887: 233) justified the vast costs of modernizing Rome as necessary for the Italian people, for progress and for humanity. On 14 March of the same year, he repeated his claim that the move of the capital to Rome was both to provide Italy with an eternal capital and to provide benefit for the world. Sella (1887: 273–311) urged his fellow Italians not to forget that they were all Italian by virtue of Rome.

In Sella's view, Italians were first and foremost Romans. Such a claim was far from merely rhetorical. Nor was it uncontentious (Arthurs 2010). 'Eternal Rome' was multiply written into contemporary Italian identity. As with Mazzini's vision, the civilizational benefits of the return to Rome were primarily those of the future. Sella's (1887: 325–30) Rome was to be the city of science, though, rather idiosyncratically, he also hoped that Latin would be restored to primacy in scientific discourse.

Away from the political leadership, the reaction of the men of the *risorgimento* to Rome was enthusiastic. Edmondo De Amicis (1870) reported on the liberation of Rome. He was there as the walls were breached and followed the troops into Rome. He was caught up in the celebrations as the crowds poured into the streets and soldiers, Romans, journalists and no doubt various other interested parties mingled in celebration. It was a historic moment of liberation from the Papacy and a culmination of the violent struggles of the previous two decades. If we trust his account, it was celebrated as a day of liberation and of unification.

De Amicis had no doubts that the 1861 decision to make Rome the capital was the right one. For him, all Italian history was present in Rome (1870: 5–6). He remembered that Cavour's declaration was saluted and welcomed throughout all the schools and piazzas: Italy could not achieve its great destiny without Rome (9). Although some among his companions in September 1870 had felt strongly that the capital should remain in Firenze, their experiences of the city persuaded them of the necessary primacy of Rome (71).

De Amicis and his friends were impressed by Rome. The houses, the piazzas, the churches, the fountains, the stairs, the columns and all the monuments seemed to have been made by a race of men twice what they were. The soldiers, he reported, were awed by Rome (De Amicis 1870: 63–8). The literary flavour of the reactions suggests that De Amicis may have been channelling Gibbon's (1781: 144–7) account of the entry of Constantine II into Rome, or even Gibbon's source, Ammianus Marcellinus, 15.10.13–16, in an expression of awe at the monumental achievements of the emperors and in a reflection of their own lessened state.

Yet it was not the Rome that was before De Amicis that so inspired him, but his hope for *la terza Roma*. Papal Rome was corrupt and corrupting. Its people had been enmeshed in a web of interests and fear that had oppressed them more efficiently than soldiers and cannon (De Amicis 1870: 19). The streets were bathed in the blood of the martyrs who had died for liberty and equality against tyranny and slavery (16). De Amicis was conscious of the religious devotion of the Romans and that religion was a barrier which must be overturned to make the new Rome (20). The new city of which he dreamed was a great modern European capital: it was the city of the future which the new Italian state would construct (12, 70–1). To achieve that transformation Rome had to escape the religious suffocation of tradition (13–14). Even the central archaeological sites from the Campidoglio to the Colosseum were neglected and ill-kept (69). It was the dream of Classical Rome which enthused the nationalists. Patriotic feeling was to be inspired in the youth of Italy by stories of imperial Rome and the struggle against the Papacy.

This reaction to Papal Rome continued into the twentieth century. André Maurel (1909: 2) differentiated the bustling *terza Roma* from Chateaubriand's city of tombs. The churches left him stupefied and offended (4). It was the antique in conjunction with the modern that impressed him. Rome was for him a city that aspired to the modernity of London, Paris and Berlin.

The persuasiveness of such narratives lay in their replication of the developmental histories of northern European societies. The values of the Enlightenment were generated in a civilization that was predominantly urban, capitalist, nationalistic and secular. That civilization defined itself against certain traditions of religion, Christian and other, and social and political systems which were seen as redolent of a premodern era. To designate Papal Rome as premodern was an effective way to devalue and marginalize its political culture. It also allowed the new regime to pose as a revolutionary presence. That pose was exaggerated. Rome was modernizing before 1870, but in the contemporary view it could only modernize under a liberal regime.

The repeated youthful dreaming of Rome created a form of alienation from the contemporary city. Romantic tourists came to visit the ruins of a civilization deeply ingrained in their cultures and identities. Contemporary Rome, as a 'spectacle mortuaire' was a trope that reinforced both Rome's separation from its antique glories and from modernity. The trope suited many. It was closely related to a perceived absence of bourgeois society. This absence was exaggerated, yet the story of a Rome held back by Papal hostility to the modern was too good to nuance. Papal Rome was to be rejected. *La terza Roma* was to carry the flag of a modern Italy.

The grandiose claims of Mazzini and Sella for *la terza Roma* drew on the reception of Classical Rome. Classicism offered a bridge between the various Italian pasts. Yet, there was an obvious and inherent tension between a nationalist essentialism that looked to Rome and the almost religious embracing of modernity. In the first decade of Rome the Capital, the drive to modernize was central.

Making modern Rome

Contemporary discussions of the social structures of Rome tended to emphasize 'traditional' elements, particularly the poor and aristocracy. Bersezio (1872: 454) identified university professors as a middle-class stratum and judged them insufficiently influential or numerous to drive social and economic change. Felix Giordano (1879: iii) saw the city as the product of and dominated by two interrelated groups, a hereditary nobility and an ecclesiastical aristocracy. Ugo Pesci's (1907: 155–72, 225–57) exhaustive history of the first eight years of Rome as capital spends many pages delineating the various aristocratic residents and foreign visitors presumably on the assumption that these groups constituted 'society'. He understood Rome as an aristocratic city whose elite were closely tied to the political and economic power of the papacy. This elite was ambivalent in their responses to the events of September 1870. The clergy tended to be hostile, and it may have been from them that the derogative name of 'buzzurri' (boors) was coined for the incomers (Pesci 1895: 255–70).

Rome was a more diverse city than these accounts allowed. There was a middle-class segment of the population and by the 1850s, there was a manufacturing sector, notably in cloth and tobacco. Financial services, particularly banking and insurance, were also prominent (Sanfilippo 1992: 27). Although railways, always a manifestation of modernity, came late to Rome, they did come. Stations were built at porta Maggiore (1856), porta Portese (1859) and Termini (1867) with new railways to Cittavecchia, Naples and Bologna. Termini was completed only in 1873 but was operational long before (Sanfilippo 1992: 33; Cassetto 2005: 31–2, 82).

Archbishop Xavier de Merode pushed through a series of urban reforms from 1850 onwards. Merode was from a prominent aristocratic Belgian family and brought a modernizing perspective to the Papal governance of Rome. The prison system was reformed, hospitals rebuilt and sanitation improved. He sponsored the development of a new district around Castro Pretorio and Santa Maria dell'Angeli. These new districts were to be further developed after 1870 along the line of what was to become via Nazionale. Merode's urbanism was influenced by his friendship with Baron von Haussmann (Bazin 1894: 130).

In 1870, Rome was the second largest city in Italy. Its population was 226,022, smaller than Naples with 449,000 but slightly larger than the other major centres of Palermo, Turin and Milan (Brice 1998: 13). That population had almost doubled from the 121,000 of 1811. Such growth was similar to that of other large Italian cities suggesting that Rome's urban development was not abnormal for the period (from Sanfilippo 1992: 61; Sella 1887: 233–72). Rome's growth accelerated with the transfer of the capital. Italian planners had experience of the demographic consequences of moving the capital. It had boosted the Florentine population by about 20,000 (Sanfilippo 1992: 49). Within a year of the unification, the population of Rome had increased to about 245,000 and Felix Giordano (1871: 186) calculated that Rome would acquire an extra 70,000 residents. Eight years later, estimates put the population at around 282,000 and the population was to reach 300,000 by 1881 (Castiglioni 1879).

The authorities planned for rapid growth. There was an urban planning committee by 30 November 1870. The first reports were published within a month (Calza 1911: 7). An urban plan (*piano regalotore*) was submitted for approval on 28 November 1871, though the provisions of the plan were circulating in the spring of 1871, and finally agreed in 1873.

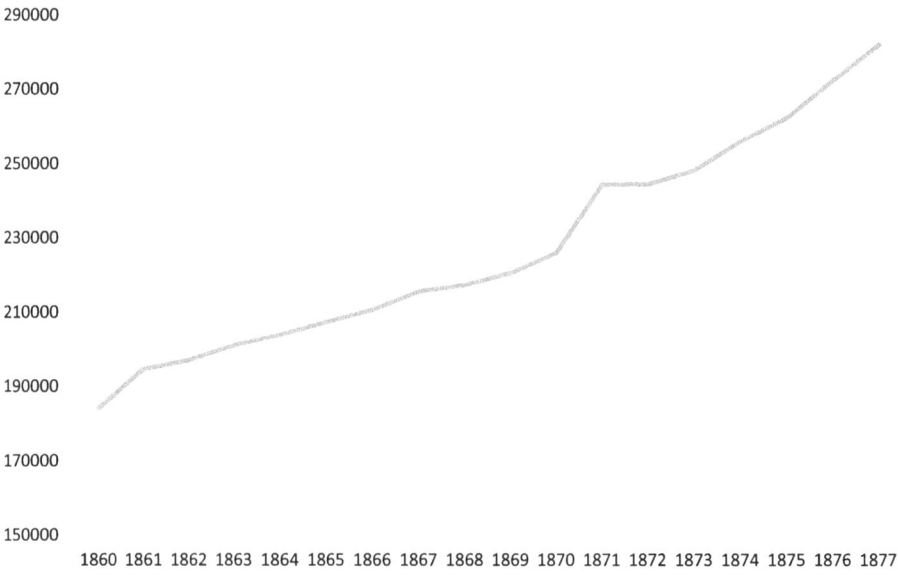

Figure 3.2 Rome's population 1860–78 (from Castiglioni 1879).

Giordano's (1871) survey gave a detailed picture of Rome and its territory and outlined plans for development and modernization. Giordano was convinced that the transfer of the capital offered the chance for 'eternal Rome' to attain a new stage as a capital of a young Italy (1871: 3). He disparaged the condition of Rome under the Papacy. Underdevelopment and governmental neglect were seen most obviously in the territory around Rome. Giordano described the suburban zone of around 200,000 hectares as 'a strange desert in the heart of Italy', denuded of habitations. It was only close to the walls that some grand suburban villas formed a transitional zone between desert and city. The dominant mode of agriculture in the region was large-scale pastoralism, which required few workers and little investment (Giordano 1871: 7). Such farms (*latifondia*) were generally seen as socially deleterious, yet they were the economic bedrock of the hereditary nobility (Giordano 1879).

Giordano (1871: 9) calculated that the city walls enclosed 1,416 hectares. Of this, gardens and vineyards occupied 780 hectares. Buildings occupied 388 hectares with streets and piazzas making up a further 180 hectares. Allowing for the Tiber itself and various watercourses, the built-up area of the city was about 40 per cent of the available intramural land. The population density stood at about 520 people per hectare, considerably less than in Naples. The quality of the housing was poor. Among the working classes, density per room was at about four people, but amongst the poorest rose to ten to twelve, with considerable consequences for health (Giordano 1871: 174–5). Giordano saw the city as falling far short of modern standards in its hygiene (compare Bersezio 1872: 302, 474). Mortality was high at about 3 per cent per annum and ran ahead of births at about 2.8 per cent. The road network was regarded as inadequate with only one major through route, the Corso. The flood defences were ineffective and in December 1870 Rome suffered a particularly severe flood that lasted into January 1871 (Giordano 1879: xlvii).

Giordano (1871: 172) listed 369 churches, sixty-one monasteries, seventy convents and nineteen other religious institutions in Rome. He described the churches as being of poor architectural style and 'decadent'. He implied that there were far too many (compare Maurel 1909: 4). In a later report (Giordano 1879: ii), he described them as sad and severe. The twin forces of Church and aristocracy were held responsible for Rome's backwardness.

Edmondo De Amicis (1870: 17–20) similarly argued that modernization would require breaking Romans' piety. This opposition between modernity and religion engaged with the symbolic spaces of the Classical. De Amicis (1870: 12–15) thought religion was entombing the Classical legacy. He viewed Papal Rome as not being the Rome of 'our people' and hoped that a Rome exposed to the 'sky and sun of liberty' would revive antique glories. Ancient Roman traditions and the ideologies of liberty and nationalism were supposedly mutually reinforcing: through their concord, Classical greatness would be resurrected (12–15).

Style entered into this debate indirectly. Giordano (1879: lxxvii) perceived Rome as a 'closed city' that would need to be opened in its revolutionary transformation. An 'open' Classical style was felt to be more in tune with the aspirations for a new city. Colonnaded façades created spaces integrated with the public areas of street and piazza and produced an aesthetic that was more inclusive of the citizen. Classical architectural style signified the new values of citizenship as well as the symbolic bond with antique Rome.

The commission for improving the city was headed by Alessandro Viviani. The *piano regolatore* of November 1871 was hugely ambitious and the *sindaco* (mayor) Luigi Pianciani scaled back some elements.[2] The plan can be considered in three aspects, the new quarters, the plans for new routes through the old city and the improvement of infrastructure, including water management. The new quarters were mostly achieved as was the management of the Tiber, but the new roads and the demolitions required to build them were more difficult. Many of the road projects took decades to bring to completion or were dropped.

Many of the additional 70,000 population were expected to be administrators or political leaders. They required a high standard of accommodation. The plan envisaged a new quarter at Quirinale along the route developed by Merode to the Castro Pretorio. This quarter covered about eighty hectares. Smaller developments covered the Oppian and Caelian hills and crossed the Esquiline to surround the archaeological park of the Domus Aurea and the Baths of Trajan. The quarters extended the city to Termini station. New blocks on the gardens of the villa Ludovisi bordered the Pincio. A further smaller quarter of thirty to thirty-five hectares was proposed for Testaccio to the south-west edge of the Aventine hill. The major development on the Vatican bank of the river was an entirely new quarter in Prati di Castello, north of Castel San'Angelo which was to be about sixty hectares (Giordano 1871: 190–2). Prati was to be connected to piazza del Popolo by a new bridge (which was to be named Ponte Regina Margherita) and through a small development of L'Oca. Further small developments were planned for the Gianicolo and Trastevere. Altogether, the new quarters planned in 1871 aimed to provide 200 hectares of housing thereby increasing the size of the city by about 50 per cent. These new areas would accommodate a further 100,000 people. In the detailed adjustments of 1873, the new housing was slightly expanded.

The plans for new roads focused on the integration of the disparate part of the city, especially the new quarters, and the provision of through routes to ease movement in the old city. One of the major elements was the completion of via Nazionale. There was some disagreement as to where it should connect with old city, either reaching piazza Colonna or stretching deeper to the Pantheon or piazza Sciarra. The plan envisaged a straightening of the Corso's access into piazza Venezia with the demolition of palazzo di Torlonia. Neither of these developments were to be completed, with the via Nazionale making an awkward sequence of turns around Trajan's column to enter piazza Venezia. The palazzo di Torlonia survived until 1903.

Viviani also proposed a major new route that would run to the west from piazza Venezia to cross the Tiber downstream of Castel Sant'Angelo. This became the Corso Vittorio Emanuele II (Kirk 2011), but was a difficult project given the buildings of artistic and historical importance along the route. It was delayed.

A further new road from the Colosseum into piazza Venezia was proposed. This was necessary to link the quarters on the Caelio and Oppio to the centre of the city. It was to

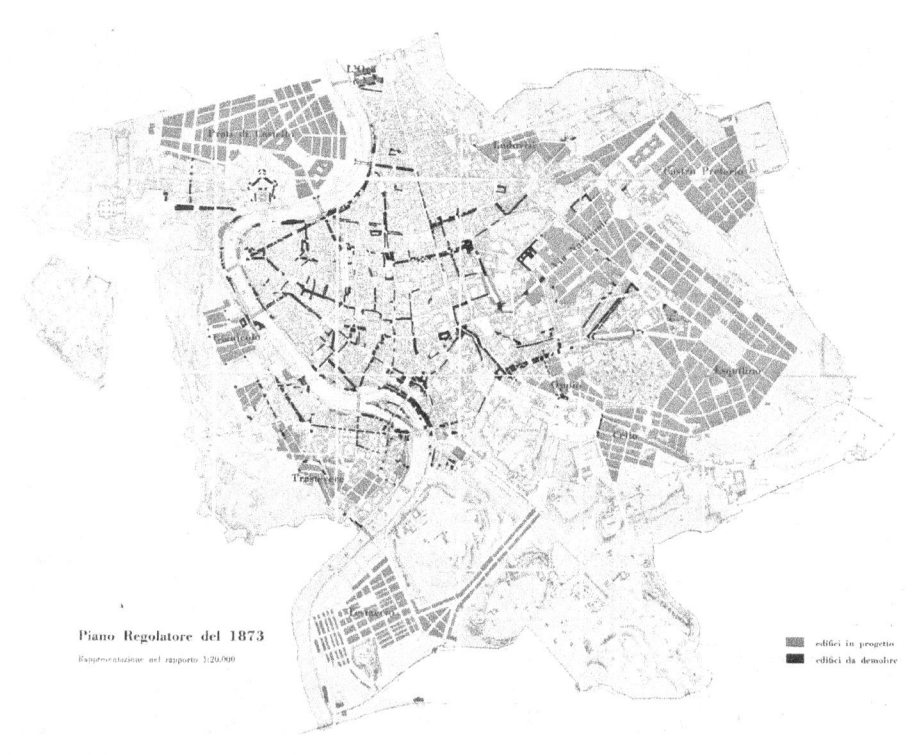

Figure 3.3 *Piano regalotore* of 1873.

perform the same function as the later via dei Fori imperiali, which was to be built in grandiose style by the Fascist urban planners. Viviani's proposed route avoided the archaeological centre. An ambitious north-south route required tunnelling under the Quirinale to join the via dei Due Macelli, which ran north into the old city, to via Nazionale and the new quarters in the south and east (Pianciani 1873: 1–10). These roads improved connectivity within the city and to the rail station at Termini.

The other major works in the old city were mainly along the Tiber banks to improve connections between the Vatican side and the old city. Bridges were expensive and there was resistance to the construction of a new bridge to Trastevere, the most industrial of the quarters of the old city. When he presented the revised plan, the *sindaco* Luigi Pianciani (1873) indignantly pointed out that the working-class residents of Trastevere paid their taxes and were entitled to the benefits of the modern city. There was clearly already a sense that the city was to be for the bourgeoisie.

The plans for the Vatican side were much less extensive. A new route was planned into Trastevere and a better connection to Gianicolo. More ambitious was a plan to connect the Vatican to the city by demolishing the small and densely occupied district of Borghi. The housing in Borghi effectively cut the piazza San Pietro off from Rome and the Tiber. The project was to get mired in controversy. It formed part of Edmondo Sanjust di Teluda's *piano regalotore* of 1909 and was finally completed with the Fascist-era construction of via della Conciliazione with Mussolini wielding the pick to begin demolitions on 28 October 1936 (Kallis 2011; Sanjust di Teulada 1908; see also p. 170).

The flood of late 1870 reinforced the need for extensive works to protect the city from the Tiber. The city also needed new water supplies and waste facilities, all of which came at a substantial cost.

Giordano (1871: 220–1) predicted that the costs of implementation of the *piano regalotore* would be about 235 million lire with an additional 85 million lire to be spent on new administrative buildings. Private investment in housing was also needed and that was estimated at 600 million lire. Giordano envisaged these costs being incurred across a fifteen- to twenty-year period. In Pianciani's (1873) report, estimates of the cost had fallen to 164 million lire spread across twenty-five years. On 24 January 1881, Quintino Sella (1887: 233–72) reported to Parliament that the work completed in Rome in its first decade together with future planned expenses would cost approximately 165 million lire. The total tax receipts for the Italian state in 1872 amounted to 1,014,000,000 lire (Houghton 1898). The redevelopment of Rome was a vast expenditure, but one which seems to have had considerable political support.

In 1881, Sella was triumphant. The Italian authorities were delivering on their promises for a new Rome. *Sindaco* Ruspoli counted 33,000 new rooms added to the city's housing stock. Rome housed around 80,000 more residents than in 1870. But the change was more significant. The census of 1881 reported that only 45 per cent of the current population had been born in Rome (Sanfilippo 1992: 54). Rome was becoming dominated by a new bourgeoisie. The replanning of the city contributed to the fierce class and neighbourhood tensions that characterized late nineteenth- and twentieth-century Rome (Herzfeld 2009).

One of the larger of the new quarters, Prati di Castello, lay to the north of the Papal fortress of Castel Sant'Angelo. In Giambattista Nolli's map of 1748, the area is one of small fields and orchards.[3] In the early photographs of the 1860s, the area is shown as flat and almost featureless: ideal for the development of a regular gridded city district. The development of a modern residential quarter contrasted with papal neglect. As Prati bordered the north, so projects along the Giancolo and in Trastevere flanked the south of the Pope's territory. The process of barricading in the Vatican from the city was completed with the construction of Calderini's palazzo di Giustizia to house Italy's supreme courts (Vallauri 2002).

The new city was not conceived as having a single focal point but was composed of relatively discrete quarters linked by avenues pushed through the city. The emphasis was on movement (circulation) rather than places of assembly and in this change, there was a subtle shift in the social form of the city. Bazin's disparaging of the evening *passeggiata* as antiquated related to the old Romans' frequenting of places of assembly rather than hurrying back to bourgeois domesticity in the new quarters of the city. In the new city, it was roads rather than piazzas which were key. Via Nazionale was a showpiece for the new Rome and a focus of architectural debate. Maurel (1909: 217) sympathized with new Romans who were criticized for their modernization of the city. For many outsiders, Rome should forever be a museum. Maurel thought the houses of via Nazionale and the new quarters were functional rather than ugly. Giuseppe Bottai (1992 [1938]), with the characteristic grandiloquence and bluster of the fascist era, regarded the via Nazionale as the only significant achievement in the first decade of national rule. In the old city, plans were ambitious, but interventions were small; there was no Haussmanization of old Rome. Rome was rebuilt as two cities, the historic centre and the dispersed quarters, with quite different urban morphologies (Zola 1896: 137–8).

The most significant building of the early period was Sella's Ministry of Finance designed and constructed by Canevari and Martinori in 1872-6 (Polla 1979). The transposition of the capital from Florence required numerous state buildings to be acquired at speed and the state expropriated various religious buildings for administrative use (Cassetto 2005: 50; Sanfilippo 1992: 90–1). The purpose-built Ministry of Finance was an exception.

The ministry was constructed on the via Venti Settembre and the via Cernaia. It was a rich archaeological site. The clearing of the site uncovered an archaic wall, a head of the emperor Titus and structures associated with the Baths of Diocletian (Polla 1979: 37). The building was spacious and imposing at 36,000 m^2 and stretching 200m along the road (Zocca 1971). It was built around a large inner court, which came to provide car parking, and was constructed on three levels with a ground-floor arcade. The design was that of a palazzo. The façade presented a row of Classicizing columns along the second storey but there was no open colonnade or imposing Classical form. There were Classical allusions in the décor, particularly in la sala della Maggioranza and the sala dei Graffiti. In the former there were painted caryatids and busts of the great Classical lawgivers, the Greeks Solon and Lycurgus, and the Romans, Numa and Justinian. Alongside the Classical heroes, there were representations of Dante and Michelangelo, Mazzini, Vico, Petrarch, Cola di Rienzo, Gioberti, Alfieri and da Brescia. It was a décor that reflected Italian culture as much as Roman (Polla 1979: 83–9).

Sella (1887: 313–24) was modest about his contribution to the design. In a speech to the Chamber of Deputies on 15 March 1881, he claimed to have taken an interest in the internal provision of the rooms, but not to have concerned himself with the façades. He was a man of numbers and science, not of art. Contemporaries saw the building as announcing a new age of bureaucratic and financial efficiency (Angeli 1932). Bazin (1894: 140), by contrast, remarked on its size but saw it as otherwise unremarkable. Zola's (1896: 135–6) character Pierre was struck by its heaviness, seeing it as a cyclopean cube in which decorative elements piled up in excess. That impression is partly a function of its location. The grand entrance on via Cernaia faces onto the relatively narrow via Volturno. There is no piazza for the building to dominate or extended vista to complete. The building seems self-contained, making no concession to its environment or the archaeological remains of the Baths of Diocletian across the street. As a symbol of *la terza Roma*, it pays little attention to Classical Rome (Kirk 2011).

The new ministry set a trend for a concentration of administrative buildings along via Venti Settembre. The ministries of war and agriculture were to follow with further ministries appearing in the early twentieth century along the same route but outside the city walls (Sanfilippo 1992: 80–1). Sella was developing the region as Città Alta (High

Figure 3.4 The Ministry of Finance.

City), central to which was the development of academic institutions. He fused the historic Accademia dei Lincei with the Società italiana delle Scienze to form La Reale Accademia dei Lincei in Rome on 14 February 1875. The foundation faced considerable and lasting resistance which focused on the over-concentration of resources on Rome and the stripping of scientific institutions from the rest of the kingdom. Sella (1879) saw the new Accademia as a counter to the intellectual influence of the Vatican. Science was to generate an 'agitation' in Rome and drive the civilizational mission of *la terza Roma*.

The Italian victory of 20 September inspired some monumental representations. The first year saw monuments to Ciceruacchio, who had proposed a constitution for Rome in the failed revolution of 1848–9, the Cairoli brothers, who had led the revolt in 1867, and monuments to the fallen of the *risorgimento*. There was a monument to Giuditta Tavani Arquati who was killed together with her family resisting Papal troops at the Ajani Wool Mill in Trastevere in 1867. A series of thirty busts to prominent Italians was placed on the terrace of Pincio. Most of these monuments were small scale and inexpensive, though there was a proposal for a larger monument to Unità (Berggren and Sjöstedt 1996: 11–16).

Monumentalization slowed after 1871 but continued to display anti-clericism, with a plaque for Galilei on the palazzo Medici, a monument to the librettist Pietro Metastasio and a plaque at the breach in the Aurelian walls in honour of the forty-eight soldiers who were killed. Further plaques honoured those killed resisting the French intervention in 1849 and in the suppression of the revolt of 1867. Perhaps the most controversial and famous monument was il monumento Bruno, established in honour of Giordano Bruno, who, like Galileo Galilei, was seen as a martyr for science in the face of enforced Papal ignorance. The monument was proposed in 1876, but Ettore Ferrari's statue was only erected on the site of Bruno's execution in the Campo de' Fiori in 1889 (Berggren and Sjöstedt 1996: 16–35).

In 1881, Sella (1887: 273–311) celebrated the success of the first decade of Rome as capital. Much of what had been planned for a generation had been achieved in a single decade. This success focused attention on the next two decades. The framework for the new civic plan centred on an agreement between the state and the Commune which became law on 14 May 1881. A subsequent law of 20 May 1881 granted the council 50 million lire from state funds and gave permission for the issuing of city bonds worth 150 million lire to fund further development (di Martino 2012). On 20 July, the Director of the Technical Office was ordered to produce a new *piano regolatore* and a commission was appointed on 12 December 1881. The Commission reported on 27 April 1882 (*Piano Regolatore* 1882). The plan was accepted in November 1883.

The new *piano regolatore* was in continuity with the previous decade. In the opening pages of the report (*Piano Regolatore* 1882: 1–5), the commissioners drew an unfavourable comparison between the Rome of 1870 and its forebears. They claimed that the liberation of 1870 established the necessary political conditions for a material improvement of the city sufficient to enable it to realize its new historical destiny. The plan focused on the further development of the new quarters at Castro Pretorio, Esquilino, the Caelio and Oppio, the Viminale and Quirinale (23–38). There was a renewed attempt to expand on the slopes of the Gianicolo and in Trastevere (38–40). The plan paid more attention to

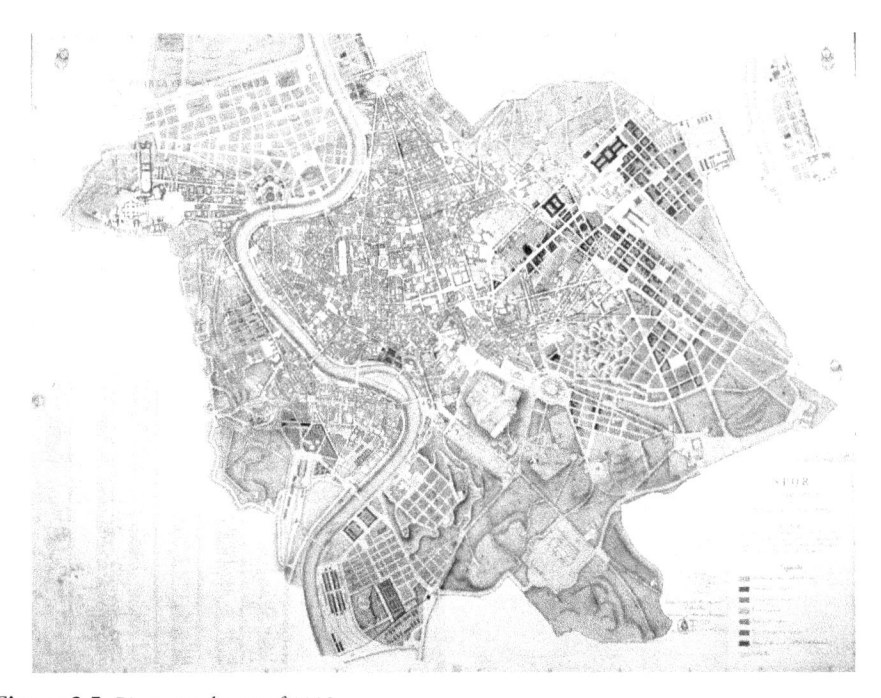

Figure 3.5 *Piano regalotore* of 1883.

railways and bridges. A bridge into the Gianicolo and a new station for Trastevere was seen as essential for the development and integration of those quarters. Testaccio was planned as a working-class service area for railway workers and for new city markets. Good riverine and rail communications allowed the in-flow of goods such as to keep industrial activity at a convenient distance from the city (40–4). Prati di Castello was to be extended and an entirely new quarter of Borgo Flaminio was to be built (44–54). These districts would be connected by another new bridge from Flaminio into the north of Prati. The plan aimed to take the total developed area of Rome to 850 hectares of which about 350 hectares were in the new quarters. The planned population was 425,000 (123–9).

The 1883 plan looked to further improve roads running north-south and develop through routes running east-west. These would allow easy communication through all parts of the city, in theory at least. The plan would have laid something close to a grid of roads on the old city. The piazza del Popolo was an existing central node for the north of the city. Improvements were proposed to all three of the main routes south, the Corso, via del Babuino and via di Ripetta. The Corso was to be extended to a large piazza on the side of the Forum, before branching to the south and east of the city. Piazza Santa Maria Maggiore was to become the hub for the south-east of the city. Via di Ripetta was to be improved to join with an extended via Nazionale near piazza Datti and the Largo Argentino (*Piano Regolatore* 1882: 64–9, 73–8). The east-west routes involved this extension of via Nazionale to Ponte Sant'Angelo (59–64). A further cross route was planned from Fontana di Trevi through an enlarged piazza del Rotonda to the piazza Navona (78–84). A third east-west route ran around the Teatro di Marcello cutting through various piazzas and streets to Bocca di Verità and then onwards to Testaccio. The plans required extensive demolition and remodelling of the city, particularly through the Ghetto. Six new bridges were envisaged and there were plans for various improvements across the Tiber, most notably the demolition of the Borghi. Yet, the planners faced the same problems in treating the intricacies of Rome's cultural heritage. The Roman and imperial fora and the Colosseum were in a line that was difficult to negotiate. Similarly, the Teatro di Marcello obstructed any putative route from piazza Venezia to Bocca di Verità. As a result, the new roads were only partially delivered.

Rome of the last decades of the nineteenth century was seen as a dichotomous city. Zola's (1896) character Pierre drew a distinction between the maze of the old city and the chaos of Trastevere and the order of the new city. Pierre was a quintessentially modern character who struggled with his faith: his journey to Rome was in part an attempt to encourage the modernization of the Church. The palazzo del Quirinale represented the new bourgeois city for Pierre–Zola. Pierre was caught between the old and the new, finding in the urban cityscape the concrete representation of his psychological troubles. The locals he met were convinced that Pierre's Catholicism misled him. The Rome he saw was a spectral presence summoned by his religious and historical sensibilities: Rome was no longer the city of the Popes but of Italy and King Umberto (Zola 1896: 137–8).

By the end of the century, trams clattered along the old streets, bands played in the gardens of Lucullus, and statues of Italian heroes were placed on the hills and parks across which the Romans took their strolls. The new quarters had the look of the major

European nineteenth-century cities. Prati di Castello had wide avenues and architectural forms familiar from Paris and elsewhere. Via Nazionale was consistently lauded as the space of the new Rome. It provided no equivalent to the piazza Colonna as a location for assembly. The focus was on movement rather than communal interaction. Maurel (1909: 5–8) claimed that one could not walk 100 metres without encountering some fragment of the ancient city. However, even among the buildings of the old city, the new economy was reshaping the urban fabric. The prospect of commercial rents was persuading the owners of the *palazzi* to rent out ground floors for shops while they retreated to the upper floors.

The ancient city played very little part in the design of *la terza Roma*. The focus was on modernization: the sewers and the street lighting, and the major arteries of communication along which the bourgeois residents of the city would travel. The new Rome aspired to be modern and scientific. The Classical city remained very much a cultural inspiration for the new Italian elite and fundamental to the nationalistic and civilizational agenda of the Italian state, but that city was fundamentally in the past.

The new city was established as an administrative and political centre. The major new districts were residential centres for the bourgeoisie. Although the *piano regolatore* of 1883 envisaged working-class areas at Trastevere and Testaccio, there was no plan for a significant industrial district. The increasingly vocal proletariats of Europe rendered the dominant liberal bourgeoisie nervous of any potential working-class incursion into their new capital. The new Rome was meant to be emphatically bourgeois (Sanfilippo 1992: 52–3). As Camillo Boito (1880: viii–ix) noted, the architectural form at the heart of the modern age was the house.

The rapid development of Rome took place in the context of the economic expansion of Italy and an extended period in which Italian tax revenues exceeded expenditures. The benefits of that expansion were felt by a substantial sector of the population: savings in banks multiplied almost four-fold in twenty-five years (Houghton 1898). Alongside vast state investments, private money flowed into Rome. The publication of the first *piano regolatore* of 1873 sparked intense speculative investment. The 1883 government's commitment of a further 200 million lire to the city sparked a triggered boom. Land prices increased by 200–300 per cent. In key areas such as Prati and the area of the via Nazionale, prices rose from 2.5 lire per square metre in 1870 to over 300 lire. The aristocratic houses of Rome were vastly enriched which, one imagines, sweetened any regrets over the fall of Papal Rome (Sanfilippo 1992: 52). The boom was a credit bubble that turned to spectacular bust in November 1889, threatening the viability of the banks and the building industry and bankrupting the city council (di Martino 2012). Yet, this merely paused the expansion of the city.

Styling Rome

The frenzy of building in Rome after 1870 provided young architects with considerable opportunities. Gaetano Koch, who was been described as '*il Padrone di Roma*', qualified in 1872 and immediately went into practice. Koch and has a good claim to be regarded as the most influential of architects in the period 1870–1910 (Meeks 1966: 320). Like many of his contemporaries, Koch worked in a conservative Roman style.

Writing about architectural style in nineteenth-century Rome raises issues of categorization. For London and Athens, the new architectures were in deliberate contrast with what had gone before. The building of the public sphere was a new and radical enterprise that was marked by a new Classical architecture. Post-1870 Rome was different. Italian architectural styles drew adaptively on the past and deployed Classical elements. Yet, architectural critics have a surprisingly firm date for the 'end' of neoclassicism in Rome, 1838 (Spagnesi 1978: 12–13). Neoclassicism gave way to *cinquecentismo*. *Cinquecentismo* adapted the style of Renaissance *palazzi* which had themselves drawn on Classical architectural elements, particularly in décor. Meeks (1966: 287) identified *cinquecentismo* as the style of new Italian nation (1865–1900), acknowledging the difficulties of definition, both stylistic and chronological. In nineteenth-century Florence, the style is associated with the architect Giuseppe Poggi. In Rome, *cinquecentismo* had been the predominant style of late Papal Rome and this preference was largely maintained into the post-1870 period.

Such continuity depended in part of the strength of the Roman architectural school at the Accademia di San Luca (Spagnesi 2015). Gaetano Koch and Pio Piacentini, on whom more below, were trained there. Rome's contemporary architecture was less eclectic than those of other cities. With the notable exception of All Saints Anglican Church (by an English architect), there is very little Gothic revival or Romanesque. The great retail arcade which was imported from Paris to Milan, Genoa and Naples was only replicated in Rome on a small scale at the Esedra. Museums and galleries, such as the palazzo delle Esposizioni Nazionale di Belle Arti and Museo Barracco, attracted neoclassical designs. Yet the new spaces of bourgeois sociability did not require an assertion of Classical citizenship values and the opposition between New Rome and Papal Rome was nuanced by Rome's architects. There were two major exceptions to this restraint: the palazzo di Giustizia and the monument to Vittorio Emanuele II. These were statement buildings designed to proclaim the new liberal political order, and they asserted theatrically the identification of nation and capital.

Gaetano Koch is best known for his palazzo della Banca d'Italia (palazzo Koch) and the piazza Esedria. He also produced a significant number of residential *palazzi* and large houses (*villini*) and made contributions to the urban design of the city. His first major project was the piazza Vittorio Emanuele II (*c.* 1880). The piazza was the largest in the city, larger than piazza di San Pietro. It appeared in the city plan as early as 1871–2 as a southern parallel to piazza del Popolo and as an entry point to the new Rome. The site was occupied by the seventeenth-century villa Palombara, which was cleared in the construction of the piazza apart from the Porta Magica, a seventeenth-century door with Egyptian 'magical' signs. The other remnant in the piazza is a third-century CE nympheum known as the Trofei di Mario, which now provides a boundary to the piazza.

By contrasting the piazza with piazza del Popolo, we can see Koch's urban imagination at work. Valadier's piazza, dominated by its central obelisk, provided a monumental and

Figure 3.6 Piazza Vittorio.

Classicizing entrance to the city. The piazza Vittorio was designed in the style of an English garden square. The residents would be able to stroll through and socialize in its communal garden. The ruins lent it a picturesque quality unusual for new Rome. The major edifices were the *palazzi* located round the edge of the piazza, the design of these was regulated by a detailed convention and their most notable features are the semi-enclosed porticos that provided spaces for small shops and offices (Manfredi 2015: 108–16).

Such *palazzi porticati* were popular in Regal Italy. The most obvious precursor is the palazzo Wedekind in the piazza Colona dating to 1838. There were prominent examples in the piazza del Duomo in Milan (1861) and piazza del Statuto in Turin (1864). They were an elegant solution to a trend in the use of *palazzi* which saw the residential and household service spaces concentrate on the higher storeys and for ground floors to be rented out for commercial purposes. The porticos blurred the boundary between public and private while the residential parts of the building became more private. Carmen Manfredi (2015) sees the design in Vittorio as blending a Piedmontese portico with Roman monumentality.

Yet, what seems most notable about Vittorio is an absence. The largest piazza in Rome had no central monument. For a piazza dedicated to the liberator-king, that absence is striking, particularly in the light of the honours that followed his death. If we read the square as a monument to the *risorgimento* and a symbol of new Rome, it would seem to represent bourgeois respectability, the integration of commerce and the cityscape, and look to English social practices.

Koch's other major urbanistic contribution was the piazza Esedra, later renamed piazza della Reppublica. The piazza is at a point of transition between Termini, the archaeological remains of the Baths of Diocletian, and the new city of vie Nazionale and Cernaia. The striking architectural element is the curved Galleria Esedra which encloses the northern end of the piazza and complements the central circular fountain. The internal *galleria* echoes on a reduced scale the great nineteenth-century *gallerie*. It is significantly monumental, especially when compared with Vittorio. There was no formal entrance to the city for those arriving by train. It was not seen as a priority in 1870 (or earlier), and it was only until 1885 that the Commune expropriated the buildings north of the piazza to provide a monumental entrance.

Koch's design was relatively moderate. The two curved hemicycles were composed of five storeys divided into three layers, the lowest two of which were bound together by combinations of pilasters and columns. The *palazzo porticato* provided a marble façade in contrast with the cream plaster of the higher levels, as if a more antique structure has been built over by a modern. Each layer is divided by entablatures. The shorter upmost unit deploys caryatids. All is topped off by curved pediments, balustrades and statue groups. Hitchcock judged the complex 'academic urbanism' that brings together 'the ancient and the modern worlds in the architecture of Rome' (Hitchcock 1958: 145). The conjunction of ancient and modern is stylistic and topographical.

The palazzo Koch which houses the Banca d'Italia (1886–92) offers a yet more restrained Classicism. The building occupies an entire block on the via Nazionale. There are three visible storeys (two are below ground). The ground floor is composed of repeating arches. Larger arches were used for the twin triportal entrances and smaller for windows. The first and second floors are composed of matching sequences of columns with corner pilasters framing large windows and balustrades across narrow balconies. The façade is completed with a restrained entablature. The symmetry, balance and disciplined design speaks of solidity, restraint and grandeur, as might be hoped for from a national bank. The interior is structured around two courts and displays a similarly restrained grandeur, especially in the broad staircases. Its extensive art collection boasts a copy of the Capitoline wolf and a Hadrianic Antinoos statue. Classicism is central to its

Figure 3.7 Koch's Galleria Esedra.

aesthetic but the inspiration appears to be the *palazzi* Farnese and Strozzi (Manfredi 2015: 135–52).

The contemporary architectural writer Misuraca (1899) judged that Koch had united a Classical aesthetic and modern utility. He reports the use of different Classical orders, the balance and restraint of the architecture, and its monumental scale. The height of the rooms at nearly five metres impressed the visitor. The sculptures included personifications of Economy, Finance and Legislation, Industry and Commerce present the drivers of modern capitalism in Classical style. For Misuraca, the building was an addition to Rome's monumental heritage. It was a building that encapsulated the modern values of the nation, expressed the potential of the Banca d'Italia to deliver the future, and reflected the fortunes, grandeur and prosperity of the nation.

The slightly earlier palazzo dell'esposizioni nazionale di belle arti on via Nazionale was designed by Pio Piacentini in a more ornately Classical style. It was a prestige building that the king himself opened on 21 January 1883. A dominating entrance composed of a deep-set arch supported by four blocks of four columns. The arch itself might recall a triumphal arch and is certainly the main ornamental element to the building. Much of the rest of the façade is composed of blank Classical-style panels, recalling Pompeian wall-panelling, punctuated by pilasters and a top frieze. The absence of any windows produces a closed effect that further focuses the eye on the ceremonial entrance.

There was considerable scope for varying degrees of Classicism in the flexibility of *cinquecentismo*. The major public architecture and the numerous private *palazzi* and *villini*

Figure 3.8 Palazzo Koch.

Figure 3.9 Palazzo dell'esposizioni nazionale di belle arti.

provided Rome with its urban imaginary. The accommodation of late nineteenth-century bourgeois culture and economy into the cityscape was compatible with traditional Roman design. The *palazzi* housed the rich new Romans as they had housed the rich old Romans. Such adaptations were a form of appropriation that allowed new Rome to establish an aesthetic hegemony. Although the class structures of the city were significantly changed by the development of Rome as capital, the predominant architectural forms could be adapted to that new social structure. Some of the public buildings leant more heavily towards the Classical. *La prima Roma* was present in *la nuova Roma* as a central element in Italy's cultural heritage. Yet, the new city was shaped by the modernity inherent in Mazzini's vision of *la terza Roma* rather than by any Romantic nationalistic essentialism which would lead Romans forward to a restored Classical age. The architecture mostly eschewed bombast and sought to assimilate with established local aesthetic norms.

One exception to this narrative is the palazzo di Giustizia housing the Corte di Cassazione, the Supreme Court of Italy. This was a monumental architectural imposition which aggressively symbolized a continued and fundamental opposition between the national state and papal secular power. Located next to Castel Sant'Angelo, the building is a colossal bastion of liberal values and national institutional power. It was topographically aligned with Prati and connected to the city along the vista generated by the ponte Umberto I. It further isolated the Vatican City by being oriented towards Prati and away from città Leonina.

The need for a palazzo for the Supreme Court was championed by Giuseppe Zanardelli from 1879. Zanardelli was an anti-clerical politician of the Italian left and a veteran of the *risorgimento*. He reformed Italian penal law through what became known as the Zanardelli code of 1889. This code eliminated the death penalty, provided some rights for workers, and encouraged the reform of convicts. The Corte di Cassazione were a central, unificatory and modernizing institution (Vallauri 2002). The law securing finance for the building was passed in 1881 and the site identified. Competitions were held in 1884 and 1886 and were won by Guglielmo Calderini (Marconi 2002).

Calderini produced a statement building that has been compared with the late neoclassicist work of Hansen and Semper in Vienna. The most immediate and obvious debt is to the Palais de Justice in Brussels, which is similarly dominant, elaborate and ornate (Pisani 2009; Marconi 2002). These associations made Calderini's design seem contemporary and international. He saw architecture as being determined by its era, a position which made more complex any historical allusions in the style (Sgueglia 2009). Calderini's (1991b) own comments on the palazzo from 20 September 1881 are imprecise and nationalistic. The building must be suited to the capital of Italy, the daughter of the ancient dominator of the world. It must be grandiose and severe. It must have its own style, the style of Rome not that of Paris, but of the successor city to that of the Caesars. This perceived need for a national style with modernity is a consistent feature of his thinking. In September 1875, Calderini (1991a) had written that the future of architecture was in unification with science. He attacked *cinquecentismo*, arguing that contemporary architecture needed to be different from that of Michelangelo and the 1500s. And yet, he wanted to avoid any non-Italian influence.

Contemporary evaluations claimed that Calderini succeeded in bridging modern European grandeur and a purely Italian style. Calderini's fellow architect, Milani (Calderini 1918: dedication), proclaimed that Calderini had revived with a new spirit the glorious tradition of Italian architecture. His crowning achievement was the palazzo di Giustizia. The palazzo was to be compared with the masterpieces of Michelangelo and Bernini and considered with an aesthetic calmness that is normally reserved for the monuments of remote epochs. Milani situates the architecture within a particular political moment, noting that liberty required new monuments and that Calderini had worked with forms which were purely national. In style, the building is described as showing a severe beauty in keeping with the models of the 1500s.

Such an assessment has not dated well and reminds us of the fundamental difficulties in writing about aesthetics. Milani's referencing of the sublime and associated notions of timelessness contrasts with the relentless activity of the architecture. Hitchcock dismissed the palazzo:

> The enormous Palazzo di Giustizia ... is an incredibly brash example of the Neo-Baroque loaded down with heavy rustication, doubtless of Piranesian inspiration. This curious (and happily unique) structure was designed ... in 1883–7.
>
> *Hitchcock 1958: 146*

The various stylistic associations – neo-Baroque, neo-Renaissance, neoclassicism – suggest a deliberate eclecticism that rendered the building heterogenous and dissonant

(Spagnesi 2015). The building exhibits theatricality and a concern with façade. Arturo Calza (1911: 30) saw it as a modern triumphal arch, perhaps focusing on the enlarged gateway in the design and an understanding of the palazzo as a celebration of 1870.

The building is composed of a long two-storey façade and a three-storey central block It has a central gateway entrance and recessed flanking sections which culminate in corner towers. The whole is given balance and unity by a repeating pattern of windows, columns, entry-ports, running balustrades, pediments and entablature. The gateway is visually dominant. Neoclassical elements are embedded within the palazzo style. The ornamentation is lavish and repeating from the small details of the windows to the second-storey neoclassical personification of Giustizia at the gate. Rustication adds further complexity to the façade. The general impression is that every surface has been used for décor, much of which is neoclassical.

The interior is luxurious. The design features long internal vistas and porticos, high ceilings, wide staircases, rich inlays and lavish use of marbles (Marconi n.d.). There are multiple statues that made present the founders of Classical law (Cicero, Licinius Crassus, Salvius Julianus, Modestinus, Gaius, Papinian) and Italian jurists and philosophers (Battista de Luca, Vico, Bartolo da Sassoferrato and Romagnosi) (Sagredo 2007: 41–60). Frescoes depict the granting of the Twelve Tables (Rome's first public law), the decree of the Senate against the worship of Bacchus (an instance of bourgeois respectability deploying law to maintain moral standards), the Emperor Hadrian appointing Julianus (establishing the legal profession), and Tribonian's presentation of the *Digest* to Justinian (Rome's major legal codification) (Kirk 2009).

The complex was completed by piazza Cavour which faced the new quarter of Prati, further associating the complex with Italian nationalism and the new city. The palazzo was by far the most theatrical of the new state buildings. It was stylistically ambitious in attempting to develop a modern Italian nationalist aesthetic. In so doing, it made frequent

Figure 3.10 Palazzo di Giustizia (from Calderini 1918).

and explicit reference to Classical culture and depicted the legal frameworks of the modern Italian state, and hence the citizenship values of that state, as directly descended from Roman models. It was a triumphal monument to secularism adjacent to the remnants of the Papal state.

A national monument: Il Vittoriano

The palazzo di Giustizia was to be dwarfed by the monument to Vittorio Emanuele II. The idea of a national monument had been under discussion when Vittorio Emanuele II died on 9 January 1878. There was an immediate question of where he should be laid to rest and how he was to be memorialized. Turin had a claim on him as his home, but Rome was the home of the nation. The king was interred in the Pantheon with a frieze proclaiming him *il Padre della Patria* (the Father of the Nation). Around 200,000 people turned out for the funeral. The Pantheon was ideal as a Classical temple which was also a Christian church. *Il Padre della Patria* translated Augustus' *Pater Patriae* and conjoined the hierarchies of nation and family (Tobia 1998: 19–22). The Augustan echo established a transhistorical link between the multiple fathers of the single nation.

The possibility of using the death to generate a new national monument was immediately attractive. The death of the king had allowed the Italian state to deploy mourning rituals as rituals of the nation. It was a sacralization of political identity that was largely new to Italy and a permanent monument to the king would not only memorialize the king but provide a quasi-religious focus for the nation. On 10 January the Commune of Rome opened a public subscription for a monument to their late king. On 4 April, Zanardelli proposed a law to fund a monument for the Liberator of the Fatherland and the 'Founder of our Unity'. The proposal became law on 16 May (Tobia 1998: 19–24; Brice 1998: 45–6).

A competition for the design was launched prematurely. The site had not been identified and the nature of the monument was left completely open. The result was chaotic. There were 293 submissions (as detailed in Brice 1998: 66–159). These ranged from isolated columns, triumphal arches, temples and pantheons, statues, to large architectural complexes. Most of the projects did not propose a location. Of the ninety-six that did make such a suggestion, the majority opted for key sites in new Rome, many close to Termini. Most avoided the archaeological areas, presumably out of respect for the ancient city.

Many of the proposals were extraordinary. Ximenes and Gallori (Project no. 209) proposed an artificial hill, surrounded by a grand sculptural frieze on the top of which was an imposing equestrian statue of the late king. Its absurd genius was to add a monumental staircase giving the impression of a helter-skelter. Columns were particularly popular solutions, normally topped with a statue. Variations gave an architectural structure to the column base which further elevated the statue, such as Mole Vittoria (project 156) or Laboremus (project 232). Other projects focused on a statue, though with elaborate settings. These had the virtue of not requiring a particular site to be identified (e.g. project 120; project 265 Italia e Vittorio Emanuele). Ceremonial gateways and arches offered the chance to combine Classical architectural elements and large statues of the king. The most ambitious were grand architectural complexes. A Pantheon-temple (project 187) comprised a three-layered dome topped with a winged Victory was one of the more restrained. Large squares with colonnades, gateways, central temple structures and columns were popular. Many of these drew on buildings familiar from Paris (les Invalides) or from Berlin (Brandenburg Gate). Almost all adopted Classical styles.

The competition was won by Paul Nénot with a large piazza centred on a column and triumphal arch (project 249). Nénot had worked on the Paris Opéra and was to build La Nouvelle Sorbonne both of which can be seen as typical fin-de-siècle urban projects. Nénot's winning design was more neoclassical and one of the more restrained proposals. Nevertheless, the project caused controversy and was eventually rejected (Acciaresi 1920). One contributory reason was that Nénot had recycled his design from a submission to a Parisian competition. That first submission had been called Ateneo (Brice 1998: 16–36). The success of a French architect in designing a national monument for Italy was also an embarrassment.

The prime minister, Agostino Depretis, rejected Nénot's scheme and launched a new competition which ran from 18 December 1882 to 15 December 1883. The area of the Capitoline was identified as the likely location. The competition was international and ninety-eight proposals were submitted (Brice 1998: 218–29). The Capitoline location effectively closed the monument so that gateways or ceremonial entrance structures (as at the Brandenburg Gate) were no longer attractive solutions. Many proposals made use of the hillside to gain elevation for the monument, which encouraged more theatrical architecture and contributed to the eventual building becoming a topographically dominant monument.

Many of the designs worked within a very similar framework. Grand staircases led to monuments structured in two or three layers. Platforms gave space for statues. An equestrian statue of Vittorio Emanuele featured frequently. There were some variations. Daniel Brade (project no. 41) and Manfredo Manfredi (project no. 83) proposed palazzo-type structures in a neo-Renaissance style. Most of the plans were neoclassical, though brazenly eclectic. Antonio Curri's proposal (project no. 76) deployed a central rotunda on an intermediate storey while on a third level a central triumphal arch was flanked by two colonnades. The whole was topped off by a massive quadrigal chariot. Bruno Schmitz (project no. 69) suggested a Roman-style temple embedded within flanking colonnades so large that they seem to dominate the central structure. Carlo Ferrario and Vincenzo Vela (project no. 57) also went for a temple structure, this time with smaller flanking structures. They further ornamented the structure with a column rising centrally from the temple on top of which was another personification. Many of the proposals seem fantastical to the point of being fevered to modern tastes.

The winning design came Giuseppe Sacconi and Eugenio Maccagnani (project no. 65). It seems more restrained than many of its competitors. A central staircase leads to a small shrine-like structure in the centre of the building. The access turns ninety degrees to flanking staircases that eventually lead up to the third level of the building. Above the shrine, there is a large equestrian statue of Vittorio Emanuele II. The statue is the central element and enormous, but when set in the vastness of the whole, it is not a dominating element. The upper layer is composed of a long central portico and flanking narrow entrance-temple structures. These reach round the statue and add to its focal quality. The twists of the staircase provide opportunities for multiple statues. The central line of columns provides a curtain backdrop that enhances the theatricality of the whole. There were considerable modifications, especially around the monumental staircase and the first level which was given a large ornamental frieze rather than the blank panels initially envisaged. Nevertheless, the building as constructed is recognizably similar to that proposed by Sacconi and Maccagnani.

Il Vittoriano was not designed to blend in. The building is a monumental shock. The architectural style is without evident local parallel. Sacconi had planned for the monument to be built from the creamy local travertine, but it was constructed in the bright white Botticino limestone. It is incongruous in its enormity. Kirk (2008) saw it as monstrous or sublime, simultaneously alienating and imposing.

Contemporary reactions were mixed. Some saw it as anti-Roman, Nordic, a symphony, a dream architecture (Racheli 1986). There is a sense of the monument as Wagnerian, out of keeping with the values of Rome and Italy. Pietro Ferrigini stressed the didactic purpose of the monument, recalling the king-soldier-liberator and providing for the uneducated an essential page of Italian history (Soprintendenza per i beni ambientali e architettonici del Lazio 1986: II 56). For Primo Levi the monument was a representation of new Rome's struggle against barbarism (Soprintendenza per i beni ambientali e architettonici del Lazio 1986: II 26–61). Angelo Conti in the influential *Nuova Antologia* 194 (March–April 1904, 386–402), saw the monument as a fitting building for the new city. Its location on the Capitoline, the scene of ancient triumphs, made it a statement of renewed national triumph. Its visibility gave it dominance over the *palazzi* and the

Figure 3.11 Sacconi and Maccagnani's design for il Vittoriano.

ancient ruins and over all the hills of Rome. It was an expression of the Italian Classical genius, a new work born from the ancient which conveyed without conscious thought the cultural achievements made possible by liberty and Italian style, atmosphere and national genius (Soprintendenza per i beni ambientali e architettonici del Lazio 1986: II 61-4). Others complained about the administrative chaos that had surrounded the project, its enormous expense, the destruction of the buildings to make space, and the length of time taken in its design and construction.[4] Nevertheless, Ojetti (1907) claimed that the balance of opinion was favourable.

Sacconi was hoping to develop a national style that projected the nobility of tradition (Druda and Signore 1986). It was not obvious that the national style would be some form of neoclassicism. Camillo Boito (1880: viii–xxvi), who was the most influential academic architectural critic of the period, favoured neo-medievalism. He found Classicism anachronistic, rhetorical and sentimental. The Italian style had to be organic and moral, by which I understand him as suggesting a style that emerged from particularly Italian cultural roots. He opposed the 'egoism' of large modern buildings, the train stations, the palazzo delle Finanze, and the palazzo di Banca d'Italia. His suggestion of the intimate relationship between architectural style and social values made him suspicious of grand interventions. Instead, he proposed that the new state opt for the architecture of the late medieval period, which was culturally and environmentally suited to the Italian nation.

Boito's preferences had no influence on the designs for il Vittoriano. Its Classicism was reinforced by the location of the monument next to the Capitoline and the Roman Forum, the symbolic centres of Classical Rome. The height of the structure favoured an association with the Acropolis and the style referenced the Erechtheion. Il Vittoriano was to be a fixed locus around which the vistas of the city were to be organized and a dominant visual symbol of the city and its culture. Critics identified Venetian, Neapolitan and Sicilian styles (Tobia 1998: 16). Some of the representative art was close to art nouveau (Dell'Ariccia 2002). Fierce argument about the statuary reflected a clash of styles between Classicism and contemporary realism (Ojetti 1907: 8; Cardano 1986). From the first, the monument was wrapped in contention and inevitably so since it represented Italy

Building il Vittoriano required major demolitions. The first stone was laid in 1885 and that year saw vast appropriations and demolitions (Calza 1911: 140–51). The palazzo di Torlonia, which had been marked for destruction since 1871 disappeared (Giordano 1871: 211). The convent of Aracoeli, a tower built under Paul III and an associated viaduct, and a host of workshops and small houses were demolished together with the vie Giulio Romano, Pedacchia, Marcel de'Corvi, Marforio and San Marco (Sanfilippo 1992: 46-7). Sacconi cleared the area to the bed rock and there encountered geological faults that considerably added to the cost of the building (Acciaresi 1920: 17–20). There was an inevitable reaction to the destruction of architectural and archaeological heritage but honouring the new Romulus was more important (Racheli 1986).

From the initial proposition on the death of Vittorio Emanuele II to its completion, the ambitions behind the structure had expanded. The first proposal envisaged a budget of 9 million lire, but by 1884 the expropriations alone were expected to cost king; it became a monument to the nation and an exercise in patriotic pedagogy (Tobia 1991: v). The remit was extended to honour the heroes of the *risorgimento* (Piantoni 1991). Its significance was enhanced by the inclusion of L'Altare della Patria in 1911. This allowed ritualized and repetitive national ceremonial to be staged at the monument. Il Vittoriano was the theatrical backdrop to the quasi-religious performance of national identity (Kirk 2011). The influential *sindaco* of Rome (1907–13), Ernesto Nathan, suggested that the statue of Vittorio Emanuele was both of a conquering liberator and the Defender of the National Faith (Tobia 1998: 15).

Sacconi's original plan had been to create a hall of honour in which the statues of Italian cultural and political heroes would be displayed, perhaps on the model of the statues of illustrious Romans that had adorned the niches of the nearby Forum Augusti. The eventual sculptural scheme emphasized the allegorical. There were personifications of cities, statues of political values (Force, Concord, Sacrifice, Law), national slogans (Liberty, Unity) and arts (Sculpture, Fine Art, Architecture and Music) (Acciaresi 1920).

The monument represented Rome as the symbolic centre of Italy. At the inauguration of l'Altare della Patria, 5,000 mayors of Italian cities were invited to Rome to dine. Even if 'the Romans of Rome' survived in the city, with their local cuisine of gnocchi and tripe, *i buzzurri, gli italiani* or *i piemontesi*, or whatever nomenclature was applied to the incomers, dominated the city. Rome by 1900 was an expression of the state (Dau Novelli 2011: 42–3, 61).

Unlike most other urban buildings, il Vittoriano is pure political scenography. Its only function was as a stage for the rituals of the nation. As Meeks puts it:

> There can be very little question that this monument achieved its purpose . . . It is breathtaking in its rich intricacy and variety of form, thus testifying in an inescapable manner to the least artistic passerby the vast wealth lavished cheerfully on such a supremely non-utilitarian building. It is a triumphant statement of faith in a material future. A memorable image has been created.
>
> Meeks 1966: 346

The reception of the building is inextricably connected to views on the fin-de-siècle Italian ultra-nationalism it depicts and, more broadly, on the Italian state. The massive demolitions damaged Rome's cityscape and displaced many working-class Romans. Its dominance of the cityscape renders it inescapably a symbol of the oppressive bourgeois nationalism that brought it into being. Mocked in its grandiosity and pomposity, tarnished by fascist nationalism, it is an easy target for subversion, not least by the Romans themselves in their regular, perhaps structural, estrangement from national and civic government (Atkinson and Cosgrove 1998).

Classicism is key to the symbolic significance of the building. Its location drew the building into conversation with Rome's Classical heritage. The references to the Acropolis suggest a bid for sublime and transcendental architecture, supposedly achieved if we trust Sacconi's eulogists. The contiguity with the symbolic centres of Classical Rome and a thematic link with the nearby Forum of Augustus conjured a continuity that is essential to the nationalist myth. Il Vittoriano established piazza Venezia as the symbolic heart of the city and can be seen as rendering monocentric the polycentric nineteenth-century city. In that morphological shift, it became possible to assert a unitary character to the city. Il Vittoriano provided Rome and Italy with a singular monument which in its every feature, declares Rome Italian and Italy Roman.

Even if some of the elements of its ideological scheme are present within the idea of *la terza Roma*, il Vittoriano was out of keeping with the monumental tradition of post-*risorgimento* Rome. Garibaldi had been honoured with a major monument on the Janiculum in 1895, but the Garibaldi monument is a statue group with some minor architectural framing and is located on the fringes of the city (Piantoni 1991). The piazza Vittorio Emanuel II had been constructed without a large monument. Il Vittoriano, by contrast, dominates the city and mythologizes the state. The fascist performance of power at l'Altare della Patria was more systemic and totalitarian than anything seen under the national governments (Brice 1998: 301–66; Tobia 1998: 95–7; Lerner 2010) but the conjoining of the Classical and imperial past with the contemporary and the almost colonial expression of state power through architectural dominance are resonant with those later representations of the Italian nation.

Il Vittoriano shares with the palazzo di Giustizia a legibility in its monumentality, but the purism of the scenography differentiates it from anything that has come before. It is theatrical, didactic, and fantastical. Its incongruity separates it from the everyday. It is an

Figure 3.12 Il Vittoriano.

attempt to make tangible the mythic unrealities of ultranationalism. Il Vittoriano stands in violent contrast to the city it would dominate.

Conclusions

The European middle and upper classes were profoundly engaged with Classical Rome: it was central to their understanding of their place in history, society and culture, and hence to their identities. Their experiences of visiting Rome were focused less on seeing the remains of the imperial city than in encountering its absence. They read that absence as symbolic of death and civilizational fall in ways which questioned the absolute values of their own Classical educations but also reinforced their confidence in their personal Classicism. It was a solipsistic and egotistical reading of Rome which emphasized the solitary experience of the viewer and the bourgeois individual as the bearer of civilization in a hostile universe. In the psychodrama of their encounters with Rome, visitors rejected the contemporary city as sepulchral, literally and metaphorically the tomb enclosing the Classical civilization of which they were the inheritors.

The trope of Rome as a tomb proved attractive to the men of the *risorgimento*. Their commitment to modernity drove them to differentiate their Rome from the contemporary papal city. Their ambition was for a modern Rome that they closely associated with bourgeois commercial and cultural values. Elements of a bourgeois Classicism were built into the city but *la terza Roma* was built as a modern bourgeois city.

The Classicism of il Vittoriano emerged violently on the Roman landscape as the aesthetic of an authoritarian, imperial ultranationalism. And yet, il Vittoriano was an exception and a contentious and often problematic and authoritarian presence in *la terza Roma*. Of the various contrasting and contentious dreams of Rome, it was this ultranationalistic vision that was to influence the fascists. Il Vittoriano, with its imperialistic Classicism and nationalistic fervour, makes visible the paradoxes and tensions in bourgeois nationalism.

CHAPTER 4
FASCIST ROME: SCENES OF FANTASY, 1922–1943

In this chapter, I focus on the development of fascist Classicism. I trace some of the main lines of political thought as manifested in architectural developments in Rome in the period. Those ideas invoked nationalism, imperialism and modernity, and grew out of the ideologies of the late nineteenth-century (Gentile 1929; Sternhall 1994; Laqueur 1996). Nevertheless, fascism was different in that its commitment to the Italian nation had a quasi-religious intensity that required citizens' ideological uniformity and demanded repeated performances of loyalty.

Nineteenth-century utopian thought imagined a close relationship between an urban environment and the processes by which the ideal citizen was formed (Alston 2012). This correlation inspired aspirational urban interventions. Yet, the inadequacy of a reliance on architectural form for delivery of the desired versions of the future citizen/city/nation is obvious (Beaumont 2012: 3; Raban 1976: 1–21). The citizen is formed in the conjunction of cultural, economic and social forces, in inequalities and power relations, in cultural interchanges and experiences, in the rules of family and society, and the struggles of social reproduction. In the face of such complexity, the fascist regime committed to the power of the symbolic (Mosse 1996). Mussolini's Rome was a theatrical and performative space in which the symbolic dominance of the regime, as expressed in architecture and ritual, was intended to produce the new citizens who would in turn deliver fascism's fantasy of a new Roman Empire.

This theatricality was mythic. The gigantism of the interventions, the repetitious colonnades, the large, emptied spaces, the smooth, hard surfaces, the monumentalism with its projection of long superhuman vistas, and the explicit decorative quotations from the Classical can all be seen as distancing elements that removed the individual from the everyday and located them within a civilizational, dehumanizing landscape (Marcello 2017). The architecture is unsubtle. It is scenographic rather than functional. Its legibility lessens the ideological power of major architecture: it is no longer a cultural form which shapes the everyday and integrates its symbols and structures so as to create a world that appears natural, but it offers a polemic in stone that cries out for the world to be as the regime wishes it to be. Two generations before Las Vegas was recognized as the City of Scenography, fascist Rome enclosed its people in an elaborate symbolic framework overwhelming in scale (Venturi, Brown and Izenour 1972; Rattenbury and Hardingham 2007). Its spectacle worked to disassociate and alienate the individual from the everyday. In the face of a general political and ideological disaffection, fascism offered the citizen a mythic signification in which the individual's quotidian struggles were given purpose within a civilizational, historical and heroic narrative. Such narratives encouraged an identification with and subordination to the regime's fantasies and the fantastical narratives were made concrete in the architecture (Falasca-Zamponi 1997; Debord 1992).

Fascist architecture presented the regime's ideals of citizenship, the contribution of its leader, its understanding of the past, its mythography and a promise of a future. The regime invested heavily in prestige projects, most notably the Forum of Mussolini in the north of the city, and the ambitious plan for a centre for a universal exhibition in 1942 at what became EUR. It reshaped the old urban centre and changed the relationship of the city to the archaeological zone.

There is an element of 'the emperor's new clothes' to this urbanism. These were spaces to be seen and visited rather than inhabited. As a result, the visitor had a choice: to see this constructed vision as a real world and commit to its ideological untruth or to turn to the messy, complex spaces of the other city. Architects and citizens alike could calculate the material advantages of adherence to fascist unrealities. Undoubtedly, fascist narratives of identity had a considerable appeal in the uncertain economic and political times of the period. The disciplinary apparatus of fascism was ferocious; it was in the nature of fascism to offer a dichotomous understanding of politics in which the world was divided between enemies and friends who were engaged in an existential struggle. Being a friend was not only safer but often rewarding.

This chapter traces fascist extremity through several brief sections without attempting a compendious coverage of the aesthetics and architecture of the period. In the next section, I examine the peculiar understanding of time and history in fascism. This paradoxical positioning sets the scene for the contradictory architectural aesthetics of fascism (Griffin 2007). In marked contrast to Nazi Germany, an agreed fascist style never emerged. Fascist buildings ranged through high modernism and Classicism and sometimes a union of both (Whyte 2017; Kallis 2018; Rifkind 2012; Fortuna 2020). Yet, the lure of Imperial Rome was inescapable (Kallis 2016), and the following sections will examine the shift from 'organic' or communitarian views of urbanism to a focus on scenography and symbol.

Myth, history and architectural form

Fascism was a belief system. It had a quasi-religious understanding of the nation and world (Gentile 1996). Its aesthetics excluded or obfuscated the materiality of social and economic inequality (Benjamin 1968) in favour of a spiritual conjoining with nation and *il Duce* (Mussolini 1932; Gentile 1929). To find one's home in that cultural system required a commitment of faith to the mythic discourses of nation and state. Alienation from the everyday was essential to that imaginative leap.

In their employment of Classicism, the fascists postulated an essential identity of imperial Rome and the fascist present. Whereas most historical philosophies from the eighteenth century onwards regarded the present as resulting from a historical process of multiple semi-discrete stages, fascism located the present within a very long and possibly eternally recurring sameness (described as palingenetic) (Fogu 2003a; 2003b; 2005; 2015). In fascist propaganda, the fascists were not like the ancient Romans, they were the ancient Romans. It was within this ideological framework that they asserted that their leader was not analogous to Caesar or Augustus but was at a fundamental level the same as Caesar and Augustus. This palingenetic conception of Italian/Roman culture is seen by Griffin as the key element in fascist ideology (compare Griffin 2002).

> Fascism is a genus of political ideology whose mythic core in its various permutations is a palingenetic form of populist ultranationalism.
>
> Griffin 1991: 26

The great propagandistic exhibitions, the *mostra della rivoluzione fascista* (1932–4), the *mostra di Roma nell'ottocento* and the *mostra augustea della romanità* (1937–8) were a display of this fundamental historical unity of Italy (Fogu 2005; Marcello 2011; Arthurs 2017; Rinaldi 1991; Andreotti 2005; 2010). Ancient Rome was united with Italy by Augustan reforms. The modern Italian nation was liberated from foreign domination and medieval fragmentation by Garibaldi's nineteenth-century Red Shirts as Mussolini's Black Shirts saved Italy from the communist threat and liberal corruption. These emergences of the true Italian essence were encapsulated in fascism. Fascism was thus present in the *risorgimento* and Augustan Rome (De Francisci 1940: 5–29). This essence was conceptualized as *romanità* (the quality of Romanness). *Romanità* might be supressed but was always present, awaiting the opportunity to re-establish its global civilization

This radical denial of history countered an understanding of modernity in which the dynamic processes of capitalist change melted away all traditions. As Marx put it:

> Constant revolutionising of production, uninterrupted disturbance of all social conditions, everlasting uncertainty and agitation distinguish the bourgeois epoch from all earlier ones. All fixed, fast-frozen relations, with their train of ancient and venerable prejudices and opinions, are swept away, all new-formed ones become antiquated before they can ossify. All that is solid melts into air, all that is holy is profaned, and man is at last compelled to face with sober senses his real conditions of life, and his relations with his kind.
>
> Marx 1848

In this view, modernity stripped away existing false ideologies and left the human to realize her plight in the material conditions of her existence. For Marx, modernity was alienating since it removed the ideological bonds of community and its metaphysical associations and replaced them with contract. Such perceptions of the rootlessness of the modern condition animate much of the writing on modern urbanism (Berman 1983; Raban, 1976; Sennett 1978).

In fascism, alienation was countered by a nationalist metaphysics. *Romanità* was identified as characteristic of the Italian nation and citizen. Mussolini was proclaimed *civis romanus* (Gentile 1996: 76). A profound nationalistic identification of self and nation had been deepened in the Italian experience of the First World War. Social differences and complexities of identities supposedly dissolved in the simple binaries of the conflict. Ultranationalists claimed that the eternal verities of masculinity and nationhood were performed in war (Marinetti 1909).[1] For the fascists, the battle of Caporetto (1917) led directly to the foundation of fascism and the rediscovery of *romanità* as the essential characteristic of the true Italian (Fogu 2003a). The idea of war as a transcendent experience that made the masculine citizen was central to Mussolini's ideology (Gentile 1929: 30; Mussolini 1932). The fascists aimed at a continuation of the political and communitarian dynamic of war (Togliatti 1978: 9–10). They committed to maintaining the memory of the war and honouring veterans and the fallen. They assimilated their battles against the socialists and communists to the 1915–18 conflict (Falasca-Zamponi 1997: 35–41). Once in power, fascism staged 'battles' against perceived socio-economic and political ills. These battles imbued everyday societal issues with mythic power and the connotations of existential struggle. Fascist masculinity would triumph in these perpetual conflicts even if those 'battles' were for births or economic growth (Berezin 1997; Ben-Ghiat 2001). The agonistic essence of the Italian needed to be performed in repeating conflicts since it was only through struggle that *romanità* was empowered.

After 1922, the primary fascist ambition was to realize the long-held desire for an Italian empire. The struggle required the commitment of new citizens to the imperial nation. These imperial citizens were not a present reality but an aspiration for a fascist future in which the Italian people would become as they had been in Roman times. The true citizen had to be formed through ritual, mass assembly, mass media, education, social discipline and, above all, in struggle.

In this agonistic mythology, the people were one across time and space. Pietro de Francisci (1940: 3–13) identified the Augustan father at work in the fascistic son. Giovanni Gentile (1929: 9–11), fascism's premier philosopher, overcame the problem of the long historical gap between Rome and the rise of Italian nationalism with an assertion that the Italian spirit was always there, an invisible omnipresence in Italian society. Mussolini proclaimed in April 1922, on the supposed foundation date of Rome, that fascism was Rome both reborn and immortal:

> Rome is our point of departure and reference. It is our symbol or, if you wish, our myth. We dream of a Roman Italy, that is to say wise, strong, disciplined, and imperial. Much of that which was the immortal spirit of Rome rises again in Fascism: the fasces are Roman; our organization of combat is Roman, our pride and our courage is Roman: civis romanus sum. It is necessary, now, that the history of tomorrow, the history we fervently wish to create, not be a contrast or a parody of the history of yesterday. The Romans were not only warriors, but formidable builders who could challenge, as they did challenge, their time.
>
> *Mussolini 1956: 160–1; trans. Painter 2005: 3*

This mythological identification proposed a perpetual presentism of the national spirit (Fogu 2003b; 2015). As in other ultranationalistic movements, that future was to be made through the past, but not as a replication of that past. In the speech of April 1922, Mussolini was wary of being trapped into historical reproduction. His immortal reborn Romans were to create the history of tomorrow. None of this stands up to critical scrutiny, but fascism never owed its power to ideological coherence, and, indeed, never claimed to do so.

Ernesto Laclau (2005: 67–128) argues that populism and fascism work through a chain of equivalences between political groupings. For him, each political grouping is defined by its demands and needs and these tend to be specific to sociological circumstances (by class, region, etc.). Populism extends a specific demand through association so that an economic demand dovetails into a cultural demand and then further dovetails into a different economic or social demand in a chain of equivalences. The demands in any chain are often irreconcilable and contradictory and can only be united into a chain of equivalences through a symbolic association, such as opposition to 'elites' or minorities, who are responsible for the failure of each specific demand to be met. As the chain of equivalences grows, so the content of demands is attenuated. The notional demands of a unitary people conjoin the sectional, varied interests of citizens, and the delivery of that unity somehow guarantees that demands will be met. The purpose of the movement becomes to deliver a symbolic unity that will obscure internal contradictions and subsume sectional interests. The resulting manifesto centres on the symbolism of belonging which is what binds the group together. Such belonging, alongside violence, deters individuals from pursuing sectional interests. The demands of irreconcilable sectional interests can be forgotten or rendered inimical to the state and made the mark of enemies. This ideological emptiness and incoherence generated arbitrary dichotomies that rendered fascism difficult to combat (Gramsci (1978 [1921]; 1978 [1924]; 1978 [1925]; Togliatti 1978: 1–15; Gagliardi 2016). When wedded to an overarching and dominant symbolic, the violence of the dichotomy encouraged citizens to acquiesce in fascism which was in its political presentation primarily symbolic.

This morass paralleled that of Marinetti's pre-war Futurists. The Futurists were a revolutionary artistic movement with much in common with French artistic radicals. Indeed, Marinetti's (1909) founding manifesto was published in French in *Le Figaro* on 20 February. They were influential in the artistic circles at the foundation of fascism, particularly through the intercession of Margherita Sarfatti. Sarfatti founded the *Novecento* movement which was committed to modernism in art, architecture and literature (Adamson 2001). Perhaps her most prominent protégé was the painter Mario Sironi, on whom more below. Sarfatti's influence in Milan and with Mussolini (they were lovers) encouraged the regime's commitment to high modernism or rationalism. As early as 1914, Antonio Sant'Elia had published *Manifesto dell'architettura futurista* which called for a new architecture of reinforced concrete freed from stylistic conventions. He imagined an architecture of grand hotels, immense roads and gates, and the house as a machine.[2]

The Futurists' future would sweep away the past and social convention (Adamson 2001; Mosse 1990). Unlike other modern technological movements, the goal was not social justice or universal prosperity, but a new setting for the performance of epic masculinity (Spackman 1996). Cultural heritage was a death from which the Futurists would release the Italian people. Museums and the gangrene of professors were to be excised in war and violence. Libraries were to be burnt. The hypermasculine individual would triumph in a new epic which, of course, recalled Classical epic. Such individualism was antithetical to socialism: Marinetti had led an attack on the Milan offices of the socialist newspaper, *Avanti* (Bowler 1991). It was also deeply misogynistic (De Grazia 1992: 31–2).

Fascist confidence in this future free from the past drew on Futurists' perception of past greatness (Griffin 2007). Fascist modernity was welded onto a past that was essential to the ideological construction of the future. That past was in no recognizable sense historical: it was symbolic and mythical. That mythical content had to be drawn into the symbology of the regime. This inherent incoherence in the fascist revolution meant that it was difficult to devise a definitive symbolic architectural language. Nevertheless, the overwhelming stress on the symbolic and the unity of the Italian people made such a language necessary.

The fascist period saw a major investment in public building. Modernist (Rationalist) groups were influential (Kallis 2018), particularly in northern Italy. Two major groupings, Gruppo 7, whose most important building is Terragni's Casa del Fascio in Como (1936), and the Movimento Italiano per l'Architettura Razionale (MIAR) (Italian Movement for Rationalist Architecture) founded in 1930 (Vannelli 2010: 20 for the MIAR manifesto), grew out of Sarfatti's Milanese circle.[3] Their engagements in architectural debates were often polemical. In 1931, Pietro Maria Bardi presented the *Tavola degli orrori* (the Table of Horrors) at a MIAR conference which depicted in photomontage examples of recent neoclassical architecture. The architectural establishment was offended. Its political muscle was such that MIAR was virtually dissolved. Although some of the Rationalists were removed from positions of importance, most continued to get work and to employ a Rationalist style and Rationalism remained a characteristic element in fascist architecture.

Fascist contributions to the world fairs and architectural competitions advertised the aesthetic values of the regime. The pavilions stressed modernity, particularly in relationship to the technologies of speed which had been lionized by the Futurists. The Italian pavilion at the Chicago World Fair of 1933 was designed by Adalberto Libera, Antonio Valente and Mario De Renzi to recollect ocean liners and aircraft (Fortuna 2020). The interior exhibition celebrated Leonardo da Vinci's flying machines, Italy's global ambition and Classical Roman architecture. Right at its heart was a severe depiction of Mussolini as 'DUX'. The association was reinforced by the arrival of a flight of the Italian air force led by General Italo Balbo.[4] Mussolini was so pleased by the press attention that he presented Chicago with a monumental column from the excavations at Ostia.

High modernism was employed polemically. The *mostra della rivoluzione fascista* (1932–4) was staged in Pio Piacentini's palazzo dell'esposizioni (see pp. 145–6). But the palazzo's neoclassical façade was obscured by a new elaborate plaster frontage designed by Libera and De Renzi. The frontage was constructed in four basic elements, two blank flanking boards topped with enormous Xs, referencing the ten years since the march on Rome; a red central rectangle which gave dominating height; four metallic pillars shaped as fasces; and the huge conference sign which crossed most of the frontage (Fogu 2003b: 135–64). The whole structure could have dropped on the centre of Rome from the

Fascist Rome: Scenes of Fantasy, 1922–1943

Figure 4.1 The Italian Pavilion at the Chicago World Fair, 1933.

imagined future cityscapes of Fritz Lang. Inside, Mario Sironi's design deployed the latest techniques in display, photomontage, and typography (Andreotti 2010).

The *mostra della rivoluzione fascista* was succeeded by the *mostra augustea*. This vast exhibition celebrated the 2,000-year anniversary of the birth of Augustus (Mostra Augustea 1938; Rinaldi 1991; Liberati 1990). Its political agenda was to associate Augustus and Mussolini (Arthurs 2017). The director of the exhibition, Giulio Quirino Giglioli, welcomed Mussolini proclaiming that Mussolini had enabled a spontaneous

Figure 4.2 Façade at the *mostra della rivoluzione fascista*.

connection with the Romans of two millennia before. The Augustan achievement was to manifest the imperial nature of a unified Italy which was now restored by Mussolini, the modern *civis romanus*. A play of substitutions between the two dictators allowed each to reinforce the standing of the other in fascist myth-history (Marcello 2011). Over a million visitors paraded through its halls (Gentile 1996: 77). Libero and De Renzi's plaster frontage was replaced by another plaster construction designed by Alfredo Scalpelli, who was one of the urbanists responsible for the fascist new town of Sabaudia. His design was modelled on a Roman gateway or triumphal arch. The frontage gave the appearance of being constructed from blocks of stone. To the left of the entrance, the façade repeated 'REX' to honour the king, and to the right, 'DUX', for Mussolini and/or Augustus. The use of Latin conjoined fascist and Roman worlds.

The ultramodernism of the Rationalists and their commitment to a revolutionary break with the past was in tension with the fascist ultranationalist understanding of the Italian past. Although these two tendencies might seem irreconcilable, a pathway was found for the groups to work together. In May 1931, Marcello Piacentini (1931a) published an article in *Il Giornale d'Italia* in defence of Italian architecture. He began with a polemical attack on Rationalist architecture, which he saw as a dominant contemporary style. Rationalism was North European. It was Bolshevik. It was Hebraic. It was utilitarian and hostile to beauty. It eroded the differences between buildings so that the house was indistinguishable from the Church, the school and the theatre. The polemic then shifted. It was possible to have a national Rationalism. Classicism was exhausted with il Vittoriano. Youth would construct a new architecture and a new Italy in which the Italian genius would find clear and serene forms that represented the national spirit and soul.

Piacentini's racist, spiritual language reflected a confidence that Rationalism could be united with Italian traditionalism. He envisaged a unified architectural symbolic to represent fascism and deliver an ultranationalist, palingenetic Italian cityscape. Piacentini co-ordinated the major urbanistic projects around the city of Rome and was to a considerable extent able to deliver that unified architectural style. The wider social and historical ambitions were, of course, fantasies.

From the organic to the symbolic city

The fondness of Rome's architects for Renaissance styling established a connection with decentralized forms of political and social power. In common with much late eighteenth- and early nineteenth-century architectural theory, emphasis was placed on 'organic' forms which emerged from local tradition and were appropriate to the natural environment (Sitte 1889; Geddes 1915). Such organic cities were conservative in that they looked back to medieval and early modern communal values and visions of social solidarity.

Gustavo Giovannoni was perhaps the most influential exponent of these views in early twentieth-century Rome. As Dean of the Architectural School of the Scuola Normale in Rome, he influenced a generation of architects. He is recognized today through his commitment to the conservation of the architectural heritage of Italy.

Giovannoni's *Vecchie città ed edilizia nuova* (1995 [1931]), the first version of which was published in 1913, is regarded as the earliest Italian work on urbanism. He imagined a debate between the conservators and the innovators (3–7). For the innovators, the city could not be a museum or an archive and the needs of the modern city were completely different from those of the old. The conservators argued that beauty was encapsulated in the old city, and it was through the old city that traditions of nation and community were inculcated. Giovannoni (7) sought authority in a Mussolini quote and so claimed that his architectural conservation was in keeping with fascist ideology.

Giovannoni saw national values as resting in traditional Italian communities. The preservation of national culture in the city required a suburban recreation of the rural community (Giovannoni 1995 [1931]: 67). The preservation of vernacular Italian architecture was in resistance to international style, by which he meant Classicism and Rationalism (119). The aim was to create the picturesque by avoiding long vistas and grandiosity in favour of short streets, curvilinear design, and variegated aspects (123–4). His model city was one of village-like suburban centres linked by rapid transit systems.

Giovannoni was influenced by Anglo-Saxon urban theorists, particularly Ebenezer Howard (1898; 1902). Howard's *Garden Cities of Tomorrow* (1902) became an international success since his garden city concept seemed to provide an escape from the social and political problems of the industrial city. The schemes attempted to realize the utopian provisions of Peter Kropotkin's (1892) anarchism with its focus on small communities and pre-capitalist production. The garden city movement preferred the local and regional to the national, connecting cities to their immediate environments. Their model communities were small medieval cities or the *poleis* of Classical Greece (Morris 1891; Reclus 1905). These movements were hostile to grandiose Classicism, particularly in its Roman forms (Alston 2012).

The opportunity to move from theory to reality came with the pre-fascist development of Rome's garden suburbs, notably Garbatella. Planned in 1917, Garbatella's construction began on 18 February 1920 under the patronage of the Vittorio Emanuele III. It was a maritime and industrial workers' village. In Giovannoni's and Piacentini's designs, the working classes of the new neighbourhood were to be accommodated in a mix of houses (*villini*) and small, individually-styled apartment blocks (*palazzini*). The houses were designed to cluster into micro-neighbourhoods. Some of the houses were slightly larger than others and some had private gardens (Costantini 1922). The height of the *villini* was limited to three storeys. They were designed to reproduce a village community (Stabile 2022). The *palazzini*, intended for a middle-class population, were up to five storeys. Designs of both types of residence were varied. This faux-rustic *romanità* contrasted with the more uniform 'Piedmontese' *cinquecentismo* urbanism of Prati and the other new districts (De Michelis 2010). G.C.'s (1925) report claimed that these peri-urban garden settlements were designed to ensure a collective and communal life in which traditional civic values were inculcated. The style was known as *barocchetto*.

The ideal faced challenges. Mussolini's antipathy to the informal settlements (disparaged as *villaggi abissini* (Abyssinian villages)) that fringed Rome and his demolitions in the most densely settled regions of old Rome (see below) generated a housing crisis to which Garbatella and the borgo of Quarticciolo were the answer. By 1930, Garbatella was one of the most densely populated districts of the city. Smaller individual houses and tenement or block housing provided for the displaced population (Gentile 2007: 75). These housing units were often without even the most basic facilities and the provision of civic services was negligible. It was only after the war that the inhabitants of Quarticciolo were able to use their political muscle to secure some infrastructural provision (Cianfarani 2020).

In Garbatella , the huge *albergo rosso* designed by Innocenzo Sabbatini for the Istituto Case Popolari (ICP) provided barrack-like living for those transferred to Garbatella. Its multistorey design differed fundamentally from the private *villini* and the more communal *palazzini*. Modernist in style, though not aggressively so, it was an institutional imposition on the suburban landscape (Kallis 2017; Kallis and Gilfoyle 2020). And yet it also laid claim to a distinctive *romanità*. The contemporaneous excavations at Roman Ostia were uncovering large well-decorated apartment blocks and Sabbatini saw his block as being within that Classical Roman tradition (De Michelis, 2009).

Giovannoni's preferred aesthetic was both unclassical and unimposing. Its political message was communal rather than civilizational. In the *Vecchie città* essay (Giovannoni 1995 [1931]: 170), he attacked one of the core elements of fascist policy in Rome, the *sventramento*, the 'disembowelment' in which the old quarters of the city were demolished. The systematic destruction of houses was, he proclaimed, a destruction of public riches, equivalent to the burning of a forest, the destruction of a mine, or the devastation of an earthquake. This systematic destruction was undermining his garden city by creating a housing crisis but was also antithetical to his faith in organic communities.

And yet, Giovannoni remained within the fascist establishment. He co-authored a catalogue of the architecture at the *mostra augustea*, commenting reverentially on his Classical precursors (Giglioli and Giovannoni 1937). The fascist architect, artist and intellectual, Alberto Calza Bini, who was responsible for the *sventramento* around the Theatre of Marcellus, wrote a glowing introduction to the *Vecchie città* in which he related Giovannoni's essay to the 'renewal that fascism was undertaking in the Italian cities' and to the education of a new generation of fascist citizens (Giovannoni 1995 [1931]: v). Although the nationalism of *Vecchie città* is evident, it is difficult to see how Calza Bini reached such conclusions.

Giovannoni's stylistic preferences situated him within a vibrant tradition of Italian architectural criticism. The most significant figure in that tradition was Camillo Boito. Boito divided architecture into the organic and symbolic. Organic architecture grew out of, represented and reinforced the community. Within liberal Italy, the particular focus, according to Boito (1880: viii–xxvi) should be on domestic residences (relating him to bourgeois sensibilities) and his model is the late medieval or early Renaissance palazzo. Boito was critical of symbolic architecture. He saw the desire to build big as a form of egoism (Boito 1880: ix). The models favoured by Boito and Giovannoni advertised the values of small-scale social units, the household, village and community, rather than states, empires and civilizations.

Fascism, however, was fixated by the symbolic. Its mix of philosophical origins led to an emphasis on the triumph of culture over nature, of the will over history, and of the image over the real (Benjamin 1968; Falasca-Zamponi 1997; Gentile 1996). Industrial cities and urban architecture presented the fascists with a problem: they were focal points of the class economy. They were not evidently closely related to the 'natural' or traditional national environment. They fostered social relations in which economic exploitation, alienation and social and political conflict were undeniable. True Italian identity was to be found in the villages and among the farmers in the connection to the land. As with other far-right movements, fascism had a significant anti-urban strand.

One response to the urban issue was to move city populations onto the land (Caprotti 2007b; 2008). New rural settlements were ideological echoes of Classical Roman colonies (Caprotti 2007a). Such agro-towns were not organic in Boito's sense, nor did they adopt the faux-ruralism of the garden city movement. Instead, they were monuments to state power in the rural environment (Mariani 1976). In places such as Littoria (inaugurated in December 1932), Sabaudia (1934), Pontina (1935), Aprilia (1938) and Pomezia (1939), the urbanistic model was the Roman military camp. Sabaudia, for instance, was split into quadrants, with rectilinear street patterns and a central area dominated by the *casa di fascia*, a clock and bell tower, the *torre littoria* and a post office. The style is Rationalist, with the geometry of the plan being reflected in the squared-off buildings and smooth faces of the concentre designs. In the first stages of the town, when the vistas were not cluttered with other buildings, the contrast between the flatness of the reclaimed land and the verticals of the building was such to make obvious the artifice of the city. The colonization programme aimed not just to transform the landscape but also the former inhabitants of the industrial city into new Italians (Ghirardo 1989: 1–66; Caprotti 2008). Although Sabaudia became home to elements of the radical intellectual left after the war who denied the political content of the architecture, Littoria, renamed Latina, and other towns of the Agro Pontino retained a powerful emotional attachment to fascism and their founder, Mussolini (Fuller 2020).

The Futurists' glorification of speed was a key element in Mussolini's Rome. Fascist planners pushed major roads through the interior of the city, notably the vie del Mare and dell'Impero which were completed in 1932 in celebration of the tenth anniversary of the fascist coup (Mulè 1932). The via dell'Impero destroyed more than 5,500 residences (Bottai 1992 [1938]) and caused huge damage to the archaeology (Kallis 2012). In Mussolini's vision, fascist Rome was to be experienced by motorcycle or car (Baxa 2004; 2010). In the city of speed, the monuments could be viewed cinematically. The viewer would take moments to get from the Colosseum, through the imperial fora to Piazza Venezia, to swing across the side of the Capitoline by the Theatre of Marcellus, down to the Forum Boarium and then along the Tiber out of the city to speed along the autostrada to Ostia Antica and the sea. The new roads were imperial, connecting the archaeological sites with the symbolism of the new Italian empire. For Mussolini, the road to the sea was a materialisation of imperial ambition and success (Mussolini 1926).

Giovannoni's vision of a network of organic communities was countered by a cinematic city to be viewed from a fast car. Inevitably, such a city was predominantly a symbol. In the cinematic projection of fascist Rome, the experience of the city was not one of social interaction, but that of the viewer, who read the meaning of the city from monumental constructions. The shift from urban participant to urban viewer turned the city-dweller into audience.

The apogee of this re-imagining of the city as symbol was Hitler's visit to Rome in May 1938. The visit was planned to an exceptional degree, with every sight to be experienced by the Nazi dignitaries considered, surveyed and, when necessary, improved. Nearly 23,000 flags, Italian and German, were positioned along the route (Baxa 2007).

Hitler's train was ushered into stazione Ostiense. Ostiense was itself a symbol of fascist Italy, connecting the city to the sea and Ostia Antica and further to the Italian Empire. Stations were symbols of modernity and attracted Rationalist designs, nowhere more obviously than at stazione Firenze di Santa Maria Novella. Ostiense similarly had a sleek Rationalist design composed of rectilinear forms with extended, blank flanking walls. The modernist cuboid of the ticket office has a tall glass entrance that is hidden behind squared off columns that lead into a long, shaded portico that runs across the front of the building. The Classicizing elements of columns, portico and pediment are delivered in modernist style. All was built to an impressive height that diminished the human scale and the station was set into an emptiness that enhanced its architectural grandeur. The décor includes Francesco Nagni's heroic bas-relief of Bellerophon and Pegasus and a series of black and white mosaics depicting imperial Rome's myth-history.

The German party arrived at night, enhancing the drama of the performance. Moving by horse and carriage, the Germans passed the pyramid of Cestius, before coming to the cleared Circus Maximus. The party then made its way down the via del'Impero, allowing Hitler to view the remains of Rome's Classical Empire rendered visible by newly installed electric lighting. Finally, they arrived in the symbolic centre of Rome and Italy, the piazza Venezia.

The Circus Maximus had been ornamented by an Axumite stele, normally, if inaccurately, described as an obelisk. The stele had been looted from Ethiopia and was placed in front of the Ministry for Italian Africa in 1927. The obelisks scattered round the city symbolized imperial conquests. Most were Egyptian, extracted by Rome's emperors. Italy's conquest of Ethiopia led to a parallel relocation of Axumite heritage (von Henneberg, 2004) that connected the fascist and Roman imperial cities.

Hitler's entry to the city was the prelude to a visit which was mostly architectural tour. The great museums were interspersed with monuments to Italian unity, including il

Figure 4.3 Stazione Ostiense in 1940.

Vittoriano and the projections of fascist Rome, including Foro Mussolini, città università and the piazza Augusteo. Interlaced with these sites were displays of Italian military might and of fascist youth's dedication to their leader. The visit was theatre and Rome was the stage. That stage linked the Classical heritage and the fascist remodelling of the city. Hell (2019: 313–37) suggests that Hitler's visit provoked a need in the German dictator for imperial *mimesis*. Hitler's urge to replicate Roman grandeur mirrored Mussolini's palingenetic vision.

Coming immediately after the *Anschluss,* the ceremonials projected Hitler and Mussolini as the balanced powers in a European civilizational axis. It was a triumph of the symbolic that promised or threatened a Romano-Germanic renewal of European imperialist civilization. That fantasy of a Rome revived was to be resolved in the global war craved by the fascist ideologues.

Liberating the spirit of *romanità*

On 21 December 1925, Mussolini announced a shift in policy on the city of Rome from a programme focused on necessities to one focused on grandeur. Claiming to have resolved the immediate problems of the city, he committed the authorities' energies to the symbolic in order to unleash the ardent spirit of *romanità*. Mussolini claimed that:

> My ideas are clear; my orders are precise and it is certain that they will become a concrete reality. In five years, Rome must appear marvellous to all the peoples of the world, vast, ordered, powerful, as it was in the time of the first empire of Augustus.
>
> *Mussolini 1925*

New/old fascist/Augustan Rome was to be made visible through the clearing of the Theatre of Marcellus, the Campidoglio and the Pantheon from the accretions of the centuries of supposed decadence. The temples of Roman Christianity were to be freed from their surrounding parasitic and profane constructions. The giant monuments of Roman history required their solitude. And a great road (which seems to be both metaphor and reality) was to be built to access a second Mediterranean empire via the reborn Ostia. Fascist Rome was to become a message to the world. Rome would again become a political and moral ideal. Mussolini was the builder of this new Rome (Bottai 1927; Muñoz 1935) and in the propagandistic contemporary receptions of the city, Rome was honoured with the epithet Mussoliniana (Schüller 1943; Piacentini 1931b).

The divesting of the Classical and Christian monuments of their 'parasitic accretions' was presented as a liberation, paralleling the rhetoric of liberation of 1922 (Bottai 1992 [1938]). This liberation would enable the monuments to fulfil their symbolic function in their 'necessary isolation'. It was a moment of fascist refoundation that would parallel the Augustan refoundation (Ricci 1925).

Isolation is only necessary if the focus is to be on spectacle and the vista in which the monuments are placed. Spectacle rendered the city legible. Legibility emphasized the symbolic over the interactive. It reduced the city to a metaphor in an ideological narrative. If the fascists wished Rome to represent their version of a singular *romanità* to a global audience, as Mussolini insisted, the cityscape needed to reflect that vision. In a city as complex as Rome, no single structure can determine the narrative. This polyfocal challenge was met by the visual unification of the monuments by road and vista (Kostof 1973: 14). Roads linked the Colosseum to il Vittoriano to the piazza Venezia, the Campidoglio to the Theatre of Marcellus, to the Pantheon and the Augusteo (Kallis 2014: 14–17). The picturesque and organic gave way to the scenographic and symbolic.

Buildings that interrupted this vision were to be demolished in a programme of *sventramenti*. This programme targeted densely populated districts occupied by the poorer elements of society. It provided the fascists with opportunities to remove sections of the population hostile to the regime (Gentile 2007: 1–9). Although elements of the remodelling had been under discussion since 1871, the scale of the interventions and the willingness of the regime to ignore opposition were unprecedented.

The demolitions were extensively publicized. Mussolini was fond of striking heroic poses as he engaged personally in demolitions. Achille Beltrame's cover for *La Domenica del Corriere* of 3 March 1935 shows Mussolini standing on the roof of an old and elevated housing block. He is wearing full military uniform and dramatically poised to strike a ritualistic *primo colpe di piccone* (first blow of the pick). Impressed demolition workers watch on. In the background, we see the via dell'Impero, the Forum and il Vittoriano, now united in the fascist cityscape of vistas. This imperial cityscape was brought into being by Mussolini's 'heroic fury', a fury that was filmed, photographed and illustrated for a mass audience. He battled old, ragged housing that was insurgent in his idealised Roman cityscape (Gentile 2007: 70).

Mussolini also swung the first pick in the demolition of the Borghi on 28 October 1936. This stretch of chaotic, poor housing was caught up in the fraught relationship between the Vatican and Italian government. Mussolini's personal involvement in that demolition symbolized the reconciliation between the Vatican and the Italian state and was the necessary prelude to the visual integration of the Vatican and Rome along the vista of the via della Conciliazione (Kallis 2011; Kirk 2006).

The demolitions were themselves monuments to the regime. Mario Mafai's paintings captured the Roman urban landscape in transformation. His 1936 *Demolition of the Augusteo* sets exposed domestic stairways and interiors, semi-ruined upper storeys, a belltower and a ragged assortment of buildings as a foreground to the about-to-be liberated Augusteo. The picturesque neighbourhood was a counterpoint to Augustan/fascist monumentality. The significantly titled *Demolition of the Villages* (1930) shows a colourful four-storey building with its front ripped away to expose elaborate baroque décor. The quietness of the scenes transmits ambivalence, but Mafai's paintings suggests a fascist Rome in which ruination and Classical monumentality are symbolic of an emergent *romanità* rather than civilizational fall.[5]

Mussolini's striking down of 'parasitic' buildings delivered Rome from a supposedly chaotic communitarianism to make visible the fascist scenography of the imperial city (Marcello 2017). Local communal histories were willed out of existence. Agnew (2010)

Figure 4.4 *Mussolini Wields the Pick* (Achille Beltrame).

argues that the complexity of those memories undermined the new cityscape. Yet, the fascist problem was fundamental: any attempt to reduce the city to a single message clashed with the complexity and density of urban processes innate to cities. Further, the spectral memory of the denigrated localities had to be preserved in the memorialization of the *sventramenti* as one of the multitude of battles against the anti-types of fascist Rome.

The attempt to convert the city into symbol encouraged grandiosity. Armando Brasini, an early favourite of Mussolini and resident architect at il Vittoriano from 1924, had proposed a major reshaping of Rome before 1922. He was encouraged by Mussolini to imagine an ambitious monumentalization of the city's centre (Marcello 2017; Kallis 2012). Brasini (1925) proposed a huge new piazza, called the Foro Mussolini, that would unite the Pantheon, piazza Colonna, the fontana di Trevi and the palazzo Montecitorio. It was described as the *umbilicus urbis novae*, a new symbolic centre of empire (Brasini 1979: 76).

Figure 4.5 Brasini's (1925) plan for piazza Colonna.

Brasini also proposed pushing a new through road across the city, starting at the ponte Milvio in the north, entering the old city through a new Foro Pinciano alongside piazza del Popolo, stretching to the Augusteo and a Nuovo Foro dedicated to the house of Savoy, passing a new Arco di Trionfo alle Vittorie d'Italia, to turn alongside the palazzo Borghese and join a new via Vaticana. The road then bifurcated with the easterly branch running to the Pantheon and the new Foro Mussolini before heading to the city walls at San Giovanni in Laterano. The westerly branch was to run out alongside the Tiber. This via Imperiale was to be 1.4 km long and 40 m wide. These new roads would have turned Rome into a processional way (Brasini 1979: 7–98).

The levels of destruction envisaged in Brasini's master plan were prohibitive. The *piano regolatore* of 1931 was radical enough, envisaging the widening of roads along the north-south lines of the old city and planning to make the piazza Augusteo a significant traffic hub for the northern central sector of the city. The planning commission included establishment architects and archaeologists, such as Corrado Ricci, Antonio Muñoz, Marcello Piacentini and Gustavo Giovannoni, who were conscious of the cultural consequences of major urbanistic interventions (Baxa 2004).

The replanning of the centre of the city was an exercise in totalitarian state power. Its point, in part, was the performance of that power. Fascism's urbanists attempted to turn the city into a single period site in which the Classical and contemporary were fused into the mythic everlasting now of fascist ultranationalism. Such hubristic plans matched perfectly the regime's sense of its global historical importance.

New Romes

It was evident by 1931 that any plan to produce the complete fascist cityscape would be the work of generations. Delivering the required theatrical settings would be much quicker on a new site. Various schemes around the city were demonstrating the potential of such an approach. These schemes enabled ideological cityscapes to be created without interfering further with Rome's architectural heritage (Marcello 2017). Piacentini suggested a new Rome to the east of the existing city. His plan would leave the old city in 'tranquillity' and provide for an extended archaeological park. The new city would have a monumental Foro Littorio, grand avenues and governmental and cultural centres. His envisaged city conformed to late nineteenth-century urbanism (Piacentini 1925; Vannelli 2010). But fascist Rome required a more radical style.

The Foro Mussolini was constructed in the north of the city in a riverine wetland across the ponte Duca d'Aosta (Painter 2005: 40–9). Work began in 1928 under the direction of Enrico del Debbio and continued after 1935 under the direction of Luigi Moretti. It had several distinct buildings with different architects but the whole was designed to provide a unified aspect. Some of those buildings have become text-book examples of Rationalist design, such as Moretti's casa delle armi (Gentile 2007: 104) and the *colonia elioterapica* on the nearby Monte Mario, which was a therapeutic sun-house and swimming pool.[6] The use of concrete and glass, the large open interior spaces, the blank façades and open aspects, the studied geometry and combination of flat and curved surfaces are archetypal of modernist and Rationalist design. The Rationalist spaces were frequently decorated with Ostian-style Classical mosaics. There was a distinct Classicism across the site in the clarity of architectural and monumental forms, the decorative features and the borrowings from villa architecture (Ciucci 1989). Foro Mussolini was a park-garden-villa complex for youth with a focus on sport, militarism and the party.

The Foro Italico provided a ceremonial entry to the complex. It exploited an extended vista from the ponte Duca d'Aosta into the heart of the site. The entry point is marked by a white obelisk inscribed 'MUSSOLINI DUX'. The obelisk stands at the end of a processional way which is framed by low cuboid markers. These look like statue bases, but further verticals which would have competed with the obelisk. Instead, they are left as blocks onto which fascist slogans were inscribed. The visitor is drawn to the fontana del Globo. This was composed of a white globe set in a shallow basin decorated with more black-and-white Ostian-style mosaics. Water ran across the surface of the globe. The composition emphasized primary coloration (black and white) and simple geometric design with the verticality of the obelisk leading to the linearity of the avenue, framed with the inscribed cubes, and culminating in the circular fountain and its spherical centrepiece. In the contemporary photographic guide to the Foro (*Foro Mussolini* 1937), the primal forms recall the mythic, uncanny emptiness of a De Chirico landscape. The floor mosaic voices youth's sinister commitment to the leader: 'DUCE LA NOSTRA GIOVINEZZA A VOI DEDICIAMO' ('Duce, we dedicate our youth to you').

The stadio dei marmi (Stadium of Marbles) sits to the north of the Foro Italico and slightly off-line from the processional way. It is a small athletic circuit on the model of a Classical amphitheatre. The marbles are fifty-five statues of athletes. These are slightly raised above the stadio floor by nine shallow steps. Each is raised further on a low base. The statues are of nude male athletes in heavily muscled Hellenistic form. The mythology of fascism extended from its historical unification with imperial Rome, through the utopian architectural form, to the hypermasculine body.

Figure 4.6 The Foro Italico (Foro Mussolini 1937).

The university of La Sapienza was provided with a grand new campus in 1932–5. This was designed by a team of architects led by Piacentini. The new campus linked Rationalist and Classical styles in the manner promised by Piacentini in his 1931 newspaper article. Arnaldo Foschini designed the main entrance. This is a Rationalist interpretation of a distinctly Classical form, a propylaeum, formed by six rectangular pillars between two flanking blocks. The central building is the Rettorato, which was

Figure 4.7 Stadio dei marmi (Foro Mussolini 1937).

designed by Piacentini. The building has an imposing grandeur generated by its height, 25.2 m from floor to roof, and its 179 m regular façade. That façade centres on a porch raised from a piazza on a 28 m wide flight of steps. The porch comprises four squared pillars that stretch to the full height of the building. The porch frames a statue of Minerva, with shield and spear, by Arturo Martini.[7]

The interior was adorned by Mario Sironi's mural *L'Italia tra le Arti e le Scienze* (1935), which has become something of a classic of fascist art. It was sufficiently discomforting after 1945 that it was painted over. The mural was not thereby destroyed, and it was restored in 2017 and became a focal point in the on-going disputes in Italy over the legacies of fascism. Simultaneously, its political power is denied and confined to history and lauded by right-wing figures as an essential and valued element in Italy's cultural heritage. Right-wing politicians proclaim fascism's death, while repeating fascist slogans and admiring fascist art (Bodenschatz 2020).

Sironi's early urban landscapes captured an industrial desolation that was the perceived battlefield of the fascist street fighting of 1918–22 (Antliff 2002; Braun 2000; Ferrari 1998a; 1998b). In his fascistic period, Sironi's art focused on the mythic and symbolic. His irregular figures, often personifications, seem as if they had been hewn from the rocky environments in which they are set. They are elemental and timeless (Braun 1996; Schnapp 2004; Antliff 2002). The use of Classical symbols, such as standards, columns and clothing, and Latin labels, as deployed in the *La Giustizia tra la Legge, la Forza e la Verità* (1936) from the palazzo di Giustizia, Milan, connect the fascist contemporary to the Classical.[8] *Il Lavoro Fascista* at the palazzo del' Informazione, Milan, combines Sironi's particular non-naturalistic, figurative style with Classical personifications of Iustitia, Lex, and Victoria. Classical Rome is represented by a Dioscoros and horse, an eagle and a Classical column. An archaic Italian figure and accompanying dog are set alongside Eve and Adam. In the centre a bald masculine stylisation of Mussolini offers a prayer towards Italia who points to the fascist slogan '*Credere, Obbedire, Combattere*' ('Believe, Obey, Fight').[9] The style contrasts markedly with Augustan Classicism and the smooth perfections of the parallel Italia frieze on the Ara Pacis and yet embeds Classical motifs in its modernist mythic representation.

The largest fascist project was EUR '42 which was situated on a marshy, green-field site to the south-west of Rome. Like the Foro Mussolini, individual architectural projects were blended into an overall aesthetic under the supervision of Piacentini. The aesthetic drew on villa architecture, particularly in the large water features. The formal unity of the site was provided by long vistas and a grid-plan redolent of the new town designs from the Agro Pontino which in turn echoed Roman military encampments. In style, the Rationalism took a Classical form. Italy was labouring under economic constraints and a shortage of steel required the architects to avoid long spans and very high buildings. The arch and colonnade were attractive means of overcoming such constraints. Yet, whatever the technical constraints, the recollection of Classicism was evidently central to the aesthetic.

The design was quasi-colonial. It symbolized the state's ability to create *de novo* an ordered urban environment (Fuller 1996). It was display architecture, attempting to fulfil

Mussolini's wish for a Rome inspiring for a global audience. The 440-hectare site was intended for the World Exhibition. Mussolini had secured the right to hold the exhibition in 1936. The Esposizione Universale di Roma (EUR) was initially planned for 1941 but was delayed so that it could become the centrepiece in celebrations of the twentieth anniversary of the 1922 coup (Kallis 2016). The new show-city would monumentalize the historical achievements of Mussolini (Notaro 2000). The modern Augustus was constructing a technocratic Rationalist and Classical future. It was urbanism at its most propagandistic (Muntoni 1995).

The brochure for EUR advertised fascist universalism, proclaiming a will to progress, peace and faith in the future (*Esposizione universale* 1939: 16). Such modernizing sentiments contrast with the frontispiece which is a stylized image of Classical sculptural and architectural fragments in ruins. The new Rome was also fundamentally the Rome of ruins, a correlation that suggested the historical and cultural significance of EUR as a site of future ruination. The site was advertised as a *mimesis* of imperial Rome, a central stage for Mussolini's re-presentation of the fascist unity with its Classical predecessor, but without any sign of the existential angst that had gripped other modern ruin-gazers or practitioners of imperial *mimesis*.

EUR was linked to the old city by road. The viale Imperiale was intended to run from the central piazza Imperiale in EUR, now piazza Guglielmo Marconi, to the Foro Mussolini. Thus, the two new fascist centres could have been seen as 'framing' the old city to the north and south, even though the distances between the two sites made their connectivity notional rather than real (Testa 1971).

Figure 4.8 Colonnade of the museo della civiltà romana, EUR.

Fascist Rome: Scenes of Fantasy, 1922–1943

EUR employed a variety of stylistic elements but managed to assimilate Rationalist and Classical features. In some cases, individual buildings exhibited a Classical gigantism. The Museo della civiltà romana was part of the original scheme for EUR. There was a need for a new museum to hold the exhibits collected for the *mostra augustea*. Its main feature is an immense colonnade designed by Pietro Aschieri and Gino Peressutti, which effectively provided a boundary to EUR. The massively tall columns are pressed together to create a narrowing effect that reduces the human scale. If we read the column in a Vitruvian sense as a representation of the human, the pedestrian is diminished and overawed in the presence of giants.

The palazzo dell'Archivio dello Stato, designed by Mario De Renzi, Luigi Figini and Gino Pollini is similarly grandiose. These three were leading Rationalist architects. The frontage is composed of two colonnaded storeys composed of plain columns. In the main building the upper colonnade is matched by a lower colonnade of square pillars. The Rationalist simplicity is given grandeur by the extension and repetition of the form in a way which recalls Burke's discussion of the architectural sublime.

Arnaldo Foschini, who had designed the propylaeum at La Sapienza, was the lead architect on the Basilica dei Santi Pietro e Paolo. The design combined traditional and non-traditional elements. It was based on a central cube with a cupola which was extended to a cruciform by porch structures. This gave the building multiple lines of symmetry. The plain externals are in contrast to its prominent location on the raised ground above EUR and at the end of one the longest vistas of the town. Perhaps more

Figure 4.9 Vista from the Basilica dei Santi Pietro e Paolo.

Classicism and the Construction of Capital Cities

significant than its architecture was the presence of a church in the secular utopia of the fascist city. The basilica referenced the cultural contribution of Christian Rome to the grand and unified narrative of Italian civilization and Mussolini's *rapprochement* with the Pope.

The palazzo degli Uffici was one of the first buildings to be finished on the site. Designed by Gaetano Minnucci, it featured characteristic square form columns which were used to create a long colonnade that opens onto a small piazza with a pool and fountain. The building is notable primarily for its décor, particularly a sculpted frieze depicting the building of Rome by Publio Morbiducci. The frieze offers an interpretation of Roman history. The first layer depicts the building of Classical Rome and the second Renaissance Rome. The third layer centres on Mussolini himself. He is at the centre of the arrangement on a horse and in full military uniform, giving the Roman salute. He is surrounded by children and three women in traditional dress, builders and soldiers. Behind are fascistic symbols, il Vittoriano and various flags. Mussolini is central to this Roman history of masculine heroism and Roman reconstruction and the spirit of *romanità*.

The architectural highlight of EUR is the palazzo della Civiltà italiana. It is an iconic building formed by a run of nine arches repeated across six floors and contained within a simple cuboid frame. Its architectural quotation of the Colosseum sits in a high Rationalist design. It's repeating open arches establish an aesthetic of emptiness, as if the building is already a ruin without function except as a symbol of the age. The lack of

Figure 4.10 La terza Roma relief, EUR.

functionality enhances its otherworldliness. It is pure symbol, and this purity had made it attractive for artists and filmmakers, sometimes contrasting its cold aesthetic with vibrant human forms. Its current use as the headquarters for the high fashion group Fendi seems particularly apposite. The association with the hyper-wealthy as consumers of the brand and through the parent company, LMVH, owned by one of the world's richest individuals, Bernand Arnault, creates an aura of unreal and unwordly wealth that mirrors its aesthetic isolation (Somma 2020). As in the Foro Italico, the eerie unreality of the building echoes De Chirico cityscapes in a mythic separation from the everyday (Loncar 2020). Although the political heritage of the building is studiously ignored by its new occupants, they cannot be unaware of its heritage and the parallel between exclusive fashion and the fascist dominance of the symbol are evident. It is difficult to escape the conclusion that the fashion house is playing a similar game of covert associations to that practised by politicians of the far right.

The building carries the inscription 'Un popolo di poeti, di artisti, di eroi, di santi, di pensatori, di scienziati, di navigatori, di trasmigratori' ('A people of poets, of artists, of heroes, of saints, of thinkers, of scientists, of navigators, of migrators'). On the ground floor, there is a sequence of statues personifying the achievements of the Italian people. Some are Classical: there is a version of Augustus and huge statues of the Dioscori and their horses. Architecture stands among her sister sciences carrying in her right hand a model of the palazzo itself, presumably her finest achievement. The superhuman bodies are hypermasculine and hyperfeminine, idealizations in the perfect world being constructed.

Figure 4.11 Palazzo della Civiltà italiana, EUR.

Classicism and the Construction of Capital Cities

EUR is utopian architecture. But it is not a utopia of community and domesticity. The human scale is unfit for its ambition. Architectural gigantism features in individual buildings with their too high columns, and in the ordered vistas and regular, repeating architectural forms. Despite the variety of architects involved, uniformity extends to the urban environment. The monumentality identifies fascist Rome with the Renaissance and Classical city. EUR proclaims its antiquity in its modernity.

The aesthetics come over today as representing an absence. This is ideological architecture that functions as a billboard for a regime that has passed. Its claims are hollow, but they always were. The dominance exercised by the symbolic gives the uncomfortable impression that one is walking around someone else's fevered dream of the world as it should be and would be if only reality could be made to submit. The architectural imposition is an attempt to overcome this reluctant reality, to advertise fascist Italy to the world, and to make people believe the myth.

A summation

The fascist remodelling of Rome appears to be a limit case in the application of the Classical aesthetic to modern urbanism. Although many of the ideas within fascism can be traced back into the nineteenth century and the parallels with other urban interventions are evident, the fascist view of history and society was unusual. In particular, whereas the Classical aesthetic had been seen in other instances to have a timeless quality that reflected civilizational achievement and excellence, this was transformed in fascism into a fundamental denial of all historical processes. The fascist city was a triumph of ideology over reality in which the symbolic was dominant. The success of fascism was in persuading or pressurizing so many to engage with its myth. The failure of the fascist city was also the failure of that ideology. The totalitarian ideologies of the twentieth century were stories which told the people what the world meant. They demanded that the people commit to a particular understanding of history. The aesthetics were a way of trying to make a reality of that understanding. Standing in a particular place at a specific time and only looking in a certain direction, the cityscape manifested the symbols of the world as the fascists hoped it to be. The fascists then asked their audience to believe that was how the world in its totality must be, irrespective of any contrary evidence. Even if Italian fascist ideology continues to be powerful, the failure of the regime exposed its fantastical nature. What remained were its symbols, as eerie bombastic spectres of a failed ideology.

EPILOGUE: CLASSICISM AND AUTHORITARIANSIM

Each of the major urban renewals covered in this book were imagined, planned and built by social and intellectual elites who were convinced that they were delivering a city which, if not ideal, was at least improved. Their urban interventions displayed specific ideological values and assumptions that were informed by their conceptions of an ideal society. Even if those developments attracted significant levels of local support, they faced some opposition and that opposition intensified over time. Ideological difference was a significant element in that opposition. Not everyone shared the same social vision and in some instances that vision was overtaken by social change.

Architecture represents ideology in a manner different from that of texts. Although one can reject a book, it is difficult to ignore a cityscape. Architecture shapes social interactions and imposes a symbolic system on citizens. Large-scale urban interventions have world-building aspirations (Sudjic 2006). However, social formations are not determined by architecture. The production of citizens and cities is multifaceted and affected by economic, social, cultural and political circumstances. Attempts to impress the citizenry into a desired form acknowledge the currently unfulfilled nature of that aspiration. The imposition of the new urban form is an authoritarian expression in opposition to existing social forms.

All major utopian interventions manifest in a substantive separation from the social and cultural realities of their cities. In the case of Classicizing cities, this gap was enhanced by specific historical associations. The identification with their Classical models was inevitably incomplete. By the early nineteenth century, there was no realistic expectation that modernity would be Classical in society, economy or politics. The new capitals were a historical fantasy. The risk of the buildings seeming out of place was mitigated by whole areas of cities being dominated by these Classical forms. But the signification was also a reference to the unreal: the *rus in urbe* and the class isolationism of London, the Athenian colonial separations, il Vittoriano, and the fantasies of history and power in fascist Rome. These projects worked partially in their isolation from the everyday and their projections of a city and nation that differed from the predominant political and social structures.

French architectural theorists asserted a universalism in Classicism through an understanding of beauty that transcended history. States and architects behaved as if architecture would generate political forms through the shaping of social interactions and the education of citizens. Since such ideal societal and aesthetic forms were supposedly rational and could be determined philosophically, those forms were seen as universal. Architecture conjoined the aesthetic and the political since the urban form was inherently political and gave representation to the city and, in the case of capitals, the nation. To oppose such forms was to oppose rationality, modernity and civilization, but to impose such forms suggested a singular and timeless form for rationality, modernity and civilization. That singular form embedded and attempted to render permanent a particular cultural and political order with its associated distribution of power and resources.

By the early nineteenth century, Classicism was acknowledged as the international style even as it was used for national self-expression. As such, it represented the relatively coherent ideology of colonial Occidentalism and an assertion of the superiority of that style over regional 'vernacular' architectural forms. Its positioning within the new republic of the US was in association with the Enlightenment neo-Roman political thought that drove the revolution and the constitutional foundation of the state (Sonne 2003; Madison and Hamilton 2017; Hammer 2008). It worked because the Classical truths were supposedly self-evident and in spite of the diversity of political forms to which those truths were applied. They could cover democratic America, oligarchic Britain, colonial Athens, liberal Italy, and fascist Rome. Colonial and imperial adoptions represented Occidental civilization, modernity and global capitalism. The extension of capitalism generated class associations when they were not already integral to the politics of the adoption of Classicisizing architectures. In the twentieth century, Soviet, Nazi and Italian fascist usages added a further authoritarian layer.

This intellectual archaeology does not suggest naivety on the part of architects nor a repeated, independent rediscovery of an original Classicism. Architects were conscious of the traditions in which they worked. Similarly, contemporary architects are conscious of the political associations of their stylistic choices. They cannot be innocent of the legacy of fascist appropriations of the Classical even if some pretend to be (Krier 1985; de la Ruffinière du Prey 1994: 265–80). These political associations partially explain why Classicism fell from fashion after 1945 and perhaps why it returns. An evidently reactionary Classicism can be detected in the arcades of Paternoster Square, London (various architects, *c*. 2000), the various townscapes of the American New Urbanism (Seaside, Celebration, McKenzie Town), Philip Johnson's Town Hall for Celebration, Florida (1996) and King Charles's Poundbury, Dorchester (Conn 2014: 277–306; Alston 2015). In such places, social and aesthetic modernity is resisted by the supposed solidity of tradition (Charles 1989). Classicism gives shape to the politics of radical social conservatism (Krier 1981; 2009).[1] The point of antique origin was always present, and always revered, but it is facile to ignore the accumulation of modern political associations, an act of forgetting that edits out much of the modern history of urbanism.

The repeated attraction of the Classical to more authoritarian regimes is notable and yet it is *prime facie* difficult to see an inherently fascistic content to a Classical column (Scobie 1990). There is a fundamental methodological objection to reading back from the fascist use of the form to earlier instances. The issue is made more complicated by architectural theorists asserting the transhistorical value of Classicism and eliding the differences between their own ages and cities and those of the Classical era. But, and obviously, the various social and political systems that supported authoritarian regimes were structured in their own eras and were not primarily intellectual responses to a

Epilogue: Classicism and Authoritarianism

Classical reception. Throughout, I have been anxious to locate the adoption of Classicizing urban forms within precise historical and cultural contexts and demonstrate how those circumstances inflected a particular urban intervention. We can discern a connecting thread in the reception of Classics and the politics of the city that stretches from nineteenth-century London to twentieth-century Rome. This thread tells us very little about the politics of architecture in the Classical period. The Classical uses of architectural style might have resonances with modern instances but would never have the same meanings.

History is a narrative in search of a meaningful ending. It is experienced without foreknowledge of that ending. The Enlightenment saw its itself as liberatory. It inspired the French Revolution and justified colonial imperialism. One can find elements of fascism and authoritarian populism in much post-Enlightenment political thought (Sternhall 1994; Laqueur 1996; Urbinati 2019). Yet, to understand the concentration camps as the inevitable outcome of the Enlightenment, as seems to be implied by Agamben (1998), is to see history as heavily determined by ideology and to ignore specific ideological and material circumstances that gave rise to fascist and ultranationalist ideologies.

Classical reception does not communicate units of fixed meaning (ideas, artefacts, texts and histories) to a receiving society. Interpretations of the prior cultural artefact will vary considerably. Furthermore, in different periods and societies, what people looked for in Classical culture changed. Different Classical texts were more popular in some period than others and even if the same texts were read, they were often read in different ways and for different ideas. Reception is shaped by the needs and concerns of the receiving community. Nevertheless, Classicism does not provide a menu of empty symbols which could be turned to any narrative purpose. There is always an original content or even a history of interpretation that cannot be assimilated or denied completely. Those histories can disrupt any appropriation.

Each version of the cities here discussed was an experiment in unreality that imagined the cities as the powerful wished them to become. Francesco Proto (2003) suggests that architecture is a dazzling mechanism to disappear reality. Architectural fixity is always in competition with social, economic and cultural vibrancy. In London, economic forces generated the social insecurities that the Regent Street development was designed to combat. Yet, history continued. The Victorian men in black replaced the dandies (Harvey 1997). Post-*risorgimento* Rome could never quite become Sella's bourgeois capital (Agnew 2010). The traces of a colonial dynamic are visible in the street plan of Athens, but Athens is a city many times transformed since the 1840s. Even EUR, which retains an unsettling affect, has its communities and vibrancy. Wandering its vistas one Saturday afternoon, I ended up a spectator at a water-polo festival. Families picnicked and played on the grassy verges of the lake. Cafés and restaurants provided lunches. The fascist utopian vision housed a living community seemingly oblivious to the landscape of signs.

There is little that would make one suspect that the urban designers were conscious of their hubris. Indeed, these urban ideological statements have shown remarkable resilience to economic, political and historical realities. The assertions of permanence were seemingly unaware that their foundational distributions of socio-economic power were temporary in the face of modernity's transformations. The buildings made natural an order that was inevitably temporary and hence associated that order with a conservatism that has frequently been reactionary. Classicism, which was introduced to represent a new order, has frequently provided the aesthetic code and an ideological support that has resisted threats to a conservative social and cultural order. It carries implications of purity, fixity and a blindness to history. Even if the falls of Classical civilizations were spectral presences in the hubristic appropriations of Classical architecture, Classicism implied a timelessness for a social order and an end to history. Classicism was perceived as essential to Western civilization and made that civilization's predominance seemingly transhistorical. That association of a current world order with an ancient counterpart was a useful story in the nineteenth century and for many it remains useful.

The appropriation of the Classical in urban architectural form makes a claim to civilizational essentialism. It sets out a particular ordering of the city as having timeless and absolute value. The aesthetic was both a mode through which power was expressed and a claim to power. Opposition was the barbarian at the gates who threatened not a redistribution of political and economic resources but an end to civilization. Classicism shielded the particular and contingent arrangements of power behind the symbolism of civilizational excellence. Whatever the distribution of political and economic resources, the Classical aesthetic laid claim to that distribution being civilizational and normative: this arrangement was the world as it ever was, or rather as it ever should have been since in each of our instances, Classicism was fundamental to a reform of an existing urban order that was judged inadequate. Even if Classicism was seen as symbolic of the new, the modern and the revolutionary, it was always to a degree conservative and authoritarian and in denial of the workings of history. It was identified with established social and political hegemonies. Particularly when the cultural references were Roman, the imperial authoritarian associations eased the transference of ancient aesthetic symbols into modern aesthetic regimes. The appropriation of the Classical was almost always a claim for excellence and a tactic to exclude those who were perceived as not exhibiting that excellence, whether that other be the lower class of London, the Greeks under a Bavarian king, or those colonized by an imperial nation. Such associations and tactical deployments explain why Classicism has so often been attractive to authoritarian conservatives.

Modern attempts to fix urban relations through a Classical aesthetic inevitably failed. The fascination of cities is their sociological complexity. They are foci of intense human endeavour. They are vibrant, confusing, and contradictory. To fix them in history is to deny that vibrancy and turn them into the billboards of a particular symbolic order. Cities can always be improved, but they will always move on, ruin upon ruin, into a future that cannot be determined by the precarious power of the present or the past.

NOTES

1 London: A Civil Society, 1800–1820

1. Figures for pre-1801 London are estimates but based on relatively good demographic data. See Finlay (1981: 51–69).
2. This figure is lower than that in the census for 1821.
3. Data from Clark 2002.
4. Stuart and Revett 1762.
5. Stuart and Revett 1787; 1794; 1816.
6. Watkin 1996: 1, claims that Soane had no coherent theory of architecture, but Soane appears to adhere to Laugier's views.
7. http://collections.soane.org/object-m1298; http://collections.soane.org/object-sc1.
8. See Arnold 2000: 25 and Arnold 2005 on the development of a landscape of rural urbanism.
9. See, for instance, Stewart's 'follies' on the Anson estate at Shugborough, such as the Athenian Tower of the Winds and the Arch of Hadrian.
10. http://collections.soane.org/object-p267.
11. https://artsandculture.google.com/asset/john-martin-the-fall-of-babylon-a-mezzotint-with-etching/wQFIF5e1q8uk8w.
12. The manuscript is entitled *Crude Hints towards an History of my House in L.I. Fields* and is transcribed and annotated in Richardson 1999.
13. This is one of the main theses of Colley 1992.
14. Appian, *Punica* 132 in which Scipio supposedly quotes *Iliad* 6. 448–9; Polybius, *Apophthegmata*, p. 200. See the discussion of ruin-gazing in Hell 2019.
15. Macaulay 1850: IV 97 in a review of von Ranke's history of the Papacy published in October 1840, imagined a visitor from New Zealand sketching the ruins of London. This was the inspiration for Gustav Doré's famous sketch of a Maori sketching London's ruins. Macaulay's point was to juxtapose the failures of temporal power with the successes of the spiritual powers exercised by the popes.
16. See Bergdoll 2000: 43 for further discussion.
17. Bill for Communications 1813: clauses Y and Z.
18. *Report from the Select Committee* 1828: 103–10. Annual rental incomes would not have come close to covering a commercial rate of interest on the investment.
19. On the picturesque and the illusory in Nash's developments, see Crook 1992.
20. See Arnold 2000: 37–9, for the shift in understanding the city.
21. https://www.collections.soane.org/ARC10637.

Notes to pp. 48–91

22. https://www.rct.uk/collection/918029/designs-for-public-improvements-in-london-westminster-design-for-a-royal-palace-to.
23. http://collections.soane.org/object-p85.
24. http://collections.soane.org/THES74344.
25. https://collections.britishart.yale.edu/catalog/tms:12035.
26. Shaw, however, had investments in the slave plantations, see https://www.ucl.ac.uk/lbs/person/view/2146666253; https://www.historyofparliamentonline.org/volume/1790-1820/member/shaw-benjamin-1770-1843.
27. This trope continued into the twentieth century, see Raban 1976.
28. *View of London* 1804. I presume that the text is plagiarized.
29. On Egan's account, see Rendell 2002.
30. Compare Walkowitz 1992.
31. These Commissioners' Churches were built following a special grant of Parliament after the Battle of Waterloo. For a list of the these churches, many of the which were built in Gothic style (especially those outside London), see https://en.wikipedia.org/wiki/Lists_of_Commissioners%27_churches.

2 Athens: The Colonization of Greece, 1830–1846

1. Hemans wrote on a variety of patriotic and imperial themes and on female behaviour. For examples of her work, see 'The Call of Liberty. May 1809' (https://www.poemhunter.com/poem/the-call-of-liberty-may-1809/) and 'The Domestic Affections' (https://www.poemhunter.com/poem/the-domestic-affections/).
2. See Ary Scheffer, *Les femmes Suliotes* (Musée du Louvre, Inv. 7857) (1827), (http://cartelfr.louvre.fr/cartelfr/visite?srv=obj_view_obj&objet=cartel_22752_24037_p0006232.001.jpg_obj.html&flag=true); Claude Pinet, *The Dance of Zalongou* (1803) (Benaki Museum) and Constance Blanchard, *Femmes grecques de Souli courant à la mort* (1838) (Musée des Augustins, Toulouse: inv. 2004.1.91). The incident also gave rise to a 'the dance of Zalongo' which is memorialized in a 1954 sculpture by George Zongolopoulos.
3. References from Byron (1986). *Childe Harold's Pilgrimage* I and II were published first in 1812, with III coming in 1816 and IV in 1818.
4. See also, 'Stanzas Written in Passing the Ambracian Gulf, November 14, 1809'.
5. See Peter Cochran's discussion of the poem at https://petercochran.files.wordpress.com/2009/03/mediterranean_poems.pdf and Byron's letter to Hobhouse of 25 September 1810, from Patras (at https://petercochran.files.wordpress.com/2010/06/byron-and-hobhouse-11.pdf).
6. Facsimile edition at http://www.hellenicparliament.gr/UserFiles/f3c70a23-7696-49db-9148-f24dce6a27c8/syn06.pdf.
7. https://commons.wikimedia.org/wiki/File:Official_entrance_of_king_Otto_and_queen_Amalia_in_Athens_1837.jpg.
8. Two calendrical systems operated in Greece in much of this period and in what follows both dates are often given.
9. https://en.wikipedia.org/wiki/File:Jean_Koletti.jpg and http://www.culture.gouv.fr/Wave/image/joconde/0639/m507704_97de17149_p.jpg.

Notes to pp. 91–175

10. https://nhmuseum.gr/en/departments/into-the-museum-s-collection/item/5042-portraitofkit sostzavelasoilpaintingoncanvasbythdrakos.
11. Greek State Archives, Ministry of the Interior, Otto Archive, file 220. Reproduced with photograph by Bastéa (2000: 71) with discussion in Biris (2005: 23).
12. Peter von Hess, *The Entry of King Othon of Greece in Athens* (1839) (Neue Pinakothek, Munich). https://commons.wikimedia.org/wiki/File:Peter_von_Hess_-_The_Entry_of_King_Othon_of_Greece_in_Athens_-_WGA11387.jpg.
13. https://commons.wikimedia.org/wiki/File:Akropolis_by_Leo_von_Klenze.jpg#/media/File:Akropolis_by_Leo_von_Klenze.jpg.
14. It is present in Christian Hansen's drawing of that year.
15. http://www.getty.edu/art/collection/objects/792/leo-von-klenze-landscape-with-the-castle-of-massa-di-carrara-german-1827/ at the Getty Museum; https://commons.wikimedia.org/wiki/File:Leo_von_Klenze_Salvatorkirche_und_Walhalla.jpg; at the Neue Pinakothek in Munich, see https://commons.wikimedia.org/wiki/File:Akropolis_by_Leo_von_Klenze.jpg
16. The population rose to 150,000 by the end of the century and 453,042 by 1920, before the great influx of refugees in 1922 (Papageorgiou-Venetas 1970: 11; Wassenhoven 1984).
17. I am grateful to Avra Xepapadakou and to Kostas Kardamis for their help in discussing early theatre in Athens.

3 Rome: City of Unity, 1870–1911

1. https://www.metmuseum.org/art/collection/search/440363.
2. http://www.archiviocapitolinorisorsedigitali.it/piante/372.htm.
3. https://www.bopen.eu/nolli_imgs/nollimap.html.
4. See the letters and articles in Soprintendenza per i beni ambientali e architettonici del Lazio 1986: II 58 from Ugo Ojetti; 58–9 from the sculptor Salvatore Grita; and 69–70 from the architect Luca Beltrami.

4 Fascist Rome: Scenes of Fantasy, 1922–1943

1. https://upload.wikimedia.org/wikipedia/commons/3/33/Manifesto_futurismo_Le_Figaro.jpg.
2. https://www.futurismo.org/architettura-futurista/.
3. https://it.wikipedia.org/wiki/Casa_del_Fascio_(Como).
4. https://chicagology.com/centuryprogress/1933fair51/. https://www.flaviamarcello.com/innovation-heritage.
5. See also Mafai's *The Roman Forum* (1930) which has a wild natural landscape imposing itself on the historical vista.
6. https://archidiap.com/opera/colonia-elioterapica/.
7. https://web.uniroma1.it/polomuseale/rettoratostoriaprogetto.
8. https://www.wikiart.org/en/mario-sironi/justice-between-the-law-and-the-force-1936/.
9. https://it.wikipedia.org/wiki/File:Palazzo_dell%27informazione,_Mario_Sironi,_Il_lavoro_fascista_01.jpg.

187

Note to p. 182

Epilogue: Classicism and Authoritariansim

1. See the latest round of argument in https://cdn.vox-cdn.com/uploads/chorus_asset/file/19700169/Draft_of_Trump_White_House_Executive_Order_on_Federal_Buildings.pdf.

BIBLIOGRAPHY

About, E. (1883), *La Grèce contemporaine*, Paris: Nachette.
Acciaresi, P. (1920), *Giuseppe Sacconi e il suo monumento a Vittorio Emanuelle II*, Rome: Tipografia Salesian.
Ackermann, R. (1808–10), *The Microcosm of London*, London: Ackermann's Repository of Arts.
Adamson, W. (2001), 'Avant-Garde Modernism and Italian Fascism: Cultural Politics in the Era of Mussolini', *Journal of Modern Italian Studies* 6: 230–48.
Adembri, B. (2000), *Hadrian's Villa*, Milan: Electa.
Agamben, G. (1998), *Homo Sacer: Sovereign Power and Bare Life*, translated by D. Heller-Roazen, Stanford: Stanford University Press.
Agnew, J. (2010), '"Ghosts of Rome": The Haunting of Fascist Efforts at Remaking Rome as Italy's Capital City', *Annali D'Italianistica* 28: 179–98.
Ainslie, R. (1836), *The Present State and Claims of London*, London: L. and G. Seeley.
Alston, R. (2010), 'Dialogues in Imperialism: Rome, Britain, and India', in E. Hall and P. Vasunia (eds), *India, Greece and Rome: 1757–2007*, 51–77 (*Bulletin of the Institute of Classics Studies*, Supplement), London: Institute of Classical Studies.
Alston, R. (2012), 'Class Cities: Classics, Utopianism, Classics and Urban Planning in Early-Twentieth-Century Britain', *Journal of Historical Geography* 38: 263–72.
Alston, R. (2015), 'The Space of Politics: Classics, Utopia, and the Defence of Order', in H. Stead and E. Hall (eds), *Greek and Roman Classics in the British Struggle for Social Reform*, 183–96, London: Bloomsbury.
Ambulator (1782), *The Ambulator or the Stranger's Companion in a Tour Round London*, London: J. Bew.
Anderson, B. (2006), *Imagined Communities: Reflections on the Origin and Spread of Nationalism*, London: Verso.
Andreotti, L. (2005), 'The Art of War: Mario Sironi and the Exhibition of the Fascist Revolution', *Architectural Theory Review* 10: 81–92.
Andreotti, L. (2010), 'The Techno-aesthetics of Shock: Mario Sironi and the Exhibition of the Fascist Revolution', in G. Hartoonian (ed.), *Walter Benjamin and Architecture*, 93–122, London and New York, Routledge.
Angeli, D. (1932), 'Il piano regolatore di Roma', *Nuovo Antologia* 1440: 193–202.
Angelomatis-Tsougarakis, H. (1990), *The Eve of the Greek Revival: British Travellers' Perceptions of Early Nineteenth-century Greece*, London: Routledge.
Antliff, M. (2002), 'Fascism, Modernism, and Modernity', *The Art Bulletin* (New York, N.Y.) 84: 148–69.
Armstrong, R. H. (2006), *A Compulsion for Antiquity: Freud and the Ancient World* (Cornell Studies in the History of Psychiatry), Ithaca: Cornell University Press.
Arnold, D. (2000), *Re-Presenting the Metropolis: Architecture, Urban Experience and Social Life in London 1800–1840*, Aldershot and Burlington, VT: Ashgate.
Arnold, D. (2005), *Rural Urbanism: London Landscapes in the Early Nineteenth Century*, Manchester and New York: Manchester University Press.
Article V (1821), 'Article V: *Anastasius; or Memoirs of a Greek, written in the 18th century*', *The Edinburgh Review* 35.69: 92–102.

Bibliography

Arthurs, J. (2010), 'The Eternal Parasite: Anti-Romanism in Italian Politics and Culture since 1860', *Annali d'Italianistica* 28: 117–36.
Arthurs, J. (2017), 'Bathing in the Spirit of Eternal Rome: The *mostra Augustea della romanità*', in H. Roche and D. Kyriakos (eds), *Brill's Companion to the Classics, Fascist Italy and Nazi Germany*, 157–77, Leiden and Boston: Brill.
Atkinson, D. and D. Cosgrove (1998), 'Urban Rhetoric and Embodied Identities: City, Nation, and Empire at the Vittorio Emanuele II Monument in Rome, 1870–1945', *Annals of the Association of American Geographers* 88: 28–49.
Bachelard, G. (1958), *La Poétique de l'Espace*, Paris: Presses Universitaires de France.
Badema-Phountoulake, O. (2001), *Σταμάτης Κλεάνθης 1802–1862. Αρχιτέκτων, επιχειρηματίας, οροματιστής*, Athens: Demos Athenaion and Demos Velventou.
Baridon, L. (2008), 'L'Architecture de Ledoux: traité, utopie ou contre-utopie', in G. Chouquer and J.-C. Daumas (eds), *Autour de Ledoux: Architecture, Ville Et Utopie: Actes du Colloque International à la Saline Royale d'Arc-et-Senans, le 25, 26 et 27 octobre 2006*, 97–116 (Cahiers de la MSHE Ledoux, No 13), Besançon: Presses Universitaires de Franche-Comté.
Bastéa, E. (2000), *The Creation of Modern Athens: Planning the Myth*, New York and Cambridge: Cambridge University Press.
Bastl, B., U. Hirhager and E. Schober (eds) (2013), *Theophil Hansen: ein Resümee: Symposionsband anlässlich des 200. Geburtstage (Symposion Der Universitätsbibliothek Der Akademie Der Bildenden Künste Wien, Juni 2013)*, Weitra: Bibliothek der Provinz.
Baxa, P. (2004), 'Piacentini's Window: The Modernism of the Fascist Master Plan of Rome', *Contemporary European History* 13: 1–20.
Baxa, P. (2007), 'Capturing the Fascist Moment: Hitler's Visit to Italy in 1938 and the Radicalization of Fascist Italy', *Journal of Contemporary History* 42: 227–42.
Baxa, P. (2010), *Roads and Ruins: The Symbolic Landscape of Fascist Rome* (Toronto Italian Studies), Buffalo, NY: University of Toronto Press.
Bazin, R. (1894), *Les Italiens d'aujourd'hui*, Paris: Calmann Lévy.
Beaumont, M. (2012), *The Spectre of Utopia: Utopian and Science Fictions at the Fin de Siècle*, Oxford, Bern, Berlin, Bruxelles, Frankfurt am Main, New York, Wien: Peter Lang.
Beaton, R. (2013), *Byron's War: Romantic Rebellion, Greek Revolution*, Cambridge: Cambridge University Press.
Ben-Ghiat, R. (2001), *Fascist Modernities: Italy, 1922–1945*, Berkeley and London: University of California Press.
Benjamin, W. (1968), 'The Work of Art in the Age of Mechanical Reproduction', in W. Benjamin, *Illuminations*, 1–26, Hannah Arendt (ed.), New York: Schocken Books.
Berezin, M. (1997), *Making the Fascist Self: The Political Culture of Interwar Italy* (Wilder House Series in Politics, History, and Culture), Ithaca, NY and London: Cornell University Press.
Bergdoll, B. (2000), *European Architecture, 1750–1890*, Oxford: Oxford University Press.
Berggren, L. and L. Sjöstedt (1996), *L'Ombra dei Grandi: Monumentai e politica monumentale a Roma (1870–1895)*, Rome: Artemide Edizioni.
Berman, M. (1983), *All That Is Solid Melts into Air: The Experience of Modernity*, London: Verso.
Berry, H. (2002), 'Polite Consumption: Shopping in Eighteenth-Century England', *Transactions of the Royal Historical Society* 12: 375–94.
Bersezio, V. (1872), *Roma: La Capitale d'Italia*, Milan: Fratelli Treves.
Bill for Communications (1813), *A BILL [AS AMENDED BY THE COMMITTEE] 'FOR, Making a more convenient Communication from the Northern parts of The Metropolis, in the Parish of Saint Mary-le-Bone, to Charing Cross in the City of Westminster'*, London: House of Commons.
Billington, J. (1834), *The Architectural Director, being a guide to builders, draughtsmen, students and workmen in the study, design, and execution of architecture*, London: John Bennett.
Biris, Kostas H. (2005), *Αι Αθήναι από του 19ου εις τον 20ον αιώνα*, Athens: Oikos Melissa.

Bibliography

Biris, M. and M. Kardamisi-Adami (2001), *Νεοκλασική αρχιτεκτονική στην Ελλάδα*, Athens: Melissa, 2001.
Blaquière, E. (1824), *The Greek Revolution; Its Origin and Progress: Together with Some Remarks on the Religion, National Character, &c. in Greece. With a Map*, London: G. & W. B. Whittaker.
Blaquière, E. (1826), *Greece and Her Claims*, London: G. B. Whittaker, 1826.
Blok, A. (1972), 'The Peasant and the Brigand: Social Banditry Reconsidered', *Comparative Studies in Society and History* 14: 494–503.
Blok, A. (1974), *The Mafia of a Sicilian Village, 1860–1960: A Study of Violent Peasant Entrepreneurs*, Oxford: Blackwell.
Blondel, F. (1675), *Cours d'Architecture*, Paris: Lambert Roulland.
Bodenschatz, H. (2020), 'Urbanism, Architecture, and Dictatorship: Memory in Transition', in K. B. Jones, and S. Pilat (eds), *The Routledge Companion to Italian Fascist Architecture: Reception and Legacy*, 54–66, Abingdon and New York: Taylor & Francis Group.
Boito, C. (1880), *Architettura de Medio Evo in Italia*, Milan: Ulrico Hoepli Editore.
Borbein, A. H. (1979), 'Klassische Archäologie in Berlin vom 18. Bis zum 20. Jahrhundert', in W. Arenhövel and C. Schreiber (eds), *Berlin und die Antike: Architektur, Kunstgewerbe, Malerie, Skulptur, Theater und Wissenschaft vom 16. Jahrhundert bis heute*, I: 99–150, Berlin: Deutsches Archäologisches Institut.
Borsay, P. (1989), *The English Urban Renaissance: Culture and Society in the Provincial Town, 1660–1770*, Oxford: Clarendon Press.
Bothe, R. (1979), 'Antikenrezeption in Bauten und Entwürfen Berliner Architekten zwischen 1790 und 1870', in Wilmuth Arenhövel and Christa Schreiber (eds), *Berlin und die Antike: Architektur, Kunstgewerbe, Malerie, Skulptur, Theater und Wissenschaft vom 16. Jahrhundert bis heute*, II: 295–33, Berlin: Deutsches Archäologisches Institut.
Bottai, G. (1927), *Mussolini Costruttore d'Impero*, Mantua: Edizioni Paladino.
Bottai, G. (1992 [1938]), 'II Rinnovamento di Roma', in G. Bottai, *La Politica Delle Arti: Scritti 1918-1943*, 122–40, edited by Alessandro Masi, from *Nouvelles Litteraires*, 12 February, Roma: Editalia.
Bourdieu, P. (1979), 'The Kabyle House or the World Reversed', in Pierre Bourdieu, *Algeria 1960*, 133–53, Cambridge: Cambridge University Press.
Bourdieu, P. (1990), 'The Kabyle House or the World Reversed', in Pierre Bourdieu, *The Logic of Practice*, translated by Richard Nice, 271–83, Cambridge: Polity Press.
Bowler, A. (1991), 'Politics as Art: Italian Futurism and Fascism', *Theory and Society* 20: 763–94.
Brasini, A. (1925), 'Progetto della sistemazione del centro di Roma', *Capitolium* 1: 32.
Brasini, L. (ed.) (1979), *L'opera architettonica e urbanistica di Armando Brasini*, Rome
Braun, E. (1996), 'Expressionism as Fascist Aesthetic', *Journal of Contemporary History* 31: 273–92.
Braun, E. (2000), *Mario Sironi and Italian Modernism: Art and Politics Under Fascism*, New York: Cambridge University Press.
Breton, E. (1862), *Athènes décrite et dessinée*, Paris: Gide.
Brettingham, M. (1761), *The Plans, Elevations and Sections of Holkham in Norfolk, the Seat of the Late Earl of Leicester*, London: J. Haberkorn.
Brice, C. (1998), *Le Vittoriano: monumentalité publique et politique à Rome*, Rome: école française de Rome.
Brownlee, D. B. (1986), 'Friedrich Weinbrunner and Kahlsruhe: An Introduction', in D. B. Brownlee (ed.), *Friedrich Weinbrenner: Architect of Karlsruhe*, 3–22, Philadelphia: University of Pennsylvania Press, 1986.
Bulwer, H. L. (1826), *An Autumn in Greece compromising sketches of the character, customs and scenery of the country*, London: John Ebers.
Burgess, R. (1835), *Greece and the Levant. Or Diary of a Summer's Excursion in 1834*, London: Longman, Rees, Orme, Brown, Green and Longman.

Bibliography

Burke, E. (1998), *A Philosophical Enquiry into the Origin of our Ideas on the Sublime and Beautiful*, edited by D. Wormersley, London: Penguin Books.
Byron, Lord (1986), *The Major Works*, edited by J. J. McGann, Oxford: Oxford University Press.
Calderini, G. (1918), *Le Opere architettoniche di Guglielmo Calderini*, edited by G. B. Milani, Milan: Bestetti and Tumminelli.
Calderini, G. (1991a), 'Michelangelo Buonarroti e l'Architettura moderna', in G. Calderini, *Scritti di architettura*, 45–63, edited by Clementina Barucci and Antonella Greco, Rome: Clear.
Calderini, G. (1991b), 'Relazione esplicativa del Progetto per il Palazzo di Giustizia in Roma', in G. Calderini, *Scritti di architettura*, 81–9, edited by Clementina Barucci and Antonella Greco, Rome: Clear.
Calhoun, C. (2007), *Nations Matter: Culture, History, and the Cosmopolitan Dream*, London and New York: Routledge.
Calotychos, V. (2003), *Modern Greece: A Cultural Poetics*, Oxford and New York: Berg.
Calza, A. (1911), *Roma Moderna*, Milan: Fratelli Treves.
Campbell, C. (1715–25), *Vitruvius Britannicus or The British Architect*, London: Campbell.
Caprotti, F. (2007a), 'Destructive Creation: Fascist Urban Planning, Architecture and New Towns in the Pontine Marshes', *Journal of Historical Geography* 33: 651–79.
Caprotti, F. (2007b), *Mussolini's Cities: Internal Colonialism in Italy, 1930–1939*, Youngstown, NY: Cambria Press.
Caprotti, F. (2008), 'Internal Colonisation, Hegemony and Coercion: Investigating Migration to Southern Lazio, Italy, in the 1930s', *Geoforum* 39: 942–57.
Cardano, N. (1986), 'Storia del progetto iconografico attraverso il dibattito contemporaneo', in Soprintendenza per i beni ambientali e architettonici del Lazio, *Il Vittoriano: Materiali per una Storia*, II, 13–31, Roma: Palombi
Carter, R. (1979), 'Karl Friedrich Schinkel's Project for a Royal Palace on the Acropolis', *Journal of the Society of Architectural Historians* 38: 34–46.
Cassetto, R. (2005), *Roma e Lazio 1870–1945: La costruzione della capitale e della sua regione*, Rome: Gangemi Editore.
Castiglioni P. (1879), 'Della Populazione di Roma dale origini ai nostri tempi', in *Monografia della Città di Roma e della Campagna Romana: Presentata all'Esposizione Universale di Parigi del 1878*, II, 187–394, Rome: Tipografia Elzeviriana.
Catalogue (1878), *Catalogue of the Library of Sir John Soane's Museum*, London: Wyman and Sons.
Chambers, W. (1791), *A Treatise on the decorative part of Civil Architecture*, London: Joseph Smeeton.
Chandler, R. (1769), *Ionian Antiquities*, London: Society of Dilettanti.
Chateaubriand, F.-R. de (1827), 'Voyage en Italie', in *Oeuvres Complètes*, VII, 145–266, Paris: Ladvocat.
Chateaubriand, F.-R. de (1849), *Memoires d'outre-tombe*, Paris: Eugène et Victor Penaud.
Chakrabarty, D. (1992a), 'Of Garbage, Modernity, and the Citizen's Gaze', *Economic and Political Weekly* 27.10–11: 541–7, reprinted in D. Chakrabarty (2002), *Habitations of Modernity: Essays in the Wake of Subaltern Studies*, 65–79, University of Chicago Press: Chicago.
Chakrabarty, D. (1992b), 'Provincializing Europe: Postcoloniality and the Critique of History', *Cultural Studies* 6.3: 337–57.
Chakrabarty, D. (2002), *Habitations of Modernity: Essays in Subaltern Studies*, Chicago and London: University of Chicago Press.
Charles, Prince of Wales (1989), *A Vision of Britain: A Personal View of Architecture*, London and Toronto: Doubleday.
Chaudhauri, A. (2009), 'Cosmopolitanism's Alien Face', *New Left Review* 55: 89–106.
Chouquer, G. and J.-C. Daumas (eds) (2008), *Autour de Ledoux: Architecture, Ville Et Utopie: Actes du Colloque International à la Saline Royale d'Arc-et-Senans, le 25, 26 et 27 octobre 2006* (Cahiers de la MSHE Ledoux, No 13), Besançon: Presses Universitaires de Franche-Comté.

Bibliography

Ciampi, I. (1870), *Vita di Giuseppe Valadier: Architetto romano*, Rome: Tipografia delle Belle arti.

Cianfarani, F. (2020), 'The Legacy of the Official Borgate: Design, Reception and Current Life of the Quarticciolo neighborhood in Rome', in K. B. Jones and S. Pilat (eds), *The Routledge Companion to Italian Fascist Architecture: Reception and Legacy*, 241–55, Abingdon and New York: Taylor & Francis Group.

Ciucci, G. (1989), 'The Classicism of the E42: Between Modernity and Tradition', *Assemblage* 8: 79–87.

Claeys, G. (ed.) (1997), *Modern British Utopias, 1700–1850*, London: Pickering and Chatto.

Claeys, G. (ed.) (2008), *Late Victorian Utopias: A Prospectus*, London: Pickering and Chatto.

Clark, G. (2002), 'Land Rental Values and the Agrarian Economy: England and Wales, 1500–1914', *European Review of Economic History* 6.3: 281–308.

Clarke, G. (2002), 'Vitruvian Paradigms', *Papers of the British School at Rome* 70: 319–46.

Cleghorn, G. (1824), *Remarks on the intended restoration of the Parthenon of Athens as the National Monument of Scotland*, Edinburgh and London: Archibald Constable and Co. and Hurst, Robinson and Co.

Clogg, R. (1988), 'The Byzantine Legacy in the Modern Greek World: The Megali Idea', in L. Clucas (ed.), *The Byzantine Legacy in Eastern Europe*, 253–81, Boulder: East European Monographs.

Cochran, P. (2010), 'Why Did Byron Envy Thomas Hope's *Anastasius*?' *The Keats-Shelley Review* 24: 76–90.

Cochrane, G. (1837), *Wanderings in Greece*, London: Henry Colburn.

Colley, L. (1992), *Britons: Forging the Nation, 1707–1837*, New Haven and London: Yale University Press.

Complete Collection (1859), *A Complete Collection of the English Poems which have obtained the Chancellor's Gold Medal in the University of Cambridge*, Cambridge: Macmillan and Co.

Conn, S. (2014), *Americans Ggainst the City: Anti-urbanism in the Twentieth Century*, Oxford and New York: Oxford University Press.

Conversi, D. (2007), 'Mapping the Field: Theories of Nationalism and the Ethnosymbolic Approach', in A. S. Leoussi and S. Grosby (eds), *Nationalism and Ethnosymbolism: History, Culture and Ethnicity in the Formation of Nations*, 15–30, Edinburgh: Edinburgh University Press.

Costantini, I. (1922), 'Le nuove costruzioni dell'Istituto per le case popolari in Roma. La borgata giardino Garbatella', *Architettura e arti decorative* 2.1.3: 119–37.

Crook, J. M. (1972), *The Greek Revival: Neo-Classical Attitudes in British Architecture 1760–1870*, London: John Murray.

Crook, J. M. (1992), 'Metropolitan Improvements: John Nash and the Picaresque', in C. Fox (ed.), *London: World City 1800–1840*, 77–96, New Haven and London: Yale University Press.

Dau Novelli, C. (2011), *La Città nazionale: Roma capitale di una nuova élite (1870–1915)*, Rome: Carocci.

Davidoff, L. and C. Hall (1987), *Family Fortunes: Men and Women of the English Middle Class, 1780–1850*, London, Melbourne, Sydney, Auckland, Johannesburg: Hutchinson.

De Amicis, E. (1870), *Impressioni di Roma*, Florence: Tipografia P. Faverio e Comp.

Dean, P. (2006), *Sir John Soane and London*, Aldershot: Lund Humphries.

De Certeau, M. (1984), *The Practice of Everyday Life*, translated by S. Rendall, Berkeley, Los Angeles and London: University of California Press.

Debenedetti, E. (1985), *Valadier: segno e architettura*, Rome: Multigrafica Editrice.

Debord, G. (1992), *La Société du Spectacle*, Paris: Gallimard.

Defauconpret, A. J. B. (1824), *Londres en mil huit cent vingt-trois ou Recueil de Lettres sur la Politique, la Literature, et les Mouers dans le cours de l'année 1823*, Paris: Libraire de Gide Fils.

De Francisci, P. (1940), *Spirito della civiltà romana*, Milan, Messina: Giuseppe Principato.

De Grazia, V. (1992), *How Fascism Ruled Women: Italy 1922–1945*, Berkeley, CA, and London: University of California Press.

Bibliography

De La Ruffinière du Prey, P. (1994), *The Villas of Pliny: From Antiquity to Posterity*, Chicago and London: University of Chicago Press.

Dell'Ariccia, A. (ed.) (2002), *Antonio Rizzi, Per le lunette del Vittoriano: Studi e disegni*, Rome: Artemide.

De Michelis, A. (2009), 'The Garden Suburb of the Garbatella, 1920–1929: Defining Community and Identity through Planning in Post-war Rome', *Planning Perspectives: An International Journal of History, Planning and the Environment* 24: 509–20.

De Michelis, A. (2010), '"Civis Romanus Sum": The Self-Conscious "Romanità" of the Garbatella', *Annali d'Italianistica* 28: 153–78.

De Quincey, T. (1853), 'The Nation of London', in T. De Quincey, *Autobiographic Sketches*, 204–9, Boston: Ticknor, Reed and Fields.

De Quincey, T. (2013), *Confessions of an English Opium-Eater and Other Writings*, edited by R. Morrison, Oxford: Oxford University Press.

Description of the View (1842), *Description of the View of Athens and the Surrounding Country*, Cambridge, MA: Metcalf, Keith and Nichols.

De Vries, J. (1993), 'Between Purchasing Power and the World of Goods: Understanding the Household Economy and Early Modern Europe', in John Brewer and Roy Porter (eds), *Consumption and the World of Goods*, 85–132, London: Routledge.

Di Martino, P. (2012), '"Rome Wasn't Built in a Day": Lobbies, Institutions and Speculation in the 1880s Building Fever', *Urban History* 39: 471–89.

Dorovinis, V. (1980), 'Capodistrias et la planification d'Argos (1828–1832)', *Bulletin de Correspondance Hellénique* suppl. 6: 501–23.

Druda, S. and M. del Signore (1986), 'Il Vittoriano e l'antico', in Soprintendenza per i beni ambientali e architettonici del Lazio, *Il Vittoriano: Materiali per una Storia* II, 117: 122, Rome: Palombi.

DuBois, P. (2008), *Slaves and Other Objects*, Chicago: University of Chicago Press.

Durand, J.-N.-L. (1817), *Précis des leçons d'architecture données à l'École Polytechnique*, Paris: J.N.L. Durand.

Durand, J.-N.-L. (2000), *Précis of the Lectures on Architecture*, translated by David Britt, Getty Research Institute: Los Angeles.

Egan, P. (1822), *Life in London or The Day and Night Scenes of Jerry Hawthorn Esquire and his Elegant Friend Corinthian Tom accompanied by Bob Logic, the Oxonian, in their Rambles and Sprees through the Metropolis*, London: Sherwood, Neely and Jones.

Egan, P. (1830), *Finish to the Adventures of Tom, Jerry, and Logic, in their pursuits through Life in and out of London*, London: G. Virtue.

Ἑλληνική Νομαρχία (1806), *Ἑλληνική Νομαρχία*, Italy.

Elmes, J. (1827), *Metropolitan Improvements or London in the Nineteenth Century*, London: Jones and Co.

Engels, F. (1892), *The Condition of the Working-Class in England in 1844*, London: S. Sonnenschein.

Esposizione universale (1939), *Esposizione Universale di Roma 1942, Anno XX E.F.*, Livorno: G. Chiappini.

Evelyn, J. (1664), *A parallel of the antient architecture with the modern; to which is added an account of architects and architecture, in an explanation of certain tearms particularly affected by architects: with L. B. Alberti's Treatise of Statues*, London: John Place.

Examen critique (1835), *Examen critique de l'ouvrage: 'De l'État acuel de la Grèce et des moyens d'arriver àsa restauration, par Mr Fréderic Thiersch'*, Leipzig: F.A. Brockhaus.

Fairburn, L. (1998), *Italian Renaissance Drawings from the Collection of Sir John Soane's Museum*, London: Azimuth Editions.

Falasca-Zamponi, S. (1997), *Fascist Spectacle: The Aesthetics of Power in Mussolini's Italy*, Berkeley and London: University of California Press.

Bibliography

Fatsea, I. (2000), *Monumentality and its Shadows: A Quest for Modern Greek Architectural Discourse in Nineteenth-Century Athens (1834–1862)*, PhD Dissertation, MIT.

Feltham, J. (1802), *The Picture of London for 1802; Being a Correct Guide to All the Curiosities, Amusements, Exhibitions, Public Establishments, and remarkable Objects, in and near London, with a Collection of Appropriate Tables*, London: Lewis and Co. 1802.

Ferrari, C. G. (ed.) (1998a), *Mario Sironi: Paesaggi Urbani*, Milan: Mazzotta.

Ferrari, C. G. (1998b), 'Paesaggi urbani', in Claudia Gian Ferrari (ed.), *Mario Sironi: Paesaggi Urbani*, 9–13, Milan: Mazzotta.

Fielding, H. (1751), *An Enquiry into the Causes of the late Increase of Robbers, etc., with some proposals for Remedying this Growing Evil*, London: A. Millar.

Finlay, G. (1836), *The Hellenic Kingdom and the Greek Nation*, London: John Murray.

Finlay, G. (1861), *History of the Greek Revolution*, Edinburgh and London: William Blackwood and Sons.

Finlay, R. (1981), *Population and Metropolis: The demography of London 1580–1650*, Cambridge: Cambridge University Press.

First Report (1812), *First Report of the Commissioners of his Majesty's Woods, Forests and Land Revenues*, London: House of Commons.

Flaxman, J (1799), *A Letter to the Committee for Raising the Naval Pillar or Monument under the patronage of His Royal Highness the Duke of Clarence*, London: T. Cadell, W. Davies and R. H. Evans.

Fogu, C. (2003a), 'Actualism and the Fascist Historic Imaginary', *History and Theory* 42: 196–221.

Fogu, C. (2003b), *The Historic Imaginary: Politics of History in Fascist Italy*, Toronto: University of Toronto Press.

Fogu, C. (2005), 'To make History Present', in C. Lazzaro and R. J. Crum (eds), *Donatello Among the Blackshirts: History and Modernity in the Visual Culture of Fascist Italy*, 33–49, Ithaca and London: Cornell University Press.

Fogu, C. (2015), 'The Fascist Stylisation of Time', *Journal of Modern European History / Zeitschrift Für Moderne Europäische Geschichte / Revue d'histoire Européenne Contemporaine* 13: 98–114.

Foro Mussolini (1937), *Il Foro Mussolini*, Milano: Valentino Bompiano.

Fortnights Ramble (1795), *A Fortnights Ramble though London, or a complete Display of all the Cheats and Frauds Practized in that Great Metropolis with the Best Methods for Eluding Them, Being a Pleasing Narrative of the Adventures of a Farmer's Son Published at his Request for the Benefit of his Country*, London: J. Roach.

Fortuna, J. J. (2020), '"Un'arte ancora in embrione": International expositions, empire, and the evolution of Fascist architectural design', *Modern Italy* 25: 455–76.

Foucault, M. (1984), 'Of Other Spaces, *Heteropias*', *Architecture, Mouvement, Continuité* 5: 56–49.

Fournier-Finocchiaro, L. (2012), 'Le mythe de la Troisième Rome de Mazzini à Mussolini', in J. C. D'Amico, A. Testino-Zafiropoulos, P. Fleury, S Madeleine (eds), *Le mythe de Rome en Europe: Modèles et contre-modèles: Actes du colloque de Caen, 27–29 novembre 2008*, 213–30, Caen: Presses Universitaires de Caen.

Fournier-Finocchiaro L. and J.-Y. Frétigné (2018), 'Prophètes et prophéte chez Giuseppe Mazzini', *Laboratoire Italien* 21: https://journals.openedition.org/laboratoireitalien/2172.

Franchetti, L. and S. Sonnino (1974), *Inchiesta in Sicilia*, Florence: Vallecchi.

Fréart de Chambray, R. (1650), *Parallèle de l'architecture antique et de la moderne avec un recueil des dix principaux autheurs qui ont écrit de cinq orders*, Paris: Edme Martin.

Freud, S. (1932-6), 'A disturbance of Memory on the Acropolis', in J. Strechey (ed.), *The Standard Edition of the Complete Psychological Works of Sigmund Freud*, XXII, 239–48, London: Hogarth Press.

Fuller, M. (1996), 'Wherever You Go, There You Are: Fascist Plans for the Colonial City of Addis Ababa and the Colonizing Suburb of EUR '42', *Journal of Contemporary History* 31: 397–418.

Bibliography

Fuller, M. (2020), 'Rural Settlers and Urban Designs: Civic Identity in the Agro Pontino', in K. B. Jones and S. Pilat (eds), *The Routledge Companion to Italian Fascist Architecture: Reception and Legacy*, 228–40, Abingdon and New York: Taylor and Francis Group.

Gagliardi, A. (2016), 'Tra rivoluzione e controrivoluzione. L'interpretazione gramsciana del fascismo', *Laboratoire Italien*, 18: https://journals.openedition.org/laboratoireitalien/1062.

Gallant, T. W. (1989), 'Greek Bandits: Lone Wolves or a Family Affair', *Journal of Modern Greek Studies* 6: 269–90.

Garnham, T. (2013), *Architecture Reassembled: The Use and Abuse of History*, Abingdon and New York: Routledge.

Garston, E. (1842), *Greece Revisited and Sketches in Lower Egypt in 1840 with Thirty-six Hours of a Campaign in Greece in 1825*, London: Saunders and Otley.

G. C. (1925), 'L'attività edilizia in Roma', *Capitolium* 1: 44–9.

Geddes, P. (1915), *Cities in Evolution: An Introduction to Town Planning and the Study of Civics*, London: Williams and Norgate.

Gellner, E. (2008), *Nations and Nationalism* (New Perspectives on the Past), Ithaca: Cornell University Press.

Gentile, E. (1996), *The Sacralization of Politics in Fascist Italy*, Cambridge, MA, and London: Harvard University Press.

Gentile, E. (2007), *Fascismo di Pietra*, Bari and Rome: Editori Laterza.

Gentile, G. (1929), *Origini e Dottrina del Fascismo*, Rome: Libreria del Littorio.

Ghirardo, D. (1989), *Building New Communities: New Deal America and Fascist Italy*, Princeton, NJ: Princeton University Press.

Giardina, A. and A. Vauchez (2000), *Il Mito di Roma da Carlo Magno a Mussolini*, Rome and Bari: Laterza.

Gibbon, E. (1781), *The History of the Decline and Fall of Roman Empire: Volume the Second*, London: W. Strahan and T. Cadell.

Giglioli, G. Q. and G. Giovannoni (1937), 'L'architettura nella mostra augustea della romanità', *Palladio* 6: 201–38.

Gilly, F. (1994), *Essays on Architecture 1796–1799*, translated by David Britt, Santa Monica: Getty Center for the History of Art and the Humanities.

Giordano, F. (1871), *Cenni sulle condizioni fisico-economiche di Roma e suo territorio*, Florence: Giuseppe Civelli.

Giordano, F. (1879), 'Condizioni topografiche e fiische di Roma e campagna romana', in *Monografia della Città di Roma e della Campagna Romana: Presentata all'Esposizione Universale di Parigi del 1878*, i–lxxvii; lxxxvii–cxxiii, Rome: Tipografia Elzeviriana.

Giovannoni, G. (1995 [1931]), *Vecchie città ed edilizia nuova*, Milan: CittàStudiEdizioni.

Goalen, M. (1991), 'Schinkel and Durand: The Case of the Altes Museum', in M. Snodin (ed.), *Karl Friedrich Schinkel: A Universal Man*, 27–35, New Haven and London: Yale University Press.

Goethe, J. W. von (1870), *Italienische Reise*, Berlin: Grote.

Gordon, T. (1832), *History of the Greek Revolution*, Edinburgh: William Blackwood; London: T. Cadell.

Gourgouris, S. (1996), *Dream Nation: Enlightenment, Colonization and the Institution of Modern Greece*, Stanford: Stanford University Press.

Gramsci, A. (1957), 'The Southern Question', in A. Gramsci, *The Modern Prince and Other Writings*, 28–51, edited by Louis Marks, New York: International Publishers.

Gramsci, A. (1971), 'State and Civil Society', in Q. Hoare and G. N. Smith (eds), *Selections from the Prison Notebooks*, 209–76, London: Lawrence & Wishart.

Gramsci, A. (1978 [1921]), 'The Two Fascisms', in A. Gramsci, *Selections from Political Writings (1921-1926)*, translated and edited by Q. Hoare, 24, from *L'Ordine Nuovo*, 25 August 1921, London: Lawrence and Wishart.

Bibliography

Gramsci, A. (1978 [1924]), 'The Italian Crisis', in A. Gramsci, *Selections from Political Writings (1921–1926)*, translated and edited by Q. Hoare, 61, from *L'Ordine Nuovo*, 1 September 1924, London: Lawrence and Wishart.

Gramsci, A. (1978 [1925]), 'Elements of the Situation', in A. Gramsci, *Selections from Political Writings (1921–1926)*, translated and edited by Q. Hoare, 67, from *L'Unità*, 24 November 1925, London: Lawrence and Wishart, London.

Grant, J. (1836), *The Great Metropolis*, Volume I, London: Saunders and Otley.

Grant, J. (1837), *The Great Metropolis*, Volume II, London: Saunders and Otley.

Greek Government (1834), *Greek Government Gazette* 22, Nauplio: 16 June.

Griechichischer Traum (1986), *Ein griechichischer Traum: Leo von Klenze. Der Archäologe (Ausstellung vom 6. Dezember 1985–9. Februar 1986 Glyptothek München)*, Munich: Staatliche Antkensammlungen und Glyptothek.

Griffin, R. (1991), *The Nature of Fascism*, London: Taylor and Francis Group.

Griffin, R. (2002), 'The Primacy of Culture: The Current Growth (Or Manufacture) of Consensus within Fascist Studies', *Journal of Contemporary History* 37: 21–43.

Griffin, R. (2007), *Modernism and Fascism: The Sense of a Beginning under Mussolini and Hitler*, Basingstoke and New York: Palgrave Macmillan.

Gunn, S. (2007), *The Public Culture of the Victorian Middle Class: Ritual and Authority in the English Industrial City 1840–1914*, Manchester and New York: Manchester University Press.

Güthenke, C. (2008), *Placing Modern Greece: The Dynamics of Romantic Hellenism, 1770–1840* (Classical Presences), Oxford: Oxford University Press.

Gwynn, J. (1766), *London and Westminster improved, illustrated by plans: to which is prefixed, a discourse on publick magnificence; with observations on the state of arts and artists in this kingdom, wherein the study of the polite arts is recommended as necessary to a liberal education: concluded by some proposals relative to places not laid down in the plans*, London: John Gwynn.

Habermas, J. (1991), *The Structural Transformation of the Public Sphere: An Inquiry into a Category of Bourgeois Society*, translated by T. Burger and F. Lawrence, Cambridge, MA: MIT Press.

Haiko, P. (2013), 'Theophil Hansens "griechischer Stil" und seine "griechische Renaissance" an der Wiener Ringstrasse', in B. Bastl, U. Hirhager, E. Schober (eds), *Theophil Hansen: ein Resümee: Symposionsband anlässlich des 200. Geburtstage (Symposon der Universitätsbibliothek der Akademie der bildenden Künste Wien, Juni 2013)*, 147–62, Weitra: Bibliothek der Provinz.

Hall, C. and S. O. Rose (2006), 'Introduction: Being at Home with the Empire', in C. Hall and S. O. Rose (eds), *At Home with the Empire: Metropolitan Culture and the Imperial World*, 1–31, Cambridge: Cambridge University Press.

Hall, T. (1997), *Planning Europe's Capital Cities: Aspects of Nineteenth-century Urban Development* (Studies in History, Planning and the Environment, 21), London, New York: E. & F. N. Spon.

Hamdorf, F. W. (1986), 'Klenzes archäologisches Studien und Reisen, seine Mission in Griechenland', in *Ein griechichischer Traum: Leo von Klenze. Der Archäologe (Ausstellung vom 6. Dezember 1985–9. Februar 1986 Glyptothek München)*, 117–212, Munich: Staatliche Antkensammlungen und Glyptothek.

Hamilakis, Y. (2007), *The Nation and its Ruins: Antiquity, Archaeology and National Imagination in Greece*, Oxford: Oxford University Press.

Hammer, D. (2008), *Roman Political Thought and the Modern Theoretical Imagination*, Norman: University of Oklahoma Press.

Hann, A. and J. Stobart (2005), 'Sites of Consumption: The Display of Goods in Provincial Shops in Eighteenth-Century England', *Cultural and Social History* 2:2: 165–87.

Harris, E. and N. Savage (2004), *Hooked on Books: The Library of Sir John Soane Architect 1753–1837*, London: Sir John Soane's Museum.

Harvey, J. R. (1997), *Men in Black*, London: Reaktion.

Bibliography

Hastaoglou-Martinidis, V. (1995), 'City Form and National Identity: Urban Designs in Nineteenth-century Greece', *Journal of Modern Greek Studies* 13: 99–123.

Hastaoglou-Martinidis, V., K. Kafkoula and N. Papamichos (1993), 'Urban Modernization and National Renaissance: Town planning in 19th Century Greece', *Planning Perspectives* 8:4, 427–69.

Haygarth, W. (1814), *Greece: A Poem*, London: W. Bulmer and Co.

Hederer, O. (1976), *Friedrich Von Gärtner, 1792–1847: Leben, Werk, Schüler* (Studien zur Kunst des neunzehnten Jahrhunderts 30), Munich: Prestel.

Hell, J. (2019), *The Conquest of Ruins: The Third Reich and the Fall of Rome*, Chicago and London: University of Chicago Press.

Hemans, F. D. (1821), *Modern Greece. A Poem*, London: John Murray.

Herzfeld, M. (1987), *Anthropology Through the Looking-Glass: Critical Ethnography in the Margins of Europe*, Cambridge: Cambridge University Press.

Herzfeld, M. (2009), *Evicted from Eternity: The Restructuring of Modern Rome*, Chicago and London: University of Chicago Press.

Hitchcock, H.-R. (1958), *Architecture: Nineteenth and Twentieth Centuries*, Harmondsworth: Penguin.

Hobhouse, J. C. (1813), *A Journey through Albania and Other Provinces of Turkey in Europe and Asia, to Constantinople, during the Years 1809 and 1810*, London: J. Cawthorn.

Hobsbawm, E. J. (1969), *Bandits*, London: Weidenfeld & Nicolson.

Hobsbawm, E. J. and T. O. Ranger (eds) (1992), *The Invention of Tradition*, Cambridge: Cambridge University Press.

Hölderin, F. (1797–9), *Hyperion oder Der Ermit in Griechenland*, Tübingen: J.G.Cotta'schen Buchhandlung.

Hope, T. (1819), *Anastasius, or Memoirs of a Greek*, London: John Murray.

Hope, T. (1835), *An Historical Essay on Architecture*, London: John Murray.

Houghton, A. B. (1898), 'Italian Finances from 1860 to 1884', *The Quarterly Journal of Economics* 3: 373–402.

Howard, E. (1898), *To-morrow: A peaceful path to real reform*, London: Sonnenschein.

Howard, E. (1902), *Garden Cities of Tomorrow*, London: Sonnenschein.

Howe, S. G. (1828), *An Historical Sketch of the Greek Revolution*, New York: White, Gallaher and White.

Hughson, D. (1805), *London; being an accurate history and description of the British Metropolis and its Neighbourhood, to thirty miles extent from an actual perambulation*, London: J. Stratford.

Hume, David (1896), *A Treatise of Human Nature*, Oxford, Clarendon Press.

Hurstone, J. P. (1808), *The Piccadilly Ambulator or Old Q: Containing the Memoirs of the Private Life of that Ever-Green Votary of Venus*, London: G. Hughes.

Israel, J. I. (2001), *Radical Enlightenment Philosophy and the Making of Modernity, 1650–1750*, Oxford: Oxford University Press.

Israel, J. I. (2006), *Enlightenment Contested Philosophy, Modernity, and the Emancipation of Man, 1670–1752*, Oxford: Oxford University Press.

Jameson, F. (2005), *Archaeologies of the Future: The Desire Called Utopia and Other Science Fictions*, New York: Verso.

Janion, E. R. (2015), *Imaging Suli: Interactions between Philhellenic Ideas and Greek Identity Discourse*, Bern: Peter Lang.

Joyce, P. (1991), *Visions of the People: Industrial England and the Question of Class 1848–1914*, Cambridge: Cambridge University Press.

Jusdanis, G. (1991), *Belated Modernity and Aesthetic Culture: Inventing National Tradition: Inventing National Literature*, Minneapolis: University of Minnesota Press.

Kaftanzoglou, L. (1839), 'Σχεδιογραφια Αθηνων', *Αιων*, 8 March.

Kaftanzoglou, L. (1994), 'Esquisse d'un plan pour la ville d'Athènes proper a remplacer le projet en execution si mal conçu et impossible a recevoir sa totale organisation', (Hellenic State Archives, Athens; Ottonian archives, Ministry of the Interior, File 124), in A. Papageorgiou-Venetas, *Athens: The Ancient Heritage and the Historical Cityscape in a Modern Metropolis*, 425–6, Athens: The Archaeological Society at Athens.

Kaldellis, A. (2009), *The Christian Parthenon: Classicism and Pilgrimage in Byzantine Athens*, Cambridge: Cambridge University Press.

Kallis, A. (2011), '"Reconciliation" or "Conquest"? The opening of the Via della Conciliazione and the Fascist Vision for the "Third Rome"', in D. Caldwell and L. Caldwell (eds), *Rome: Continuing Encounters between Past and Present*, 127–51, Farnham and Burlington, VA: Ashgate.

Kallis, A. (2012), 'The "Third Rome" of Fascism: Demolitions and the Search for a New "Urban Syntax"', *Journal of Modern History* 84: 40–79.

Kallis, A. (2014), *The Third Rome, 1922-1943: The Making of the Fascist Capital*, New York and Basingstoke: Palgrave Macmillan.

Kallis, A. (2016), 'From CAUR to EUR: Italian Fascism, the "Myth of Rome" and the Pursuit of International Primacy', *Patterns of Prejudice* 50: 359–77.

Kallis, A. (2017), 'Rome's Singular Path to Modernism: Innocenzo Sabbatini and the "Rooted" Architecture of the Istituto Case Popolari (ICP), 1925–1930', *Papers of the British School at Rome* 85: 269–301.

Kallis, A. (2018), 'Futures Made Present: Architecture, Monument, and the Battle for the "Third Way" in Fascist Italy', *Fascism (Leiden)* 7: 45–79.

Kallis, A. and T. J. Gilfoyle (2020), '"Minimum Dwelling" all'italiana: From the Case Popolari to the 1929 "Model Houses" of Garbatella', *Journal of Urban History* 46: 603–21.

Karydis, N. (2022), 'The Revival of Classical Architecture in Athens, 1830–1840: Educational Institutions Designed by Christian Hansen and Stamatios Kleanthis', in N Temple, A. Piotrowski and J. M. Heredia (eds), *The Routledge Handbook in the Reception of Classical Architecture*, 449–65, Abingdon and New York: Routledge.

Kedourie, E. (1993), *Nationalism*, Oxford and Cambridge, MA: Blackwell.

Kirk, T. (2006), 'Framing St. Peter's: Urban Planning in Fascist Rome', *The Art Bulletin* (New York, NY) 88: 756–76.

Kirk, T. (2008), 'Monumental Monstrosity, Monstrous Monumentality', *Perspecta* 40: 6–15.

Kirk, T. (2009), 'Verso l'immaginario giusto; I concorsi architettonici per il Palazzo di Giustizia, 1883–1887', in Mario Pisani (ed.), *La Corte di Cassazione: I progetti e l'architettura del capolavoro di Giuseppe Zanardelli e Guglielmo Calderini*, 29–47, Rome: Gangemi.

Kirk, T. (2011), 'The Political Topography of Modern Rome, 1870–1936: Via XX Settembre to Via dell'Impero', in D. Caldwell and L. Caldwell (eds), *Rome: Continuing Encounters between Past and Present*, 101–28, Farnham and Burlington, VA: Ashgate.

Kitromilides, P. (1992), *The Enlightenment as Social Criticism: Iosipos Moisiodax and Greek Culture in the Eighteenth Century* (Princeton Modern Greek Studies), Princeton, NJ: Princeton University Press.

Kitromilides, P. (2003), 'An Enlightenment Perspective on Balkan Cultural Pluralism: The Republican Vision of Rhigas Velestinlis', *History of Political Thought* 24: 465–79.

Kitromilides, P. (2006), 'From Republican Patriotism to National Sentiment', *European Journal of Political Theory* 5: 50–60.

Kitromilides P. (ed.) (2010), *Adamantios Korais and the European Enlightenment*, Oxford: Voltaire Foundation.

Kitromilides, P. (2013), *Enlightenment and Revolution: The Making of Modern Greece*, Cambridge, MA, and London: Harvard University Press.

Kleanthis, S. and E. Schaubert (1994), 'Memorandum on the Projected Plan for the New Town of Athens [Erläuterung des Planes der Stadt Neu-Athen, 1832]', in A. Papageorgiou-Venetas

Bibliography

(ed.), *Athens: The Ancient Heritage and the Historical Cityscape in a Modern Metropolis*, 407–9, Athens: The Archaeological Society at Athens.

Kolettis, I. (2007 [1844]), 'Τῆς Μεγάλης αυτής Ἰδέας', in *National Romanticism: The Formation of National Movements: Discourses of Collective Identity in Central and Southeast Europe 1770–1945*, II, 244–8, translated by Mary Kitroeff, Budapest: Central European University Press.

Koliopoulos, J. S. (1987), *Brigands with a Cause: Brigandage and Irredentism in Modern Greece 1821–1912*, Oxford: Oxford University Press.

Koliopoulos, J. S. (1989), 'Brigandage and irredentism in nineteenth-century Greece', *European History Quarterly* 19: 193–228.

Kolokotrones, T. (1969), *Memoirs from the Greek War of Independence, 1821–1833*, translated by E. M. Edmonds, from the Greek text of G. Tertzetis, Chicago: Argonaut.

Kondaratos, S. (1994), 'The Parthenon as Cultural Ideal: The Chronicle of its Emergence as Supreme Monument of Eternal Glory', in P. Tournikotis (ed.), *The Parthenon and its Impact on Modern Times*, 19–53, Athens: Melissa Publishing.

Korres, M. (ed.) (2010a), *Οι Πρώτοι Χάρτες της πόλεως των Αθηνών (Fauvel) 1787, (Κλεανθης-Schaubert) 1831–1832, (Weiler) 1834, (Schaubert-Stauffert) 1836, (Stauffert) 1836–1837, (F. Altenhofen) 1837, Επιτροπη 1847*, 6, Athens: Ekdotikos Oikos Melissa.

Korres, M. (2010b), 'Ο Χάρτης του L. S. Fauvel, 1787 (ή λίγο αργότερα) ΚΛ: 1: 6.646,15', in M. Korres (ed.), *Οι Πρώτοι Χάρτες της πόλεως των Αθηνών (Fauvel) 1787, (Κλεανθης-Schaubert) 1831–1832, (Weiler) 1834, (Schaubert-Stauffert) 1836, (Stauffert) 1836–1837, (F. Altenhofen) 1837, Επιτροπη 1847*, 10–12, Athens: Ekdotikos Oikos Melissa.

Kostof, S. (1973), *The Third Rome: 1870–1950: Traffic and Glory*, Berkeley: University Art Museum.

Kostova, L. (2007), 'Degeneration, Regeneration and the Moral Parameters of Greekness in Thomas Hope's Anastasius, or Memoirs of a Greek', *Comparative Critical Studies* 4: 177–92.

Koutsopanagou, G. and L. Droulia (2009), *Εγκυκλοπαίδεια του Ελληνικού τύπου 1784–1974: εφημερίδες, περιοδικά, δημοσιογράφοι, εκδότες* (Kentro Neoellēnikōn Ereunōn: 103), Athens: Institouto Neoellēnikōn Ereunōn/Ethniko Idryma Ereunōn.

Krier, L. (1981), *Drawings 1967–1980*, edited by M. Culot, Brussels: AAM Editions.

Krier, L. (ed.) (1985), *Albert Speer: Architecture 1932–42*, Brussels: Archives d'architecture modern.

Krier, L. (2009), *Drawing for Architecture*, Cambridge, MA: MIT Press.

Krinsky, C. H. (1967), 'Seventy-eight Vitruvius Manuscripts', *Journal of the Warburg and Courtauld Institutes* 30: 36–70.

Kropotkin, P. (1892), *La Conquête du Pain*, Paris: Tresse & Stock.

Kruft, H. W. (1994), *A History of Architectural Theory from Vitruvius to the Present*, translated by Ronald Taylor, Elsie Callander and Antony Wood, London and New York: Zwemmer and Princeton Architectural Press.

Kühn, M. (1979), 'Schinkel und der Entwurf seiner Schüler Schaubert und Kleanthes für die Neustadt Athen', in W. Arenhövel and C. Schreiber (eds), *Berlin und die Antike: Architektur, Kunstgewerbe, Malerie, Theater und Wissenschaft vom 16. Jahrhundert bis heute*, I: 509–22, Berlin: Deutsches Archäologisches Institut.

Laclau, E. (2005), *On Populist Reason*, London and New York: Verso.

Laqueur, W. (1996), *Fascism: Past, Present and Future*, Oxford; Oxford University Press.

Laugier, M.-A. (1753), *Essai sur l'Architecture*, Paris: Duchesne.

Laugier, M.-A. (1755), *Essay on Architecture*, London: Osborne and Shipton.

Laugier, M.-A. (1765), *Observations sur l'Architecture*, Paris: Desaint.

Leake, W. M. (1826), *An Historical Outline of the Greek Revolution*, London: John Murray.

Leake, W. M. (1835), *Travels in Northern Greece*, London: Rodwell.

Leake, W. M. (1851), *Greece at the End of Twenty-three Years' Protection*, London: John Rodwell.

Bibliography

Ledoux, C.-N. (1804), *L'architecture considérée sous le rapport de l'art, des moeurs et de la legislation*, Paris: H. L. Peronneau.

Ledoux, C.-N. (1847), *Architecture*, Paris: Lenoir.

Lefebvre, H. (1991), *The Production of Space*, translated by D. Nicholson-Smith, Oxford and Cambridge, MA: Blackwell.

Lefebvre, H. (1996), 'Seen from the Window', in Henri Lefebvre, *Writings on Cities*, edited by R. Kaufman and E. Lebas, 219–27, Malden, MA, Carlton, MN, and Oxford: Blackwell.

Leigh, S. (1830), *Leigh's New Picture of London*, London: Samuel Leigh.

Leontis, A. (1995), *Topographies of Hellenism: Mapping the Homeland*, Ithaca and London: Cornell University Press.

Lerner, L. S. (2010), 'Italian Subjectivity in the Era of "Roma Capitale" (1870–2010): The Embrace of the Empty Sign', *Annali D'Italianistica* 28: 137–52.

Le Roy, J.-D. (1758), *Les ruines des plus beaux monuments de la Grèce*, Paris: H.-L. Guérin et L.-F. Delatour.

Le Roy, J.-D. (1759), *Ruins of Athens with remains and other valuable antiquities in Greece*, London: Sayer.

Lewin, L. (1979), 'The Oligarchical Limitations of Social Banditry in Brazil: The Case of the "Good" Thief Antonio Silvino', *Past & Present* 82: 116–46.

Liberati, S. (1990), 'La Mostra Augustea della Romanità : l'allestimento della facciata, il progetto e l'organizzazione delle sale, il consuntivo della manifestazione, l'eredità', in R. Siligato, M. Tittoni and M. Riposati (eds), *Il Palazzo delle Esposizioni: urbanistica e architettura*, 223–7, Rome: Carte Segrete.

Loncar, J. (2020), 'F is for . . . Fluctuating Symbolism: The Palazzo della Civiltà Italiana and its Shifting Meaning', in Kay Bea Jones and Stephanie Pilat (eds), *The Routledge Companion to Italian Fascist Architecture: Reception and Legacy*, 92–110, Abingdon and New York: Taylor & Francis Group.

London Guide (1819), *The London Guide and Stranger's Safeguard against the Cheats, Swindlers, and Pickpockets that abound the Bills of Mortality forming a Picture of London as regards Active Life collected from the verbal communications of William Perry and Others to which is added a glossary of cant terms*, London: J. Rumpus.

Macaulay, T. B. (1850), *Critical and Historical Essays contributed to The Edinburgh Review*, Leipzig: Bernh. Tauchnitz Jun.

Mackridge, P. (2010), *Language and National Identity in Greece, 1766–1976*, Oxford: Oxford University Press.

McNeal, R. (1991), 'Archaeology and the Destruction of the Later Athenian Acropolis', *Antiquity* 65: 49–63.

Madison, J. and A. Hamilton (2017), *The Federalist Papers*, New York: Race Point.

Malcolm, J. P. (1803–7), *Londinium Redivivum or an Ancient History and Modern Description of London*, London: John Nichols and Son.

Mallouchou-Tufano, F. (1994), 'The Parthenon from Cyriacus of Ancona to Frédéric Boissonas: Description, Research and Depiction', in P. Tournikotis (ed.), *The Parthenon and its Impact on Modern Times*, 164–99, Athens: Melissa Publishing.

Malouchou, G. E. (2010), 'Plan D'Athénes en 1820: Ερμηνευτικές Σημειώσεις του Π. Ευστατιάδη', in M. Korres (ed.), *Οι Πρώτοι Χάρτες της πόλεως των Αθηνών (Fauvel) 1787, (Κλεανθης-Schaubert) 1831–1832, (Weiler) 1834, (Schaubert-Stauffert) 1836, (Stauffert) 1836–1837, (F. Altenhofen) 1837, Επιτροπη 1847*, 56–61, Athens: Ekdotikos Oikos Melissa.

Mandeville, B. (1724), *The Fable of the Bees: or, Private Vices, Publick Benefits with an Essay on Charity and Charity-Schools and A Search into the Nature of Society*, London: J. Tonson (3rd edn).

Manfredi, C. V. (2015), *L'Opera di Gaetano Koch architetto di Roma capitale: Costruzione e trasformazione della città*, Roma: Edizioni Quasar.

Bibliography

Marcello, F. (2011), 'Mussolini and the Idealisation of Empire: The Augustan Exhibition of *romanità*', *Modern Italy* 16: 223–47.

Marcello, F. (2017), '*Forma Urbis Mussolinii*: Vision and Rhetoric in the Designs for Fascist Rome', in H. Roche and K. N. Demetriou (eds), *Brill's Companion to the Classics, Fascist Italy and Nazi Germany* (Brill's Companions to Classical Reception, 12), 370–403, Leiden and Boston: Brill.

Marconi, C. (n.d.), *Fotografie e Disegni del Palazzo di Giustizia di Roma*, Roma: Gangemi.

Marconi, P. (2002), 'Il "Palazzaccio": storia e architettura', in M. Fabbri, A. Greco, P. Marconi, M. Pisani, P. Portoghesi and C. Vallauri (eds), *Il Palazzo di Giustizia di Roma*, 25–40, Roma: Gangemi.

Mariani, R. (1976), *Fascismo e 'città nuove'*, Milan: Feltrinelli.

Marinetti, T.F. (1909), 'Le futurisme', in *Le Figaro*, 20 February: 1.

Martin, G. (1971), 'Wilkins and the National Gallery', *The Burlington Magazine* 113 (June): 318–29.

Marx, K. (1848), *The Manifesto of the Communist Party*, in *Marxists Internet Archive*, https://www.marxists.org/archive/marx/works/1848/communist-manifesto/index.htm.

Maurel, A. (1909), *Un Mois à Rome*, Paris, Hachette.

Mazzini, G. (1864), *Scritti editi e inediti di Giuseppe Mazzini*, Milano: G.Daelli.

Mbembe, A. (2001), *On the Postcolony* (Studies on the History of Society and Culture), Berkeley: University of California Press.

Meeks, C. L. V. (1966), *Italian Architecture, 1750–1914*, New Haven and London: Yale University Press.

Middleton, R. (2004), 'Introduction', in J.-D. Le Roy, *The Ruins of the Most Beautiful Monuments of Greece*, translation by David Britt (Texts and Documents), 1–199, Los Angeles: Getty Research Institute.

Miliarkis, A. (1884), 'Τελετή επί της Ακροπόλεως των Αθηνών', *Εστια* 447: 461–7.

Mill, J. (1817), *The History of British India*, London: Baldwin, Craddock and Joy.

Miller, W. (1926), *The Early Years of Modern Athens*, London: The Anglo-Hellenic League.

Misuraca, G. (1899), 'Il nuovo palazzo della Banca d'Italia in Roma', *L'Edilizia moderna* 8.4: 25–42.

Mogg, E. (1806), *London in Miniature*, London: E. Mogg.

Morris, E.J. (1843), *Notes of a Tour Through Turkey, Greece, Egypt and Arabia Petraea to the Holy Land*, London: N. Bruce.

Morris, W. (1891), *News from Nowhere: or, an Epoch of Rest, being some chapters from a Utopian Romance*, London: Reeves & Turner.

Moss, D. (1979), 'Bandits and Boundaries in Sardinia', *Man* 14: 477–96.

Mosse, G. L (1990), 'The Political Culture of Italian Futurism: A General Perspective', *Journal of Contemporary History* 25: 253–68.

Mosse, G. L. (1996), 'Fascist Aesthetics and Society: Some Considerations', *Journal of Contemporary History* 31: 245–52.

Mostra Augustea (1938), *Mostra Augustea della Romanità. Catalogo 1937–38*, Rome.

Mudie, R. (1825), *Babylon the Great: A Dissection and Demonstration of Men and Things in the British Capital*, London: Charles Knight.

Mulè, F.P. (1932), 'Le Grandi arterie monumentali di Roma: Il Duce sulla via dell'Impero', *Capitolium* 11: 557–72.

Muñoz, A. (1935), *Roma di Mussolini*, Milan: Treves.

Muntoni, A. (1995), 'La vicenda dell'E42: Fondazione di una città in forma didascálica', in Giorgio Ciucci (ed.), *Classicismo, classicism: architettura Europa/America 1920–1940*, 135–8, Milan: Electa.

Mussolini, B. (1925), 'La nouva Roma', http://www.adamoli.org/benito-mussolini/pag0342-.htm.

Mussolini, B. (1926), *Roma antica sul Mare*, Milan: Mondadori.

Mussolini, B. (1932), *The Doctrine of Fascism*, http://www.worldfuturefund.org/wffmaster/reading/germany/mussolini.htm.

Bibliography

Mussolini, B. (1956), *Opera omnia. Vol. XVIII*, E. Susmel and D. Susmel (eds), Florence: La Fenice.
Nerdinger, W. (ed.) (2000), *Leo von Klenze: Architekt zwischen Kunst und Hof 1784–1864*, Munich, London and New York: Prestel.
Neumeyer, F. (1994), 'Introduction', in Friedrich Gilly, *Essays on Architecture 1796–1799*, translated by David Britt, 1–101, Santa Monica: Getty Center for the History of Art and the Humanities.
Notaro, A. (2000), 'Exhibiting the New Mussolinian City: Memories of Empire in the World Exhibition of Rome (EUR)', *GeoJournal* 51: 15–22.
Ojetti, U. (1907), *Il monument a Vittorio Emanuele in Roma a le sue avventure*, Milan: Fratelli Treves.
Olsen, D. J. (1964), *Town Planning in London: The Eighteen and Nineteenth Centuries*, New Haven and London: Yale University Press.
Original Picture (1826), *The Original Picture of London, Enlarged and Improved: being a correct guide for the stranger as well as for the inhabitant, to the Metropolis of the British Empire together with a description of the Environs*, London: Longman, Rees, Orme and Green (24th edn).
Owenson, S. (1809), *Woman; or Ida of Athens*, London: Longman, Hurst, Rees and Orme.
Pagden, A. (2005), 'Fellow Citizens and Imperial Subjects: Conquest and Sovereignty in Europe's Overseas Empires', *History and Theory* 44: 28–46.
Painter, B. W. (2005), *Mussolini's Rome: Rebuilding the Eternal City*, New York and Basingstoke: Palgrave Macmillan.
Palladio, A. (1570), *I quattro libri dell'architettura, ne' quali, dopo un breue trattato de' cinque ordini, & di quelli auertimenti, che sono piu necessarii nel fabricare*, Venice: D. de' Franceschi.
Palma di Cesnola, A. (1826), *Greece Vindicated; in Two Letters*, London: Palma Di Cesnola.
Panetsos, G. A. and M. Z. Cassimatis (eds) (2014), *Hellenische Renaissance: Η αρχιτεκτονικη του Θεοφιλου Χανσεν (1813–1891)*, Athens: Ιδρυμα Εικαστικων Τεχνων & Μουσικης and B. & M. Θεοχαρακη.
Papadopoulou-Sumeonidou, P. (1996), *Η Επιλογή της Αθήνας ως πρωτεύουσας της Ελλάδος 1833–1834*, Thessaloniki: Oikos Adelphon Kuriakide.
Papageorgiou-Venetas, A. (1970), *Athenes Majeure*, Paris: Librairie Vincent, Fréal et Co.
Papageorgiou-Venetas, A. (1992), 'Gärtner in Griechenland und der Bau der Athener Residenz', in W. Nerdinger (ed.), *Friedrich Von Gärtner: ein Architektenleben, 1791–1847: mit den Briefen an Johann Martin von Wagner*, 135–55, Munich: Klinkhardt & Biermann.
Papageorgiou-Venetas, A. (1994), *Athens: The Ancient Heritage and the Historical Cityscape in a Modern Metropolis*, Athens: The Archaeological Society at Athens.
Papageorgiou-Venetas, A. (1996), 'Η Αθηνα Πρωτευοσατης Ελλαδος ενα οραμα του Ευρωπαϊκου Κλασικισμου', in *Αθηναϊκος Κλασικισμος*, 25–45, Athens, Pnevmatiko Kentro.
Papageorgiou-Venetas, A. (2000), *O Leo Von Klenze στην Ελλάδα: Τεκμήρια για τη νεοελληνική ιστοριογραφία*, Athens: Ekdoseis Odysseas.
Papageorgiou-Venetas, A. (2001), *Αθηνα, Ένα όραμα του κλασικισμού*, Athens: Ekdoseis Kapon.
Papageorgiou-Venetas, A. (2008a), *Athens: The Ancient Heritage and the Historical Cityscape in a Modern Metropolis* (Athens: The Archaeological Society at Athens).
Papageorgiou-Venetas, A. (2008b), *Friedrich Stauffert: Städte und Landschaften in Griechenland zur Zeit König Ottos* (*Peleus*, 21), Mainz and Ruhpolding: Verlag Franz Philipp Rutzen.
Papageorgiou-Venetas, A. (2010a), 'Ο Αρχιτέκτων Eduard Schaubert (1804–1860). Η δράση του στην Ελλάδα. Τα Πολεοδομικά του Κατάλοιπα', in M. Korres (ed.), *Οι Πρώτοι Χάρτες της πόλεως των Αθηνών (Fauvel) 1787, (Κλεανθης-Schaubert) 1831–1832, (Weiler) 1834, (Schaubert-Stauffert) 1836, (Stauffert) 1836–1837, (F. Altenhofen) 1837, Επιτροπη 1847*, 12–15, Athens: Ekdotikos Oikos Melissa.
Papageorgiou-Venetas, A. (2010b), 'Χάρτης της Αθήνας του 1820', in M. Korres (ed.), *Οι Πρώτοι Χάρτες της πόλεως των Αθηνών (Fauvel) 1787, (Κλεανθης-Schaubert) 1831–1832, (Weiler)*

Bibliography

    1834, (Schaubert-Stauffert) 1836, (Stauffert) 1836–1837, (F. Altenhofen) 1837, Επιτροπη 1847, 77–8, Athens: Ekdotikos Oikos Melissa.
Papageorgiou-Venetas, A. (2010c), 'Χαρτογραφικό Σκαρίφημα της Παλιάς Αθήνας με Επισήμανση των Εκκλησιών', in M. Korres (ed.), *Οι Πρώτοι Χάρτες της πόλεως των Αθηνών (Fauvel) 1787, (Κλεανθης-Schaubert) 1831–1832, (Weiler) 1834, (Schaubert-Stauffert) 1836, (Stauffert) 1836–1837, (F. Altenhofen) 1837, Επιτροπη 1847*, 78–9, Athens: Ekdotikos Oikos Melissa.
Papageorgiou-Venetas, A. (2011a), 'Athens: Modern Planning in a Historic Context. Planning Initiatives and Their Impact on the Gradual Creation of the Cultural-Archaeological Park of the City', in A. Papageorgiou-Venetas, *In Focus: Athens/Im Brennpunkt: Athen* (*Peleus* 56), 56–89, Mainz and Ruhpolding: Franz Philipp Tutzen Verlag.
Papageorgiou-Venetas, A. (2011b), 'Bauen in Athen: Neue Wege des Klassizismus. Gesltungsprinzipien deutscher Baumeister am Beispiel der Entwürfe für die Athener Reidenz (1833–1836)', in A. Papageorgiou-Venetas, *In Focus: Athens/Im Brennpunkt: Athen* (*Peleus* 56), 15–40, Mainz and Ruhpolding: Franz Philipp Tutzen Verlag, 2011.
Parton, J. (1868), 'Pittsburg', *The Atlantic Monthly* 21.123 (January): 17–36.
Peckham, R. S. (2000), 'Map Mania: Nationalism and the Politics of Place in Greece, 1870–1922', *Political Geography* 19: 77–95.
Peckham, R. S. (2001), *National Histories, Natural States: Nationalism and the Politics of Place in Greece*, London: I. B. Tauris.
Perrault, Ch. (1687), *Le Siècle de Louis le Grand*, Paris: Jean Baptiste Coignard.
Perrault, Ch. (1692–3), *Parallele des Anciens et des Modernes en ce qui regarde les arts et les sciences*, Paris: Jean Baptiste Coignard.
Perrault, Cl. (1683), *Ordonnance des cinq espèces de colonnes selon la méthode des anciens*, Paris: Jean Baptiste Coignard.
Pesci, U. (1895), *Come siamo entrati in Roma*, Milan: Fratelli Treves.
Pesci, U. (1907), *I primi anni di Roma capitale, 1870–1878. Con 100 illustrazioni*, Florence: B. Bemporad e figlio.
Petropoulos, J. A. (1968), *Politics and Statecraft in the Kingdom of Greece, 1833–1843*, Princeton: Princeton University Press.
Philippidis, D. and G. Konstantas (1988 [1791]), *Γεωγραφία Νεωτερική*, edited by A. Koumarianou, (Nea Hellenike Bibliotheke 45), Athens.
Piacentini, M. (1925), 'La grande Roma', *Capitolium* 1: 413–20.
Piacentini, M. (1931a), 'Difesa dell'architettura italiana', *Il Giornale d'Italia* 2 May: 3.
Piacentini, M. (1931b), 'Roma Mussoliniana: II progetto del Piano Regolatore della Roma', *L'Illustrazione Italiana*, 9: 312–17
Pianciani, L. (1873), *Discorso pronunciato dal sindaco nella Tornata del Consiglio Comunale di Roma il 6 Ottobre 1873 sul Piano Regolatore*, Rome: Tip. Municiplae Salviucci.
Piano Regolatore (1882), *Piano Regolatore e di Ampliamento della Città di Roma: Relazione della Commissione esaminatrice nominate dal Consiglio Comunale nella seduta del 12 Dicembre 1881*, Rome and Florence: Tipografica Bencini.
Piantoni, G. (1991), 'Arredo urbano di Roma Capitale fra il 1870 e il 1914 come messagio politico-simbolico', in Commune di Roma, *La Capitale a Roma: Città e arredo urbano 1870–1945*, 19–27, Rome: Carte Segrete.
Pinto, J. A. (2012), *Speaking Ruins: Piranesi, Architects and Antiquity in Eighteenth-century Rome*, Ann Arbor: University of Michigan Press.
Pisani, M. (2009), 'L'architettura del Palazzo di Giustizia a Roma di Guglielmo Calderini', in Mario Pisani (ed.), *La Corte Di Cassazione: I progetti e l'architettura del capolavoro di Giuseppe Zanardelli e Guglielmo Calderini*, 101–23, Rome: Gangemi.
Pitt, C. (1818), *Comparison of the Original Estimates, with the Actual Expenditure; Extracts from the Parliamentary Reports. Conduct of Various Officers and Surveyors; Reports of*

Compensation Causes. Together with Memorials and Correspondence between the Author and the Commission. Part 1, London: C. Pitt.

Plantzos, D. (2014), 'Dead Archaeologists, Buried Gods: Archaeology as an Agent of Modernity in Greece', in D. Tziovas (ed.), *Re-imagining the Past: Antiquity and Modern Greek Culture* (Classical Presences), 147–64, Oxford: Oxford University Press.

Polla, E. (1979), *Il Palazzo delle finanze di Roma capitale*, Rome: Libreria dello Stato.

Potts, A. (1991), 'Schinkel's Architectural Theory', in M. Snodin (ed.), *Karl Friedrich Schinkel: A Universal Man*, 47–55, New Haven and London: Yale University Press.

Proto, F. (2003), 'Introduction', in Jean Baudrillard, *Mass. Identity. Architecture. Architectural Writings of Jean Baudrillard*, ix–xiii, Chichester: John Wiley & Sons.

Quinet, E. (1830), *De la Grèce moderne et de ses rapports avec l'Antiquité*, Paris: Levrault.

Racheli, A. M. (1986), 'Un monumento nella città', in Soprintendenza per i beni ambientali e architettonici del Lazio, *Il Vittoriano: Materiali per una Storia*, 27–36, Rome: Palombi.

Rattenbury K. and S. Hardingham (eds) (2007), *Robert Venturi and Denise Scott Brown: Learning from Las Vegas*, Abingdon and New York: Routledge.

Remarks (1816), *Remarks on the Buildings and Improvements in London and Elsewhere*, London and Bath: James Cruttwell.

Raban, J. (1976), *Soft City*, London: Hamish Hamilton.

Raybaud, M. (1824), *Mémoires sur la Grèce pour server á l'Histoire de la Guerre de l'Indépendence*, Paris: Tournachon-Molin.

Reclus E. (1905), *L'Homme et la terre: histoire contemporaire*, Paris: Libraire Universelle.

Reid, J. J. (2000), *Crisis of the Ottoman Empire: Prelude to Collapse 1839–1878*, Stuttgart: Franz Steiner Verlag.

Rendall, J. (2006), 'The Condition of Women: Women's Writing and the Empire in Nineteenth-century Britain', in Catherine Hall and Sonya Rose (eds), *At Home with the Empire: Metropolitan Culture and the Imperial World*, 101–21, Cambridge: Cambridge University Press.

Rendell, J. (2002), *The Pursuit of Pleasure: Gender, Space and Architecture in Regency London*, London: Athlone Press.

Report from the Committee On the Petition of the Tradesmen (1817), Report from the Committee On the Petition of the Tradesmen and Inhabitants of Norris Street and Market terrace in the Parish of Saint James, with the Liberty of Westminster respecting the new Street from Charing Cross to Mary-le-Bone Park and the Northern Parts of the Metropolis, London: House of Commons.

Report from the Select Committee (1828), *Report from the Select Committee on the Office of Works and Public Buildings*, London: House of Commons.

Ricci, C. (1925), 'La liberazione dei resti dal Foro da Augusto', *Capitolium* 1: 3–7.

Richardson, M. (ed.) (1999), *Visions of Ruin: Architectural Fantasies and Designs for Garden Follies*, London: The Soane Gallery.

Rifkind, D. (2012), *The Battle for Modernism: Quadrante and the Politicization of Architectural Discourse in Fascist Italy*, Vicenza: Marsilio.

Rinaldi, M. (1991), 'Il volto effimero della città nell' età dell' impero e dell' autarchia', in Commune di Roma, *La Capitale a Roma: Città e arredo urbano 1870–1945*, 118–29, Rome: Carte Segrete.

Rose, W. K. (1897), *With the Greeks in Thessaly*, London: Methuen and Co.

Rosen, F. (1992), *Bentham, Byron, and Greece: Constitutionalism, Nationalism and Early Liberal Political Thought*, Oxford: Oxford University Press.

Rosen, F. (1998), *Greek Nationalism and British Liberalism*, Athens: Κεντρο Νεοελληνικων Ερευνων/Εθνικου Ιδρυμτος Ερευνων.

Ross, L., C. F. Hansen and E. Schaubert (1839), *Die Akropolis von Athen nach den neuesten Ausgrabungen. 1. Der Tempel der Nike Apteros*, Berlin: Schenk & Gestaecker.

Roubien, D. (2013), 'The Origins of the "Monumental Axis" of Neo-classical Athens and its Relationship with the Antiquities', *The Journal of Architecture* 18: 225–53.

Bibliography

Roubien, D. (2017), *Creating Modern Athens: A Capital between East and West*, London: Routledge.
Russack, H. H. (1942), *Deutsche Bauen in Athen*, Berlin: Wilhelm Verlag.
Sagredo, A. M. (ed.) (2007), *La Corte di Cassazione: Le opera d'arte del Palazzo di Guistizia di Roma*, Rome: Gangemi.
Said, E. W. (1980), *Orientalism*, London: Routledge and Kegan Paul.
Said, E. W. (1993), *Culture and Imperialism*, London: Chatto & Windus.
St Clair, W. (2008), *That Greece Might Still Be Free: The Philhellenes in the Greek War of Independence*, Cambridge: Open Book.
Samiou, A. (2009), 'French Travellers to Greece and the Representation of Modern Greeks in the Nineteenth Century', *Journal of European Studies* 39: 455–68.
Sanfilippo, M. (1992), *La Costruzione di una Capitale Roma 1870-1911*, Milan: Silvana Editoriale.
Sant Cassia, Paul (1993), 'Banditry, Myth, and Terror in Cyprus and Other Mediterranean Societies', *Comparative Studies in Society and History* 35: 773–95.
Sanjust di Teulada, E. (1908), *Piano Regolatore della Città di Roma, 1908*, Rome: Stabilimento Danesi.
Schiller, F. (2016), *On the Aesthetic Education of Man; Letters to Prince Frederick Christian Von Augustenburg*, translated by Keith Tribe, Harmondsworth: Penguin Classics.
Schinkel, K. F. (1840), *Werke der höheren Baukunst für die ausführung Erfunden und Dargestellt von Dr C. F. Schinkel*, Potsdam: Verlag von Ferdinand Riegel.
Schinkel, K. F. (1848), *Werke der höheren Baukunst für die ausführung Erfunden und Dargestellt. 2*, Potsdam: Verlag von Ferdinand Riegel.
Schnapp, J. T. (2004), 'Flash Memories (Sironi on Exhibit)', *South Central Review* 21: 22–49.
Schüller, S. (1943), *Roma Mussoliniana: Roma Capitale Moderna/Das Rom Mussolinis: Rom als modern Haupstadt*, Düsseldorf, Editrice Mosella.
Schwarz, U. (ed.) (2003), *Christian Frederik Hansen und die Architektur um 1800*, Munich: Deutscher Kunstverlag.
Scobie, A. (1990), *Hitler's State Architecture: The Impact of Classical Antiquity*, University Park: Pennsylvania State University Press.
Scott, J. C. (1990), *Seeing Like a State: How Certain Scheme to Improve the Human Condition Have Failed*, New Haven: Yale University Press.
Scully, V. (1963), 'Kleanthes and the Duchess of Piacenza', *Journal of the Society of Architectural Historians* 22: 139–54.
Sechs Lithographien (n.d.), *Sechs Lithographien zu L. von Klenze's Reise nach Greichenland* (no publisher).
Second Report (1816), *Second Report of the Commissioners of his Majesty's Woods, Forests and Land Revenues*, London: House of Commons.
Sella, Q. (1879), *Dell' Accademia dei Lincei*, Bologna: Nicola Zanichelli.
Sella, Q. (1885), *Pensieri di Quintino Sella: Tratti dai suoi discorsi e dalle sue lettere*, edited by F. Casanova, Turin: Librario di il Re D'Italia.
Sella, Q. (1887), *Discorsi Parlamentari*, Rome: Topografia della Camera dei Deputi.
Sennett, R. (1978), *The Rise and Fall of Public Man*, New York: Vintage Books.
Sennett, R. (1994), *Flesh and Stone: The Body and the City in Western Civilization*, New York and London: W. W. Norton.
Serlio, S. (1545), *Reigles generales de l'Architecture, sur les cincq manières d'edifices, a scauoir, Thuscane, Doricq, Ionicq, Corinthe & Composite, avec les exemples danticquitez, selon la doctrine de Vitruue*, Pieter von Aelste.
Serlio, S. (1987 [1584]), *I sette libri dell'architettura*, Bologna: Forni.
Sgueglia, A. (2009), 'Guglielmo Calderini: La tradizione a servizion della città', in M. Pisani (ed.), *La Corte Di Cassazione: I progetti e l'architettura del capolavoro di Giuseppe Zanardelli e Guglielmo Calderini*, 125–49, Rome: Gangemi.

Bibliography

Shelley, P. B. (1964), *The Letters of Percy Bysshe Shelley*, edited by F. L. Jones, Oxford: Clarendon Press.

Sitte, C. (1889), *Der Städtebau nach seinen künstlerischen Grundsätzen*, Wien: Verlag von Carl Graeser.

Smith, A. (1776), *An Inquiry into the Nature and Causes of the Wealth of Nations*, London: Strahan and Cadeli.

Smith, A. D. (1986), *The Ethnic Origins of Nations*, Oxford: Blackwell.

Smith, A. D. (1991), *National Identity*, Harmondsworth: Penguin.

Smith, A. D. (2000), *The Nation in History: Historiographical Debates About Ethnicity and Nationalism*, Hanover: University Press of New England.

Smith, A. D. (2004), *The Antiquity of Nations*, Cambridge and Malden, MA: Polity.

Soane, J. (1827), *Designs for Public Improvements in London and Westminster*, London: James Moyes.

Soane, J. (2000), *The Royal Academy Lectures*, edited by D. Watkin, Cambridge: Cambridge University Press.

Somma, P. (2020), 'The palazzo della civiltà Italian from fascism to fashion', in K. B. Jones and S. Pilat (eds), *The Routledge Companion to Italian Fascist Architecture: Reception and Legacy*, 79–91, Abingdon and New York: Taylor & Francis Group.

Sonne, W. (2003), *Representing the State: Capital City Planning in the Early Twentieth Century*, Munich, Berlin, London and New York: Prestel.

Soprintendenza per i beni ambientali e architettonici del Lazio (1986), *Il Vittoriano: Materiali per una Storia*, Rome: Palombi.

Spackman, B. (1996), *Fascist Virilities: Rhetoric, Ideology, and Social Fantasy in Italy*, Minneapolis and London: University of Minnesota Press.

Spagnesi, G. (1978), *L'architettura a Roma al Tempo di Pio IX*, Rome: Multigrafica Editrice.

Spagnesi, G. (2015), 'Roma capitale: il disegno urbano e il linguaggio architettonico', in C. V. Manfredi, *L'Opera di Gaetano Koch architetto di Roma capitale: Costruzione e trasformazione della città*, IX–XIII, Rome: Edizioni Quasar.

Stabile, F. R. (2022), 'Shaping Early Twentieth Century Rome: the AACAR and the Contributions of Filippo Galassi and Gustavo Giovannoni', *Planning Perspectives* 37: 551–81.

Stademann, F. (1841), *Panorama von Athen. An Ort und Stelle aufgenommen und herausgegeben*, Munich: Dr Franz Wild'schen Buchdruckery.

Stanhope, L. (1825), *Greece in 1823 and 1824; being a series of letters and other documents on the Greek Revolution written during a visit to that country*, London: Sherwood, Jones and Co.

Sternhall, Z. (1994), *The Birth of Fascist Ideology*, translated by D. Maisel, Princeton: Princeton University Press.

Stobart, J. (1998), 'Shopping Streets as Social Space: Leisure, Consumerism and Improvement in an Eighteenth-century County Town', *Urban History* 25: 3–21.

Stoler, A. L. (1995), *Race and the Education of Desire: Foucault's History of Sexuality and the Colonial Order of Things*, Durham and London: Duke University Press.

Stonestreet, G. G. (1800), *Domestic Union or London as it should be*, London: J. Walter.

Strong, F. (1842), *Greece as a Kingdom or a Statistical description of the Country from the Arrival of King Otho in 1833 to the Present Time*, London: Longman, Brown, Green and Longman.

Stuart, J. and N. Revett (1762), *The Antiquities of Athens Measured and Delineated by James Stuart and Nicholas Revett, Painters and Architects*, Volume I, London: John Haberkorn.

Stuart, J. and N. Revett (1787), *The Antiquities of Athens, Measured and delineated by James Suart FRS and FSA and Nicholas Revett*, Volume II, London: John Nichols.

Stuart, J. and N. Revett (1794), *The Antiquities of Athens, Measured and delineated by James Suart FRS and FSA and Nicholas Revett*, Volume III, London: John Nichols.

Stuart, J. and N. Revett (1816), *The Antiquities of Athens, Measured and delineated by James Suart FRS and FSA and Nicholas Revett*, Volume IV, London: J. Taylor.

Bibliography

Sudjic, D. (2006), *The Edifice Complex; The Architecture of* Power, London and New York: Penguin Books.
Taine, H. (1866), *Voyage en Italie*, Paris, Hachette.
Testa, V. (1971), 'La realizzazione dell' EUR', in Unione romana ingegneri e architetti, Saverio De Paolis, Armando Ravaglioli (eds), *La Terza Roma: Lo sviluppo urbanistico, edilizio e tecnico di Roma capitale*, 41–5, Rome: Fratelli Palombi.
Thiersch, F. (1833), *De l'État acuel de la Grèce et des moyens d'arriver à sa restauration*, Leipzig: Brockhaus.
Tilly, C. (2003), *The Politics of Collective Violence*, Cambridge: Cambridge University Press.
Tobia, B. (1991), *Una Patria per gli italiani*, Rome and Bari: Laterza.
Tobia, B. (1998), *L'Altare della Patria*, Bologna: il Mulino.
Togliatti, P. (1978), *Lezioni sul fascismo*, Roma: Editori Riuniti.
Tsiomis, Y. (2017), *Athènes ä soi-même étrangère: Naissance d'une capitale néoclassiques*, Paris: Paranenthèses.
Tziovas, D. (2009), 'The Novel and the Crown: *O Leandros* and the Politics of Romanticism', in R. Beaton and D. Ricks (eds), *The Making of Modern Greece: Nationalism, Romanticism and the Uses of the Past*, 211–24, London and New York: Routledge.
Ugolini, R. (2011), 'L'Idea di Roma', in R. Ugolini, C. Strinati, B. Vespa (eds), *L'idea di Roma: Una città nella storia*, 31–40, Rome: Gangemi Editore.
Urbinati, N. (2019), *Me the People: How Populism Transforms Democracy*, Cambridge, MA, and London: Harvard University Press.
Vallauri, C. (2002), 'L'Italia al passaggio del secolo: Il bibattito sul "Palazzaccio" nella e nel Parlamento', in M. Fabbri, A. Greco, P. Marconi, M. Pisani, P. Portoghesi and C. Vallauri (eds), *Il Palazzo di Giustizia di Roma*, 11–24, Rome: Gangemi.
Vannelli, V. (2010), *Marcello Piacentini e la grande Roma: It protagonista, I progetti, gli scritt saggi, 1979–2009*, Roma: Lulu Press.
Venturi, R., D. S. Brown and S. Izenour (1972), *Learning from Las Vegas*, Cambridge, MA, and London: MIT Press.
Vidler, A. (1990), *Claude-Nicolas Ledoux: Architecture and Social Reform at the End of the Ancien Régime*, Cambridge, MA, and London: MIT.
View of London (1804), *A View of London or, The Stranger's Guide through the British Metropolis*, London: B. Cosby and Co.
von Henneberg, K. C. (2004), 'Monuments, Public Space, and the Memory of Empire in Modern Italy', *History & Memory* 16.1: 37–85.
von Klenze, L. (1838), *Aphoristische Bemerkungen gesamelt auf seiner Reise nach Griechenland*, Berlin: G. Reimer.
von Quast, A. F. (1834), *Mittheilungen über Alt und Neu Athen*, Berlin: George Gropius.
Walkowitz, J. R. (1992), *City of Dreadful Delight: Narratives of Sexual Danger in Late-Victorian London*, Chicago: University of Chicago Press.
Walston, J. (1988), *The Mafia and Clientelism: Roads to Rome in Post-War Calabria*, New York: Routledge.
Ward, E. (1703), *The London Spy*, London: J. How.
Ward, E. (1725), *The Amorous Bugbear or, The Humours of a Masquerade*, London: A. Bettesworth, J. Bateley and J. Brotherton.
Wassenhoven, L. (1984), 'Greece', in Martin Wynn (ed.), *Planning and Urban Growth in Southern Europe*, 5–36, London and New York: Mansell.
Watkin, D. (1982), *Athenian Stuart: Pioneer of the Greek Revival*, London: George Allen and Unwin.
Watkin, D. (1996), *Sir John Soane: Enlightenment Thought and the Royal Academy Lectures* (Cambridge Studies in the History of Architecture), Cambridge: Cambridge University Press.
Watkin, D. (1999), 'Built Ruins: The Hermitage as a Retreat', in Margaret Richardson (ed.), *Visions*

of Ruin: Architectural Fantasies and Designs for Garden Follies, 5–14, London: The Soane Gallery.
Whyte, I. B. (2017), 'National Socialism, Classicism and Architecture', in H. Roche and K. N. Demetriou (eds), *Brill's Companion to the Classics, Fascist Italy and Nazi Germany* (Brill's Companions to Classical Reception, 12), 404–34, Leiden and Boston: Brill.
Wilkins, W. (1807), *The Antiquities of Magna Graecia*, Cambridge: The University Press.
Wilkins, W. (1816), *Atheniensia, or remarks on the topography and buildings of Athens*, London: John Murray.
Wilkins, W. (1837), *Prolusiones Architectonicae: or Essays on Subjects connected with Greek and Roman Architecture*, London: John Weale.
Wilkinson, H. R. (1951), *Maps and Politics: A Review of the Ethnographic Cartography of Macedonia*, Liverpool: Liverpool University Press.
Wilson, K. (2003), *The Island Race: Englishness, Empire and Gender in the Eighteenth Century*, London and New York: Routledge.
Wonders (1810), *The Wonders of the British Metropolis; being an instructive and amusing sketch of London*, London: T. Tegg.
Wood, R. (1753), *The Ruins of Palmyra, otherwise Tedmor, in the Desert*, London: R. Wood.
Wood, R. (1757), *The Ruins of Balbec, otherwise Heliopolis, Coelosyria*, London: R. Wood.
Woodhouse, C. M. (1973), *Capodistria: The Founder of Greek Independence*, Oxford: Oxford University Press.
Wordsworth, C. (1836), *Athens and Attica: Journal of a Residence There*, London: John Murray.
Xepapadakou, A. (2022), 'Towards the Institutionalization of Musical Life in Nineteenth-Century Greece and Southeatern Europe: The First Steps of the Formation of New Creative and Cultural Industries', in Saijaleena Rantanen and Derek B. Scott (eds), *Institutionalization in Music History*, 15–36, Helsinki: DocMus Research Publications.
Yalouri, E. (2001), *The Acropolis: Global Fame, Local Claim*, Oxford: Berg.
Zocca, M. (1971), 'L'Urbanistica romana dal 1870 al 1945', in Unione romana ingegneri e architetti, Saverio De Paolis and Armando Ravaglioli (eds), *La Terza Roma: Lo Sviluppo Urbanistico, Edilizio e Tecnico di Roma Capitale*, 17–32, Rome: Fratelli Palombi.
Zola, E. (1896), *Rome*, Paris: Blbliothèque Charpentier.

INDEX

Acropolis, Athens
    archaeological site 95, 100, 102, 106–7, 118
    architectural influence 16, 26, 68, 118, 152–3
    clearing of 106, 119
    cultural symbol 106–9, 111, 117, 119
    palace site 104–6, 108–9
    topographical marker 95, 97–8, 101–02, 110–11
    under Ottoman rule 94, 103
    war of independence 70, 88
    see also Parthenon
Adam, Robert 26
Alberti, Leon Battista 9, 28
Agro Pontino 167
Aigina 92, 103, 117
Ainslie, Robert 19, 60, 63
Akademias 118
alienation 7–8, 56, 131, 158–9, 167
Amalia, Queen of Greece 89, 111–12, 116
Antiquities of Athens (Stuart and Revett) 14, 16–17, 26, 30
antisemitism 64
anti-urbanism 8, 68
Aprilia 167
arcadia
    London 44, 45, 49–50
Argos 71, 92
Armansperg, Count 89, 92, 100, 115
Armansperg, Countess 86, 115
Arquati, Giuditta Tavani 138
Athena Promachos 105
Athens
    capital, choice of 73, 92–4
    hotels 116–17
    Ottoman 93–5, 97, 103, 106, 111
    plan of 95–108
    population of 93, 95, 97, 114–15
    ruination of 93–6, 98–9, 103
Augustus 149, 179
    Augustan Age (Britain) 34, 43, 45
    Augustan Age (Rome) 37, 43, 55, 159
    Augustan Rome 169–70
    Augusteo 169–70, 172
    empire of 169
    Forum Augusti 153–4
    mostra augustea 163–4, 166, 177
    and Mussolini 159–60, 163–4, 176

Babylon 35, 57, 64
Bachelard, Gaston 7
Bank of England 26, 35, 37, 46
Barberini, piazza 125
Bedford, Duke of 38
Bentham, Jeremy 53, 81
Bersezio, Vittorio 126–7, 131
Bessan map 95
Billington, John 32–3, 67
Birkbeck, George 53
Blake, William 6
Blaquière, Edward 84, 92
Blondel, François 10, 14, 28, 30
Bloomsbury 21, 37–42
    Bloomsbury Square 37
    Gordon Square 38
    Queen Square 37–8
    Russell Square 38
    Tavistock Square 38
    Woburn Square 38
Bocca di Verità 140
Boito, Camillo 141, 152, 166–7
Bourdieu, Pierre 19
Borghi 135, 140, 170
Borgo Flaminio 140
Bottai, Giuseppe 137
bourgeoisie
    culture 75, 123, 155, 159
    Greek 83, 87, 113–20
    morality 65–6, 79, 107
    and nationalism 3–5, 68, 75–7, 153
    residences of 8, 41, 46, 50, 166
    in Rome 123–7, 135–6, 140–1
    spaces of 4–6, 20, 22–4, 98, 142–6
    see also public
Bracciolini, Poggio 9
Brasini, Armando 171–2
Brettingham, Matthew 25–6, 29
Britannia 47, 48
British Museum 22, 45–6
Bruno, il monumento 139–40
Buckingham House/Palace 19, 21, 44, 47–8, 55
Bulwer, Lytton 85
Burke, Edmund 10, 25–6, 30–1, 177
Burlington, Earl of 25–6
Burton, Decimus 47–8, 52, 55

Index

Burton, James 38
buzzurri 131
Byron, Lord 78–80, 82, 126

Cadbury 61
Caelio 134, 139
Calderini, Guglielmo 136, 146–7
Calza Bini, Alberto 166
Campbell, Colen 25, 29
Campidoglio 122, 129–30, 169–70
Capodistrias, Ioannis
    assassination of 81–2, 89
    President of Greece 73, 76, 85, 92–3, 98, 115, 117
    Tsarist minister 69, 91
Cairoli 138
Carlton Club, see clubland
Carlton House 19, 45, 53
Carlyle, Thomas 6
Casali 115–16
Castro Pretorio 132, 134, 139
Catholic Church 139
Cavour, Camillo Benso di, Prime Minister, 129–30
Cavour, piazza 148
Chambers, William 13, 29–30, 35
Chandler, Richard 26
Charing Cross 22, 45
Chateaubriand, François de, Duc d'Enghien
    in London 36, 64
    in Rome 125–6
Chios 71–2, 89, 101
Chiswick House 25, 41–5
churches
    All Saints Anglican, Rome 142
    architectural style 68
    in Athens 93–5, 99, 102, 118
    Basilica dei Santi Pietro e Paolo, EUR 176–7
    in London 45, 57
    in Mistras 99
    in Rome 127, 130, 133
    at Stadiou 98
    St Martin-in-the-Fields 25, 26
    St Mary le Strand 25
    St Matthew's, Brixton 68
    in Nauplio 73
    St Pancras 68
    St Paul's 19, 31, 45–6, 57–9
    St Peter's 125
    Westminster Abbey 19
    see also Catholic Church
    see also Orthodox Church
Ciceruacchio 138
cinquecentismo 124, 142, 145, 147, 165
citizenship
    Classical 23, 52, 44, 66–8, 76, 105, 142, 149
    bourgeois 14, 46, 50, 65–6

fascist 157–61
republican 6, 24–5, 33, 55, 67, 76–7, 107
urban 1, 25, 98, 124, 134, 181
class 2, 22–3
    conflict 35–6
    structure 60–2
    elite identities 21
    mobility 61
    spatial division by 21–3, 42–5, 50–2, 62–6
    semiotics of 58–61
    see also bourgeoisie
    see also working classes
clubland 4, 21–2, 45–6, 52, 54–55, 64
    Arthur's 54
    Athenaeum 54–5, 62
    Boodle's 54
    Brooks's 54
    Carlton Club 54, 62.
    Clarence 54
    Crockford's Club House 51, 54–5, 61
    Junior United Service Club 54, 62
    Oriental Club 54, 62
    Oxford and Cambridge Club 54, 62
    Reform 54
    Travellers' 54, 62
    Union 54–5
    United Service Club 54–5
    United University Club 62
    University Club 55
    White's 54
    Windham's 54, 62
clubs
    Athens 116
    architectural 14
Cochrane, Admiral Lord 86
Cochrane, George 85–9, 95, 103–4, 116
Cockerell, Charles 29, 51
Coke, Thomas 25
colonialism 1, 27, 74–6, 91–2, 120, 175, 182–3
    and Athens 2–3, 6, 105–7, 112–14
    authoritarian 82
    and development 82–4, 85–7
    literary 78–80
colonna, piazza 122, 124, 128, 134, 141, 171–2
Colosseum 126, 130, 134, 140, 167, 170, 178
Constantinople 69, 89–92, 101, 119
Constitution (Epidavros) of 1822 81
Coram, Thomas 61
Corinth 70, 79, 88, 92–3
Corinthian
    columns 51, 53
    fashion 62–4
    Kate 62–3

Index

Tom 48, 60, 62–3
Corso 126–7, 133–4, 140
country houses 6, 9, 25, 68
    see also Holkham House, Norfolk
    see also villa
crime 6, 35, 58–60

Dance, George 28, 29
da Vignola, Giacomo Barozzi 29
De Amicis, Edmondo 129–30, 133
de Francisci, Pietro 160
de Merode, Xavier, Archbishop 131–2, 134
Depretis, Agostino 150
de Quincey, Thomas 36, 56–7, 64
de Quincy, Quatremère 14, 30
De Renzi, Mario 162, 164, 177
di Cesnola, Palma 83, 88, 82
Dickens, Charles 6
Dodwell, Edward 30
Dulwich Picture Gallery 28
Durand, Jean Nicolas 28, 110

Egan, Pierce 48, 56, 59–63
Elgin, Lord 79, 92, 105, 107
Elmes, James 29, 33–5, 43–4, 48–51, 55, 57, 64
Empire 23
    British 3, 22, 24, 34, 43–4, 46–7, 50, 64
    end of 31, 34–7, 64
    Italian/fascist 157, 160, 167–9, 171
    Ottoman 71
    Roman 31, 168
    wealth of 64
Engels, Frederick 6
Enlightenment, the 5–6, 14–15, 32, 74–6, 130, 183
    Athens 74, 91–2, 99–100, 103–8, 110
    and education 102
    English 34, 44
    and fascism 2, 183
    Greek 76–7, 80–2, 84, 119
    monarchy 17, 83, 112
    politics 2, 182–3
    Scottish 52
    utopianism 12
Esedra 142–4
Esquilino 127, 134, 139
EUR 158, 175–80, 183
Evelyn, John 10, 29

fascism 2
    architectural style of 3
    citizenship 158
    discipline 157
    ideological system 158–64
    war 160

Fielding, Henry 35–6
Filiki Etaireia 71
Finlay, George 71–2, 91, 101
Flaxman, John 47
Forum of Augustus, *see* Augustus, Forum Augusti
Foschini, Arnaldo 174, 177
Fréart de Chambray, Roland 10, 28
freedom
    aesthetics 13–16, 31
    political 85, 74, 78, 81, 84, 112
    of worship 81
futurists 161–2, 167

Galaxidi 71, 117
gambling 51, 54–5, 59, 61–2
Galilei, Galileo 138–9
Gandy, Joseph 35, 37, 55
Garbatella 165–6
gardens 30
    Amalia's garden, Athens 112
    Athenian house 97
    Athens 97–8, 100, 102–3, 105, 110–11, 118
    city as garden 51, 109, 165–7
    Edenic 25, 78–80
    garden squares 38, 99, 143
    garden suburb 165–6
    Kensington 45
    of Lucullus 140
    Pincio 127–8
    Rome 124, 126, 133–4, 173
    rus in urbe 8, 46, 109, 181
    Vauxhall 26, 45
    see also arcadia
Garibaldi 121, 154, 159
Garston, Edgar 110, 115–16
Gaskell, Mary 6
Gentile, Giovanni 160
George III, King of England 53
George IV, King of England/Prince Regent 33–4, 43, 53–4, 64
George V, Patriarch of Constantinople 89
Germanos, Bishop of Patras 69–70, 85
Germany
    Nazi 158
Gianicolo 134, 136, 139–40
Gibbs, James 26
Giglioli, Giulio Quirino 163–4
Gilly, Friedrich 14–15, 98
Giordano, Felix 131–3, 136
Giovannoni, Gustavo 164–7, 172
Goethe 125
Gogos Bakolas 88
Gothic 29, 32, 68, 116, 125, 142
Gouras 88–9

213

Index

Greece
    Byzantine 74, 81, 92, 99, 106–7, 116
    cultural achievement 15–16
    finances 72, 102, 113
    folk traditions 74, 84, 107, 119
    foundation of modern state 72–3
    and freedom 13, 74, 78–9, 81, 84
    Muslims in 69–71, 81, 89, 103
    women of 78–80, 82–3, 85–7, 103, 107, 113–14, 117
Greek war of independence 69–74
    language controversy 119
    massacres during 71
    religious war 71–2, 78, 84–5, 89–90
Grivas 89
Grote, George 53
guidebooks
    London 45–6, 57–62
Gutensohn, Johann 104
Gwynn, John 24–6, 29, 33

Hansen, Christian 15, 117–18
Hansen, Theophil 15, 117–18, 147
    Parlamentsgebäude 6
Haygarth, William 78
Hemans, Felicia 78
history 123, 125, 155, 175, 182
    Ancient 30, 75, 79, 83, 91
    Athenian 100, 104, 106–7
    Byzantine 106–7
    of architecture 30, 67
    and colonial mentalities 107
    end of 8–9
    fascist 4, 158–64, 175, 180–1
    Italian 125, 151
    of Rome 123–5, 168, 176
    and ruins 16, 169
    transcendence of 31, 105, 184
Hitler, Adolf 168–9
Hobhouse, John Cam 82–3
Hölderlin, Friedrich 78–80
Holkham Hall, Norfolk 25, 29
Hope, Thomas 13–14, 67–8, 78
Howard, Ebenezer 165
Howe, Samuel 84
Hugo, Victor 6
Hume, David 61
hut, primitive 12–14, 30–1
Hyde Park 41, 44
    entry to 26, 46–9
    promenade in 46, 59–60, 62
Hydra 70, 87
Hyperion 78, 80

Ibrahim Pasha 71–2
imperialism 23–4

Inwood, Henry 29–30, 68
Ionic
    columns 48, 51, 118

Jupiter Stator, Temple of 28

Kaftanzoglou, Lysandros 98–9, 102, 117–19
Kalavryta 69
kapitani 76, 81–9, 91, 110
Karaiskakis 86–8
Karlsruhe 98
Kew Gardens 35
Kleanthis, Stamatios 15, 92
    Arsakeio school 117
    house of 114–15, 117
    houses designed by 115–16
    plan of Athens 92–3, 95–108
klefti 76, 81, 84, 87–9, 91, 103, 110, 120
Koch, Gaetano 141–5
Kolettis, Ioannis 90–2, 100
Kolokotronis, Theodoros 70, 72, 86
Korais, Adamantios 77, 80–1
Koroni 70, 72
Kropotkin, Peter 165

Laclau, Ernesto 161
Langhans, Carl Gotthard 14
Laugier, Marc-Antoine 10–14, 28, 30–1, 67–8
Leake, William 80, 83, 91, 11–12
Ledoux, Claude-Nicolas 11, 13, 28
Le Roy, Julien David 14, 26, 30
Leverton and Chawner, architects 39–40
Libera, Adalberto 162
Littoria 167
Liverpool, Lord 36–7, 66
Liverpool, St George's Hall 6
L'Oca 134
Louvre, the 10–11, 53
Ludwig of Bavaria 73–4, 86, 93, 100, 106, 110, 112
luxury 24–5

Maccagnani, Eugenio 150–1
Mafai, Mario 170
Malcolm, Admiral 101, 116
Malcolm, James 38, 57, 64
Manchester 6
Mandeville, Bernard 25
Mani 87, 89, 119
Mansion Benizelou 115
Marble Arch 47
Marble Hill House, Twickenham 25
Marinetti, Filippo Tommaso 161–2
Mavrokordatos, Alexandros 81–2, 85, 93
Mavromichalis, Petros 70, 72–3, 87
Mazzini, Giuseppe 121, 123, 128–9, 131, 137, 146

Index

mechanics, *see* working classes
megali idea 76, 90–1
Megara 70, 92
Menidi 70, 88
Mesolongi 71–2, 87, 89, 117
Mill, James 53
Ministry of Finance, Rome 137–8
Minnucci, Gaetano 178
Mistras 70, 84, 99
Modon (Methoni) 70, 89
Moisiodax, Iosipos 80
Moretti, Luigi 173
Morris, Edward 113, 116–17
Morris, Roger 29
mostra augustea della romanità 159, 163, 166, 177
mostra della rivoluzione fascista 159, 162–3
mostra di Roma nell'ottocento 159
Movimento Italiano per l'Architettura Razionale (MIAR) 162
Muñoz, Antonio 172
Mussolini
    architect of Rome 167, 169–70, 172–8
    demolitions in Rome 136, 165, 169–71
    depictions of 162, 171, 174
    Forum of 158, 169, 171–4, 176
    relation to history 159, 161, 169, 175–6
    ideology 160, 165
    imperialism 167, 169
    as Roman 159–60, 163–4, 176
    and Sarfatti 161

Napoleon, Louis 121
Nash, John 39–45, 47–52, 55, 61, 65
Nathan, Ernesto, *sindaco* 153
National Gallery, London 22, 52–3
National Library, Athens
nationalism 2–3, 5, 15, 74–7
    English/British 33, 66–8
    fascism 157–60, 172
    Greek 69, 119–20
    Italian 123–9, 148–9, 153–5, 166
Nauplio 71, 73, 86, 89, 92–3, 115, 117
Navarino, battle of 72
Nazi 2, 6, 168, 182
Nénot, Paul 150
Newcastle 6
newspapers 4, 75
    British 107
    Greek 73, 76–7, 93, 114, 117
    Italian 162, 174
    London 62, 65
New Street, *see* Regent Street
Novecento 161

Odysseus 88
Oppio 134, 139

Orthodoxy
    Church 81, 85, 89–90, 103
    culture 81, 86, 103, 117
    national communities 69–71, 76–9, 81, 89–91
Ostia 167–9
    antiquities 162, 166, 173
Otto, King 73
    in Athens 86–7, 89–90, 101, 103, 106–8, 117
    marriage, *see* Amalia
    palace 103–6, 108–12
    revolution against 114
    rule 73, 79, 89–92, 99, 117
Ottoman
    architecture 112, 116
    traditions 81, 83–4, 101, 119
    rule in Greece 69–73, 77–9, 81, 86–9, 91, 94
Ottonopolis 98, 103, 108
Owenson, Sydney 78–9

palazzi porticati 143–4
palazzo degli Uffici 178
palazzo della Banca d'Italia, *see* palazzo Koch
palazzo della Civiltà italiana 178–9
palazzo delle Esposizioni Nazionale di Belle Arti 142, 145–6, 162
palazzo di Giustizia, 136, 142, 146–9, 154
palazzo Koch 142, 144–5, 152
palazzo Wedekind 143
palichari, see *klefti*
Palladio, Andrea 9, 28
    see also villa, Palladian
Palmyra 26, 30
Paris 11–12, 20, 91, 123, 126, 142
    centre of architectural education 14–15, 30, 110, 150
    fashions of 87, 107
    revolutionary 36
    rival to London 22, 31–3, 45
Parthenon 104–6, 108, 113
    marbles 48, 53, 55
    modern experience of 17
    modern versions 17
    Stuart and Revett drawings 16
    see also Acropolis
Patras 69–71, 89
Perrault, Charles 10
Perrault, Claude 10, 12, 28
Peta, battle of 88
Peterloo 66
Peyre, Marie-Joseph 14, 28
Phanariotes 69, 84, 100–1, 115
Philhellenism 72, 74–5, 79, 88, 82, 108
physics of perception 10, 25–6, 30–1
Piacentini, Marcello 164–5, 172–5
Piacentini, Pio 142, 145, 162
Pianciani, Luigi, *sindaco* 134–6

215

Index

Pincio 127–8, 134, 138
Piranesi, Francesco 29
Piranesi, Giovanni Battista 29, 35, 126, 147
Pius IX, Pope 121
Pittsburg 6
Poggi, Giuseppe 142
Polytechnio, Athens 118
Pomezia 167
Pontina 167
Popolo, piazza del 127–8, 134, 140, 142, 172
Poros 73
Prati di Castello 134, 136, 140–1, 146, 148, 165
prostitution 45, 56–7, 59–60, 63–4, 82
Psara 70–1, 89
public, the 8, 23, 33, 40, 68, 112
    public benefit 31, 40–1, 45, 52, 56
    public opinion 72
    public sphere 37, 52–3, 56, 65–8, 75–7, 134, 142
Pugin, Augustus 29

Quarrel of Ancients and Moderns (Querelle des Anciens et Modernes) 9–10
Quinet, Edgar 83–4, 93
Quirinale 134–5, 139–40

Rationalism (architectural) 162–4, 173, 176–8
Regent's Park 22, 34, 37, 39–41, 43–51
Regent Street 22, 41–6, 50, 55, 57, 65, 183
Repton, Humphrey 38
Repubblica romana 121
Reshid Pasha 71
Revett, Nicholas 14, 26, 106
    see also Antiquities of Athens
Riou, Stephen 28–9
Rododafnes Castle 115
Romanticism
    civilization 36
    Greek 77–80, 110
    landscapes 32, 109–10, 112
    liberal 71, 74
    Rome 124–8, 131
    ruins 34–7, 94, 105, 112, 131
Rome
    cost of development 136, 141, 152–3
    la terza Roma 122–3, 128–31, 137–8, 141, 146, 154–5, 178
    piano regolatore 132–3, 135–6, 139–41, 172
Ross, Ludwig 106, 118
ruins, aesthetic of
    Athens 16–17, 79–80, 83–4, 93–4, 99, 103, 115
    London 34–7, 185, n. 15
    Rome 105, 123–7, 143, 152, 170, 176–8
Ruspoli, Emanuele, *sindaco* 136
Rustici, Cencio 9

Sabaudia 164, 167
Sabbatini, Innocenzo 166
Sacconi, Giuseppe 150–3
St James's, London 19, 21, 24, 40, 44, 55, 59, 61
Saline de Chaux 11–12
Sanjust di Teluda, Edmondo 135
Sarfatti, Margherita 161–2
Schaubert, Eduard 15
    archaeologist 188
    house of 115, 117
    plan of Athens 92–3, 95–108
Schinkel, Karl Friedrich 14–15, 92
    and the Acropolis 103–6, 108–10, 112
Sella, Quintino 121–2, 129, 131, 136–9, 183
    Ministry of Finance 137–8
schools
    architectural school Athens 118
    architectural school Rome 142, 164
    Arsakeio school 117
    in Greece 80, 84, 99, 102, 114, 119
    Hills' school 117
    London 57
Shelley, Percy 81, 126
shops
    bourgeois identity 4, 20, 22
    London 42 44–6, 49, 51–2, 60–1, 63
    Rome 141–3
Serlio, Sebastiano 9
sex
    Orientalism 79, 86, 126
    urban 22, 59–64, 68
Sironi, Mario 161, 163, 175
Smirke, Robert 29, 46, 53, 55, 106
Smyrna 89
Soane, Sir John 13–14, 26–32, 48–9, 61
    and the Bank of England 26, 28, 48
    Hyde Park 48–9
    lectures 28, 30–2
    library 28–30
    and ruins 35, 37
Society of Dilettanti 26, 29
Sophie de Marbourg, Duchess of Plaisance 115–16
Souli 71, 78
Soutsos, Panayiotis 79–80
Soutzos, Michael 69, 101
Spetses 70, 82
stazione Ostiense 168
Stonestreet, George Griffin 34, 37
Stuart, James 14, 26, 106
    see also Antiquities of Athens
Syros 92–3

Taine, Hippolyte 124–5
Tavistock, Marquises of 38

Index

Termini
    piazza 122, 126, 143, 149
    stazione 131, 134–5
theatre 4, 20–2, 45, 46
    Adelphi Theatre, London 62
    as sites of sexual encounter 59, 63
    Athens 98, 103, 107
    Boukoura Theatre, Athens 116
    King's Theatre/Italian Opera, London 41, 64
    of Marcellus 166–7, 169–70
    Opéra, Paris 150
    Rome 128
    Skontozopoulos Theatre, Athens 116
Thiersch, Frédéric 85, 89–90
Tombazi, Admiral 86
Tower of the Winds 17, 50
Trafalgar Square 43, 62
Trastevere 121, 124, 134–6, 138–41
Treaty of London 72
Trikoupis, Spyridon 93
Tripolitsa 69–71, 84, 89, 92
Tzavelas, Kitsos, Greek Prime Minister 89, 91

Ude, M. 61
USA 5, 182
university
    La Sapienza 174–5
    University of Athens 103, 110–11, 114, 117–18
    University of Bonn 52
    University College London 22, 46, 52–3, 55
    in Rome 131
    University of Virginia 52
utopia 4, 7–9, 12, 14, 157, 165, 173, 181
    Athens 74
    EUR 180, 183
    fascist 173, 178
    London 27, 34, 37, 49

Valadier, Giuseppe 127–8, 142
Valente, Antonio 162
Van Aelst, Pieter Coecke 9
Vasos, Kapitanos 88–9
Vauxhall, *see* gardens
Velestinlis, Rigas 77, 81
Venezia, piazza 124, 128, 134, 140, 154, 167–8, 170
Versailles 98, 109
via della Conciliazione 136, 170
via dell'Impero 167, 170
via del Mare 167
via di Ripetta 140
via Nazionale 132, 134–7, 140–1, 144–5
Vienna 6

villa 8, 25, 30, 173, 175
    English villa 50
    Hadrian's villa 28, 105
    Palladian 9, 11, 14, 25, 68
    Pliny's villa 105
    Regent's Park 39, 44, 50
    Roman 104–5, 112
    suburban Roman 132
    Villa Borghese 127–8
    Villa Ilissia 115–16
    Villa of Julius II 125
    villa Palombara 142
    villa Ludovisi 134
Vitruvius 8
    De Architectura 8–10, 12, 28, 30
    Vitruvian architecture 8–10, 68, 177
    New Vitruvius Britannicus 29
    Vitruvius Britannicus 14, 25, 29
Vittoriano, Il 123, 142, 149–55
Vittorio Emanuele II, King 121–2, 149, 152–3
Vittorio Emanuele III, King 165
Vittorio, piazza 142–4, 154
Viviani, Alessandro 134–5
von Gärtner, Friedrich 15, 110–12
von Hess, Peter 103
von Heideck 92, 115
von Klenze, Leo 15, 98
    on the Acropolis 106–8
    and landscape 109–12
    paintings 105, 109
    palace 108–9
    plan of Athens 100–3
von Maurer 92
Voulgaris, Evgenios 80

Ward, Edward 59–60
Westminster 19, 21, 22, 24, 41, 45–6
Wilkins, William 30, 52
    National Gallery 53
    University Club 55
    University College 52–3
Winckelmann, Johann Joachim 29
Wood, Robert 26, 30
Wordsworth, Christopher 88, 93–4, 103, 111
working classes 23, 30, 44
    city of 24

Ypsilanti, Alexandros 69
Ypsilanti, Demetrios 69

Zanardelli, Giuseppe 146–7, 149
Zappeion 118
Zola, Emile 128, 137, 140